King of the Gumballs

An Entrepreneur's Spiritual Journey Building a Business While Raising Eight Kids and Surviving the Feminist Movement and a Fifty-Year Marriage

Maury & June
Here's a copy of my book. Hope you like it and if you do please tell others.
Thanks
Lyle

By

Lyle M. Becker

First Edition

ISBN: 0-9661143-0-2

Content: 1) Family/Child Care/Relationships
2) Spiritual Growth/Religion
3) Business/Entrepreneurship
4) Self-Actualization/Self-help
5) Feminist movement

Library of Congress Catalog Number: 97-094643

Printed and bound in the United States of America

Published by
Caliana Publishing Co.
P.O. Box 1459
Appleton, WI 54913

Dedication

To my wife Dolores and our eight children
who gave so much so I could be successful in business.

Thanks

To writing instructors Cork Milner and Richard O'Connor of the Santa Barbara Adult-Ed Program, Paula McCarty and Mike Shaw, two great young journalists who helped critique the book, my editor, Marcia Lorenzen, and my son Jonathan, who designed the cover.

All Profits

From this book will be donated to the Caliana Foundation to help the less fortunate in the world, in loving memory of Callie and Anna, two very caring women, mothers of Dolores and Lyle Becker.

Prologue

"I don't get it. You can afford to fly around the country visiting customers and now you're flying on business to Hong Kong, and all you do is sell gumballs?"

"We sell a hell of a lot of gumballs," I said, with a chuckle, sipping my Canadian Club and water.

She was a young woman in marketing for Black and Decker in the seat next to me on Singapore Airlines on her way to visit the Black and Decker plant in Singapore.

"And you sell them through these little penny gum machines, the ones put out by the Kiwanis clubs?"

"No, our machines are mostly in supermarkets and vend more than gumballs. We also have machines that vend small toys and novelties packed in clear plastic capsules. I'm on my way to Hong Kong to buy toys for our machines."

"So you're the guy responsible for my kids hounding me for quarters to play the gum and toy machines at the supermarket?"

I looked at her over my reading glasses and said rather sheepishly, "We don't have all the machines out there, only the ones with Toy 'n Joy on them. Some mothers really get upset about these gum and toy machines."

"You must have a lot of machines to make it profitable to go all the way to Hong Kong to buy toys," she said as she held out her glass for more champagne as the attractive flight attendant came by in her formal gown.

"Yes, we have them in all 50 states."

"Are you connected with the Mafia?"

"Are you kidding? Life's too short for that! If the Mafia were involved I'd get out of this business."

"Is this your own business?" She seemed quite interested.

"Yes, I've been in it for more than 50 years."

"Really? How did you ever get started in the gumball machine business?"

Good question. It was a long time since I thought back to 1941 when this shy kid of 18, with little self-esteem and no sales ability, started in business with 300 peanut machines.

She settled back on her pillow, sipping her champagne, and turned to me in her window seat looking like she was ready for the story of my life.

Like the colors of the gumballs in our machines, there were yellow days when the sun shone on the business with success, blue days of discouragement, and black days of failure. Then there were the red and orange days with the excitement of new ideas and new hope.

Looking back on my life, it was an exciting 50 years—married to Dolores, building a family business, raising eight kids, and struggling through the feminist movement while Dolores claimed her personhood, wondering whether our marriage would survive.

Finally, it dawned on me that our family life and my business life were combined on a spiritual journey. Building the business taught me what I thought to be failures were instead stepping-stones to the next plateau of success. In our family life I also learned there weren't any failures, only growing experiences.

Then came the insight that I wasn't making this journey alone. God was there beside me, guiding me, co-creating a peaceful and happy life for our family.

Chapter 1

"You know, Lyle, dollar for dollar there is more money in penny peanut machines than in candy and cigarette machines." Herman Plous and I were sitting across from each other at the double desk in his office in Green Bay, Wisconsin. Plous had purchased my dad's cigarette vending business in the summer of 1940. A few years before my dad had been appointed postmaster in Brillion, a town of 1,200 in Wisconsin. It was a political appointment. He was a dedicated Democrat, and this was his "retirement job." He was sixty-years old and couldn't yet depend upon social security, since it only started five years before as part of Franklin D. Roosevelt's "New Deal."

I was 17 and had just graduated from high school. I decided to move the 30 miles to Green Bay to become Herman's bookkeeper and part-time serviceman for his candy and cigarette vending business. I felt like my dad was selling me with the business. I wanted badly to attend college to study business and accounting, but my dad had just put three of my brothers through the University of Wisconsin, and they had trouble finding jobs. Times were tough during the Depression of the 1930s.

"Maybe you'll want to go into your own business someday," my dad said to me when I was considering taking the $50 a month job Plous offered me. "Why not get some business experience," he advised. My dad, who had been in business for 40 years, had 12 kids. I was number 12. Not one of them followed in his footsteps and took over the family business. I think he had a secret desire that I go into business someday to carry on the family tradition. He probably saw more of a future for me in business than in my going to college and struggling to find a job. I felt I was being cheated out of a college education, but I didn't have many options, so I took his advice and went to work for Plous.

During my school years I helped my dad with his office work, doing the ordering, paying bills, making the bank deposits. I also helped my brothers service our cigarette vending machines on Saturdays and during summer vacations. I did well in my bookkeeping class in high school, and I felt I could handle the job with Plous as bookkeeper and part-time serviceman.

Hermy, as Plous preferred to be called, had the confidence of a progressive businessman, but he didn't look the part. I never remember seeing him in a business suit. Usually, he wore a pair of slacks and a long-sleeved dress shirt with the cuffs turned up to his elbows. Being rather short, with a wide nose, he wasn't a handsome man, but his smile made up for it. He seemed to be always smiling and laughing as he was talking. I wanted to learn all I could from Hermy.

The learning process of a different nature started soon after I began to work in his storefront office and warehouse on Cherry Street. I was going through the stuff in the glove compartment of Hermy's Studebaker. He had asked me to go to his car and get a map. I was shocked. I came across a bunch of pornographic pictures, actual photographs of naked young men and women in all sorts of deviant sexual acts. It was sexually exciting, but also abhorrent. I couldn't believe what I was seeing really took place, but someone had to have taken the photographs of this orgy. After looking at them for a while, I found the map he wanted, then shoved the photos under the other maps and slammed the glove compartment door. I didn't tell anyone about my experience. With my strict Catholic upbringing I felt it was sinful to look at those pictures.

Another unexpected maturing experience came a few weeks later. There were several houses of prostitution in Green Bay. We called them cathouses. They were good locations for cigarette machines as the women employed there smoked a lot of cigarettes. Sometimes the machines would go empty between regular service calls, and as the part-time serviceman, it was my job to fill them. So, I drove to the Golden Shoe in the red-light district a few miles out of Green Bay. I thought a house of prostitution would be a house, not a rectangular one-story building without any kind of a name or sign. The front door was locked. I felt like I was breaking the law, and probably was, by ringing the doorbell. The woman who opened the door—I don't know if it was the madam or one of the girls—must have been expecting a customer rather than the cigarette guy. She was in shorts with a halter top that should have been tied in the front, but wasn't, and no bra. I had seen my share of "girlie" magazines at Barnard's Drug Store in Brillion when I was growing up, but there's nothing like the real thing, close up.

"Ah…I…I came to service the cigarette machine," I stammered, staring straight ahead. The sickening smell of heavy perfume permeated the air.

"Well sonny, you came to the right place. We're plum out," she said as she stepped aside to let me in with my box of cigarettes.

I know why she called me sonny—a gangling kid of 17, 120-pounds, with my ears sticking straight out from my crew cut. I'm sure my face was red with embarrassment.

"Could you tell me where the cigarette machine is?" I blurted.

"It's in here," she said as she pointed to a room near the front door. The building had a corridor down the center with six rooms on either side. I went into the tiny 6 x 8-foot room furnished with a black leather couch and a small table with a lamp. There was hardly enough room for the cigarette machine. The other rooms seemed to be furnished the same way.

"I'll only be a few minutes," I said as I opened the machine and started to fill it.

"That's okay. Just shut the door when you leave dearie," she said as she walked down the hall.

I was shocked. My hormones were raging and I couldn't get out of there fast enough. My palms were sweating and my knees weak. As I drove back to Hermy's office I thought about those women, wondering whether they chose this lifestyle or were forced into it by the lack of jobs in these depressed times.

I enjoyed living in Green Bay, rooming with two other boarders in the home of a delightful elderly German couple. Even though the beef was usually boiled and tasteless, the $20 a month rent included the old man waking me in the morning with a smile, tweaking my toes through the blanket.

Hermy was very considerate. He let me use the delivery van to go home to Brillion on weekends and didn't charge me for the gas.

I had been working for Hermy for almost a year, and we were sitting across the desk from each other in his office when he made the statement that there was more money in peanut machines than in candy or cigarette machines. He was bouncing ideas off of me. I was flattered he used me as a sounding board and was floored with his statement because he only had a few peanut machines. Candy and cigarette machines were the mainstay of his business. It didn't make sense to me, so I asked him about it.

"It's the investment in the machines and the margin of profit that counts," he said, taking a Lucky Strike out of the pack in his shirt pocket and lighting it. "Peanut machines cost $5 or $10 each depending upon the model you buy and cigarette and candy machines cost $50 to $100, ten times as much. I make 4 cents on a 15 cent pack of cigarettes and a little more than a penny on a nickel candy bar, about 25 percent. But every time someone pulls the lever on a penny peanut machine I make a half-a-cent, 50 percent. A high margin of profit on a low-cost machine is better than a low margin on a high-cost machine," he concluded.

"It makes sense," I agreed.

That night, lying on my bed in the boarding house listening to the Big Bands on the radio, I thought about the conversation with Hermy, and I dreamed of being in my own peanut business. I serviced the peanut machines Hermy had in Dehn's and Oliver's ice cream stores in Green Bay. They emptied almost every week. At 50 percent profit it wouldn't take very many machines for me to make more than I was earning working for Hermy. My problem, even if I could get my dad to finance me in the business, was my insecurity. A meek young kid, self-conscious, I was never comfortable talking with strangers. It scared me to think about asking someone about putting one of my peanut machines in their place of business, even though the machines are put in on a commission basis at no cost to the owner. I was afraid of rejection. I wasn't a salesman and had no desire to be one. I knew I could service the machines once they were on location, but there was no way I could put them out. Was there something in my childhood that caused my insecurity, and could I overcome my fear?

My father, a cigar maker by trade, moved 24 miles from Manitowoc to Brillion in his early '20s and started his own cigar factory. There were fewer than 500 people in Brillion in 1900. His cigar business thrived, producing 1 1/2 million hand-rolled cigars a year with 30 employees. The Becker family became one of the wealthiest in town. My dad bought into several other businesses in town and invested heavily in the burgeoning stock market, buying many stocks on margin. It was the Roaring Twenties.

Four years before I was born in 1923, my father was struck down with tuberculosis. A highly contagious disease, and a killer, it was through my mother's determination and 16-hour workdays that he recovered, and no one else in the family became infected. Taking care of eight kids, keeping up a six-bedroom house, and pregnant with my brother Harold, she had to climb two flights of stairs every time my dad pounded on the floor with a cane and needed help.

Everything that came out of his bedroom had to be sterilized, and the boiling water had to be heated on a wood or kerosene stove.

Six years after Harold was born, my sister Louise drowned in Lake Winnebago in a bathing accident while attending nurses training in Oshkosh. She was only 18.

In 1929 the stock market crashed. People on Wall Street jumped out of windows because they lost everything. The stocks my dad invested in so heavily on margin were worthless because the price dropped so low that he owed the brokerage house more than the stocks were worth. He lost everything except our home and the cigar factory. I was six-years-old. The Great Depression of the 1930s had begun. I was a depression kid, and we were poor.

My dad was down to only a few cigar makers, as handmade cigars were now in competition with machine-made cigars and cigarettes. Cigarettes sold for 10 to 15 cents for a pack of 20. Most people couldn't afford his Brilliant Harvest and Becker Havana Plantations, even though they retailed at 5 and 10 cents each.

No longer able to support his family with the cigar business, he went into the wholesale candy and tobacco business. He bought two large trucks and loaded them with candy bars, chewing gum, smoking and chewing tobacco, cigarettes and Becker cigars. He hired my brother Eugene and my brother-in-law Dick to call on the grocery stores, restaurants, and taverns in the surrounding counties to sell the merchandise.

There was a lot of competition in the wholesale business from similar companies in Manitowoc and Green Bay. Cigarettes brought in most of the money from the routes, so to secure the locations, my dad went into the cigarette vending business. He knew that controlling the key to the vending machines meant getting all the cigarette business in the taverns in which they were placed. He bought machines on a time-payment plan and soon could boast of having the first cigarette vending machines in central and northern Wisconsin.

In thinking back on my early years, I wondered if there was something in my childhood that caused my insecurity. Not only I, but the five youngest kids seemed insecure; my older brothers and sisters were much more outgoing and assertive. Maybe it's because they were raised in the good times and we during the Depression. When I thought of all the catastrophes my dad and mother suffered—his T.B., my sister drowning, the stock market crash, raising 11 children (one died at birth), half of them during the Depression—I could see why they didn't have time for us individually. I can't remember my father ever hugging me, taking me on his lap or playing a game with me. He must have been too preoccupied making a living for his family. Also, I don't ever remember that he spanked me. But, I never doubted his love for me.

The five youngest kids all seemed to be afraid of our father. A stoic, strict disciplinarian, of German descent, with a quick temper, he was a believer in the old adage that children should be seen and not heard. I remember going with my parents to visit my aunts and uncles. Most of them were farmers. They talked together for what seemed like hours. It was like we were invisible to them.

Besides the strict discipline I got at home from my father, I also got it at St. Mary Catholic Grade School, which was across the street from our home. Kids who were discipline problems were sent to the principal, Sister Albertine, who struck them on their knuckles with a ruler for misbehaving.

I hated to be called in from hide-and-seek on a fun evening to go to May devotions. Living only a block from church, it seemed my parents expected me to be in church every time the lights were on. Of course, they were there too. I said my prayers before I went to sleep at night, prayers I had memorized like the "Our Father," the "Hail Mary," and the "Act of Contrition." The last prayer was very important, lest I died that night with a mortal sin on my soul I hadn't confessed and would go to hell. In church, I read prayers from my prayer book while the priest was saying Mass in Latin, which was okay because I couldn't understand it anyway. Only on Sunday did the priest talk to us in English, in a sermon. In our daily Mass before school and on Sundays he kept his back to us most of the time. I liked to go to communion because I got to take a fried egg sandwich to school and eat it after Mass, because we had to fast from food and even water from midnight the night before.

Right and wrong and confessing my sins really bothered me. I hated confession. I went because the nuns lined us up in church once a month and we went, whether we needed to or not. According to the list of sins in my prayer book, all mine were venial sins. We were taught in religion class that it wasn't necessary to confess venial sins, as they would be erased when we went to communion, but it was recommended we tell them to the priest anyway.

To tell the priest how many times I looked at dirty pictures—those "girlie" magazines at Barnard's Drug Store—or how many times I had impure thoughts or actions with myself was embarrassing. There was a question in my mind whether masturbation might be a mortal sin and that really worried me. With mortal sins on your soul when you died you would to go hell—forever. I was constantly in fear of sinning, not getting to confession, dying, and going to hell. The nuns talked about the fire of hell; it would be eternal, and you would burn forever. What a terrible thing to lay on a kid—or an adult.

In my prayer book under mortal sins they listed eating meat on Friday, missing Mass on Sunday, or killing someone.

Certainly killing someone would be a serious offense against God, but what kind of a God would send me to hell for eating meat on Friday or missing Mass? And in the next breath the nuns would tell us that God was a loving Father. What a millstone of fear to carry around all my life.

We were told by the nuns and the priests not to read the Bible; we needed the clergy to interpret it for us. Religion for me was a burden, not a pleasure. The bible stories I read in school and remembered gave me the impression that God was forever punishing his people. The stories also talked about faith, but it was hard to have faith in such a harsh God. I felt God was like a man with a whip who wielded it to keep us in line. It was hard to believe the nuns when they told us that God loved us.

When we were to consider marriage, we were cautioned to marry a Catholic. If we married someone from any other religion, the spouse must agree to raise the children Catholic, not just Christian, but Catholic.

I don't remember a thing that happened in school, where I sat in any of my classrooms or who any of my teachers were from the first day of school—when my mother took me to school and I followed her home—until the seventh grade when Sister Francis George taught me that school could be fun. Those formative years must have been so horrible that I completely blocked them out of my mind.

My childhood experiences left me with a fear of adults, especially those in authority. Now I had a business venture in mind, which I hoped my dad might finance, but I was too scared to make the simple sales presentations necessary to put out the peanut machines that could start me in business, and put me on the road to success.

Chapter 2

Chuck Buckman started working for Hermy as a serviceman for his cigarette and candy machines around the time I was hired. A fun guy with a round red face, in his mid-twenties, he was always clowning around. He didn't seem to have a care in the world. I think I related to him because his ears were bigger, and stuck out even more than mine. Chuck's wife Caroline kept tabs on him since he liked to hang out at taverns, with his brother Ward, drinking beer and talking smart.

One hot June afternoon, after I'd worked for Hermy for about a year, Chuck returned from the cigarette route and I asked him if he wanted to stop for a beer after work. Even though he was quite a bit older, he seemed to like me and I considered him a friend. Green Bay was full of taverns and there were no laws against selling beer to minors. I liked beer, learning to drink it when I went with my brothers on the cigarette route. I didn't like hanging out in taverns, but this was a chance to get to know Chuck better. Chuck had a gift of gab and I wondered whether he might be my ticket into the vending business, maybe a partnership where my dad would finance the machines and Chuck would put them out.

We stopped at the Ten-O-One Club on Main Street. We pulled up two stools at the bar and I ordered a couple of mugs of Schlitz.

"How do you like working for Hermy?"

"Oh, it's a job," Chuck said, taking a big gulp of beer, the foam leaving a ring on his upper lip.

"That's about the way I feel, too. What did you do before you started with Hermy?"

"I worked for my dad and my uncle, who were partners, servicing their cigarette machines. Hermy bought their machines about the same time he bought your dad's." Chuck took a Camel from his silver cigarette case, tapped it on the bar and lit it with his lighter. A Big Band tune was playing on the jukebox.

"Did you have a chance to go to college?" I asked.

"I went to the University of Wisconsin for a couple of years. I worked summers selling bandage to pay for my tuition, room and board."

"You sold bandage? What's that?" I was interested in any sales experience Chuck had.

"Al Kantor, a neighbor and a good friend of mine, and I started selling bandage the summer we got out of high school. Al also needed money for college."

"What's bandage?" I asked, again.

"Didn't you ever see it? It comes in a roll. You cut off a piece and wrap it around your finger. It sticks to itself. (Band Aids weren't invented yet.) My cousin knew a guy who handled the stuff, so we started selling it in Green Bay. We earned enough for our first year at the University of Wisconsin; then the following summer we bought a beat-up Model A Ford and headed for the big cities," he said as he crushed out his cigarette in the ashtray on the bar.

"We hit pay dirt in the office buildings in Milwaukee and Chicago. There were 'no soliciting' signs in most of the buildings, but when they kicked us out, we'd just go to another floor or another building. Everybody was trying to sell something those days to make a buck during the Depression."

"Who did you sell to in the office buildings?"

"The secretaries. We'd ask them to stick out a finger. We'd quickly wrap a piece of bandage around it to show them how it stuck to itself, but wasn't sticky to the touch. We showed them how it made a smooth compact bandage that didn't get in their way when they were typing. We asked 50 cents a roll or whatever we could get," Chuck said with a laugh. "It cost 10 cents a roll, so we made big bucks. We wore out two Model A's in three summers running around the country. We even went out to New York City to sell it. It was great experience and a hell of a lot of fun Back-er, but I've got to get going. Thanks for the beer."

For some reason he always called me Back-er.

That night I turned down the music on the radio beside my bed, my mind wandered to my first recollection of what I thought was God's intervention in my life. As a kid I was fascinated with the penny punchboard at Barnard's Drug Store. The 4 x 6-inch board, about an inch thick, had 1,000 eighth-inch holes drilled into it, each containing a folded slip of paper with numbers from 1 to 1,000. It cost a penny to punch out a number with a metal punch. If the number ended in zero, you were entitled to a candy bar. Other special numbers entitled you to two candy bars, or the grand prize of five candy bars. For all other numbers you received nothing. It was a gamble, so I said an "Our Father" and a "Hail Mary," as I walked the block from my home to the drug store with a few pennies. I thought about the miracles in the Bible, like Peter getting out of the boat and walking on the water to Jesus and then sinking as his faith wavered. I really tried to have faith that I would win. This was my first experience in gaining faith in God through prayer. Praying to win worked. It was like multiplying the loaves and fishes in the Bible, only I was multiplying my pennies into nickel candy bars.

Lying there on my bed, thinking, in my boarding house home away from home, and my radio tuned to Big Band music, I wondered again whether Chuck Buckman might be the answer to my getting into the peanut vending business. He seemed honest and I was pleased to hear of his sales experience, going around the country selling bandage. Maybe we could go into partnership. Again, I thought about the possibility of my dad financing us. Chuck could become a 50-50 partner without any investment, just for putting out my half of the machines. It sounded like a good idea. I decided that night I would go to Brillion the following Saturday to talk to my dad about my going into business with Chuck.

I was a little anxious approaching my dad about financing Chuck and me in the peanut business, but my dad seemed mellower during his years as postmaster. He made a good salary, by Depression standards, and must have been relieved by not having the anxieties of trying to make money in a business.

He seemed more pleasant to me during my high school years, and I felt fairly comfortable talking with him. Some evenings I helped him sort the evening mail that was delivered by train to the post office. After I was 16, and had my driver's license, he let me use the family car for special occasions, like the junior prom and dates when I was a senior.

After supper, Dad and I went into the living room. I told him I had something I'd like to talk to him about. He sat in his black leather adjustable chair, tilting it back to make it more comfortable and lit up a White Owl, not a Becker brand; the last cigar maker departed from the now abandoned cigar factory several years before. As I sat on the davenport near him he seemed calm and in a good mood. He looked good for 63, although it seemed like his skin was wearing out, it looked so thin and red. He was always rather bald, but the gray hair he had left made him look distinguished.

"How's the job going with Plous?" he asked.

"That's what I wanted to talk to you about." I said, as I rubbed my sweaty palms together. "I've been working for Plous for almost a year now. He gave me a $25 raise to $75 a month. I guess he didn't want to lose me. A friend of his, Izzey Mednikow, who owns the largest grocery store in Green Bay, was kidding Plous saying I should come work for him."

Dad seemed pleased. "I guess you must be doing a pretty good job."

I explained to Dad that Hermy discussed with me how there was more money per dollar invested in peanut machines than in candy or cigarette machines. The cost of the machines was a lot less, $5 to $10 each, and the margin of profit was about 50 percent, double that of candy and cigarette machines.

"Do you think Plous is unhappy with the cigarette machines he bought from me?" Dad seemed concerned.

"He never said he was. Plous has only a few peanut machines around Green Bay, mostly in ice cream stores and busy gas stations that I service for him, and they seem to do very well. He also has machines he services on his way to Iron River, Michigan, when he goes home on weekends. He said they pay for his trip. He figures you can buy 10 or 15 peanut machines for the cost of one candy or cigarette machine. I've been thinking about going into the peanut vending business and I'd like to talk to you about it." I forced the words out of my mouth, trying to show as much confidence as possible.

"I see," he said, pulling the lever to straighten his chair, knocking the ash from his cigar into the free-standing metal ashtray next to his chair.

"I know at 18 I'm pretty young to go into business for myself, but I feel confident I could service the machines once they are on location. For years I went along with my brothers on the Saturday cigarette route and I've been servicing some of Plous' candy and cigarette machines as well as his peanut machines over the past year. The only thing I don't feel confident about is finding locations for the peanut machines, but there's a fellow who works for Plous, Chuck Buckman, that I'm considering as a partner. I feel he has the confidence and the sales experience to place the machines."

"How old is Chuck?" Dad asked. "Have you talked to him about this?"

"No, I haven't, I wanted to talk to you first. Chuck is 25. I feel he's honest, he has an outgoing personality and sales experience. He spent several summers traveling around the country with a friend selling bandage. He made enough money to put himself through a couple years at the University of Wisconsin." I knew Dad respected young people who worked their way through college.

"What's bandage?" Dad asked, re-lighting his cigar with a wooden match, puffing on it several times to get it going.

"I think we used to have a roll of it around the house. It's that bandage that sticks to itself, but isn't sticky to the touch."

"Yes, I remember, and he made enough money on that stuff to put himself through two years of college? That's amazing."

"He said he and his friend Al made $10 to $20 a day (which was a lot of money in the '30s). I figured he could put out my half of the machines south of Green Bay and Chuck could place his in Green Bay and north. Then we'd each service our own."

"How many machines would you need?"

I was excited that he was interested. "I don't know, maybe 200. We'd both sign notes for what we owed you and pay you interest." I said.

"It might be a good idea," he said, "but let me sleep on it."

"That's great. I'm glad you're interested." I got up, so excited I went over and shook hands with him. I felt like hugging him, but our family didn't show affection that way.

The next morning we discussed it again and he said it sounded like a good idea as long as Chuck was willing to put out the machines. I thanked him. I was anxious to get back to Green Bay to see if Chuck was interested.

The following Monday, when it was time to leave work, I

asked Chuck if he'd like to stop for a beer on the way home because I had something to talk to him about.

"What's up, Back-er? You seem excited about something."

"Sorry, it'll have to wait until we each have a cold one in front of us," I said as we left Hermy's office.

We met at the Ten-O-One and I ordered a couple mugs of Schlitz. Someone had plugged some nickels in the jukebox and it was playing a Wisconsin polka.

"So what gives, Back-er? What are you all bug-eyed about?" Chuck asked.

"How would you like to go into the peanut vending business with me?" I blurted. I couldn't wait to break the news.

Chuck put down his beer as his jaw dropped. "You crazy or something? What do you mean—go into the peanut business? I don't have any money."

"You don't need money. My dad will finance us," I said with a grin.

"You gotta be kidding." He still looked stunned.

"I'm not kidding. I already talked to my dad about it."

"Why the peanut business?"

"Hermy says there's more money in peanut machines than in candy or cigarette machines and they're a lot less expensive."

"Yes, I heard him say that, too. He must know what he's talking about, but you've got to be kidding, Back-er," he said again.

"No, I'm not. I talked to my dad over the weekend and he said he would be willing to back us in a partnership. There's a catch though. You've got to help me place my half of the machines."

"That shouldn't be a problem. Bartender, give us a couple more beers and a couple bags of chips; we're celebratin'."

"I've been thinking about this for a while. I always hoped to be in a business for myself some day. I grew up in the Depression like you; I hate being poor," I said.

"Wait until I tell Caroline about this—me in my own

business! She won't believe it." Chuck said. "I've got to get home to break the news."

Chuck thanked me and shook my hand so hard I thought it would come off. He was grinning like the cat that swallowed the elephant as we parted outside the tavern. I was pleased that Chuck was interested. With him putting out my machines there should be no problem in getting started.

That night even the boiled beef tasted good. Again, that evening, lying on my bed with the music down low, I thanked God, imagining what the future would be like in our new business. I thought of a name for the business, B & B Vending Service, for Becker and Buckman, of course. I thought about being my own boss and about all those peanut machines out there making money for us day and night, even while we slept. All we had to do was put the peanuts in and take out the money.

I thought about the freedom I'd have. I could start work and finish when I wanted to. I could take time off without asking anyone. I would be my own boss, and I'd make a lot of money.

Chuck and I made plans for quitting our jobs and getting started in business. Since Chuck had a wife to support, I said I'd quit first and look into purchasing the machines, then when the machines and merchandise arrived, Chuck could give his notice to Hermy. I planned to check out both the Northwestern and the Silver King machines. Both were advertised in the *Billboard* magazine Hermy subscribed to and both factories were in northern Illinois, about a four-hour drive. We figured that maybe within a month or so we'd be ready to start placing machines.

I gave Hermy two-weeks notice and told him I was going into the peanut vending business. He looked surprised, but was supportive. He wished me success in the business. He said he didn't plan to expand his peanut machine business. I didn't ask him why, I wasn't open to any thoughts that might derail our plans.

Chapter 3

My dad took a day off from work and we drove to Northwestern Corporation in Morris, Illinois, where Hermy purchased his machines. Ray Greiner, sales manager of the company, showed us around the plant and took us to lunch, which impressed me. I also felt an obligation to buy some machines, which I suppose was the idea.

Northwestern had the best quality machines on the market with porcelain bodies and coin mechanisms that eliminated most slugs. We bought 90 Model 39 Bell machines at $10 each. Every tenth play, when the bell in the machine rang, you received a free portion of peanuts. That sounded like a great idea to me. We also bought 10 Triselector Models at $30 each. They were beautiful console floor models that took both pennies and nickels, with a selection of three different kinds of nuts or candy-coated peanuts. I thought these would be great for the ice cream stores.

Chuck's brother Ward, a handsome brute about my age, who seemed to have a lot more self-confidence than I, went with me to the Silver King factory a week later. Silver Kings with a baked enamel finish and at $5 apiece looked like a bargain. We bought 200 of them. They had a less expensive finish and a simplified coin mechanism. Our total cost for the 300 machines was $2,200.

Dad helped me pick out a used 1936 Chrysler sedan for $300. What a thrill to own my first car. It was elegantly upholstered and I thought it was great that the front end bounced when I pumped the brakes. I didn't realize it probably needed shocks.

Chuck gave Hermy a couple weeks notice and told him he was going into the peanut vending business with me. He said Hermy was nice about it.

Chuck and I formed B & B Vending Service, a 50-50 partnership. We signed 6 percent promissory notes payable to my dad for what we owed him. He said as long as we paid the interest regularly we could pay off the notes as we made money in the business. I appreciated this; there was no pressure on us for monthly payments.

The machines arrived at our warehouse, which was the old cigar factory in Brillion. The peanuts I ordered from Peanut Specialty Company in Chicago showed up about the same time. I removed the glass domes and set the portion wheels so they would vend what I thought to be a generous portion for a penny. I filled some of the machines with Spanish peanuts, the small round ones with the red skins, and the other machines with Virginias, the large yellow ones made popular by Planters.

The machines were ready to go, but not my partner Chuck. This was the day we would start placing machines and I was depending on him to place them. Chuck didn't arrive until shortly after noon. Ward came along with him. Gene, who was about Chuck's age, and had serviced Dad's cigarette machines offered to come along, too, as he didn't have anything else to do that day. We wouldn't be short of manpower on this operation.

"Think fast!" Chuck yelled as he tossed one of our glass-domed Silver Kings from the top of the concrete cigar factory steps, to Ward who was down below about ten feet away.

"You crazy bastard," Ward laughed, catching it just in time. Then came another and another.

"Wait a minute," I shouted. "You guys will have broken glass and peanuts all over the sidewalk."

Chuck and Ward were always clowning around. That's what

I liked about them. They were fun to be with and didn't seem to have a care in the world. Chuck continued to toss the machines down the stairs and Ward caught all 15 of them and placed them safely in the back of Chuck's Chevy Carryall.

"Now we're in business, Back-er," Chuck said to me.

"Not until we get these dang things out making money for us," I said. I knew I wasn't going into the locations myself to place the machines.

"Let's go," Ward said as he hopped into the driver's seat. Chuck sat next to him with Gene and me in the seat behind.

There were three or four taverns, a couple grocery stores, a restaurant and a gas station in Brillion. The taverns would be the only possible places for our machines and they were small. I was thinking of ice cream stores and busy gas stations for our machines, like Hermy had. I suggested we drive to Chilton, 15 miles to the south, a town several times the size of Brillion. I had ulterior motives for not stopping in Brillion. I was afraid of rejection. If anyone turned us down in my hometown, I would have a hard time facing them later.

We drove through Potter and Hilbert, both smaller than Brillion, each with a couple of small taverns like the ones in Brillion.

The talk in the carryall was not about placing machines, it was stupid talk. No one suggested we stop anywhere in Potter or Hilbert, so we headed straight for Chilton. This town had some larger taverns and a drug store with a soda fountain, the closest thing to an ice cream store, but again, nobody said we should try to place some machines there. I was getting concerned. They were still goofing off and telling stories.

We had driven through New Holstein and were approaching Kiel. Nobody suggested we stop at any of the taverns in New Holstein. I felt I was with the Three Stooges, rather than on a business trip to put out machines. I couldn't push them, since I wasn't willing to go into any of the locations myself to try to place a machine.

Kiel was pretty much like the other small towns we had gone through, and still nobody suggested we stop. I was worried. I wondered whether they all might be as afraid as I was. Finally, I got up my courage as we were leaving Kiel and headed toward Elkhart Lake.

"We've got to stop in Elkhart Lake," I said, "otherwise we'll end up in Milwaukee and that's 100 miles from Brillion."

"I guess you're right, Back-er," said Chuck. "There aren't any towns between Elkhart and Milwaukee."

"It looks like taverns are our best bet," I said. "There were no ice cream shops or big gas stations in any of the towns we went through."

"Guys, this is it," Ward said stopping in front of the only tavern in Elkhart Lake. This town was smaller than all the others we went through and this tavern was about the smallest, too.

We all got out of the carryall and stood on the sidewalk in front of Joe's Place.

"Well, Wardie, you going in to talk to Joe about taking a machine?" Chuck said with a grin on his face.

"No, I don't think so, Charlie," Ward said, chuckling. Chuck and Ward called each other these endearing names when they were teasing each other.

"I know I'm not going in," I said seriously.

"You going in Gene?" Chuck asked, smiling at him.

Gene took a couple steps back, ran this hands through his hair and said, "Naw, guess I'll go get a haircut!"

That cracked us up and everyone burst out laughing. It broke the tension.

"Get a haircut!" Chuck said. "Well I'll be a son of a bitch."

I wondered what I got into with this bunch of clowns. Didn't they realize this was serious business? We had a lot of money invested. I was scared. I thought Chuck would get the machines out in a breeze, but now I figured Chuck was probably as frightened as I was, to try to place the machines.

"I guess that leaves me," Chuck said as he put the Silver King filled with Spanish peanuts under his arm and went in to see Joe.

It seemed like forever. I could feel the sweat running down my back. Why is it taking so long? I figured the guy didn't want it and Chuck was trying to talk him into it. Finally, Chuck came out smiling, no machine under his arm.

"You did it, you did it." I yelled, excitedly. I felt like jumping up and down and throwing my arms around Chuck.

"Well, Back-er, now we're in business," Chuck said, beaming.

"We're not really in business until we get all the machines out," I said.

"Did you have a hard time selling him?"

"He said he wanted two. I told him I could only spare one," Chuck said, slapping me on the back, kidding as usual.

"It must have been easy," Ward said. "You weren't in there more than two minutes."

"Boy, am I relieved," I said. "I was worried because we weren't stopping anywhere on the way down here."

"Well, let's go back and get those other taverns we passed on the way. I'm hot now," Chuck said, grinning.

On the way back to Brillion we stopped at what looked like the most prosperous taverns in each town. Chuck put out a total of nine machines that afternoon. Even though they wouldn't be hot locations like Hermy had, they'd be out making us some money.

I figured Chuck would be able to place 15 or 20 machines a day and he'd have my half of the 300 machines out in a few weeks.

It wasn't to be. I had a difficult time getting him to come to Brillion to go out with me.

Instead of having my 150 machines out in the first month, which I expected; I had only 40 of them out. I was getting more frustrated each day. Chuck said he had his own machines to get out to make a living for himself and Caroline. I couldn't blame him for than, I didn't have any living expenses, I got free room and board at home.

The day of reckoning came. I finally made up my mind that if I wanted my machines out I was going to have to place them myself. After going into prospective locations with Chuck I learned what to say. Chuck also taught me that if you make enough calls you'd put out some machines. Some days he landed about one out of two calls, other days he did worse, some days better. I told Chuck I would feel they were rejecting me if they didn't take the machine. He said it wasn't me they were rejecting, they just didn't want the machine for some reason.

Nothing in my past seemed as difficult as the thought of making that first sales call. I got up my courage and chose Manitowoc, a nice-sized city about 25 miles from Brillion, for my first try at salesmanship.

I pulled up at a tiny two-pump gas station on a side street thinking the smaller the business the more the owner needed the profit from the machine. I sat in the car, my hands shaking, trying to overcome my fright. I mouthed the words I was going to say. I had them memorized. Finally, taking a deep breath, putting the machine under my arm, I said a little prayer and went in.

The 8 x 10-foot shop I entered had a counter with a cash register on it. Tires were piled in one corner and on the shelves behind the register were cans of oil, boxes of spark plugs, and a green card of perfumed car deodorizers. To the right was a door to a one-stall garage where a guy, I presume the owner, was lying face up on a dolly under a car.

"Good morning," I called out as cheerfully as I could. He poked out his head, smudged with grease, from under the car as the dolly's wheels scraped on the concrete floor.

"What can I do for you?" he asked.

"I'd-like-to-leave-this-ah-peanut-machine-on-your-counter-at-no-cost-to-you-on-a-commission-basis-and-I'll-come-back-regularly-to-clean-and-fill-it-and-pay-you-20-percent-of-the-money-it-takes-in." The words sputtered out of my mouth like a blast from a machine gun.

I wiped a smudge off the clear-glass dome with my sleeve and held the machine toward him. It looked great, a brand-new red Silver King with shiny fresh redskin peanuts begging to be purchased.

"I don't think it would do much business," he said still lying on his back. "I'm the only one here. I don't get many gas customers. I do mostly repair work."

It made sense that this would be a lousy spot for a machine. I remember Hermy saying most of the peanuts sold in a gas station were bought by the employees who pumped the gas. But I wanted my first presentation to be a success, so I pressed on.

"If you don't mind, I'd like to leave it for a few weeks and see how it does."

"It's up to you," he replied, as he rolled himself back under the car. "It's no skin off my nose."

I set the machine on the counter next to the cash register and said, loud enough for him to hear under the car, "Thanks a lot, see you in a few weeks."

I got out of there as quickly as I could. I didn't want to give him a chance to change his mind. I knew it would be more like a month before I'd be back, but I told him a few weeks because I didn't want him to think the peanuts would get stale.

"I did it! I did it!" I shouted to myself when I got outside. It was a lousy location, but he didn't say "no!"

What a feeling of accomplishment I had! If I could do it in one place, I could do it in others. I stopped next at a tavern. I was not quite as nervous this time. The owner let me leave the machine. I was on a roll! The next call was another tavern, and after I gave my sales pitch the owner said he didn't want it on his bar. Since there was no other place for it, I thanked him and left. I tried to remember what Chuck said, the guy wasn't rejecting me. The next place was a gas station and he took it. I lived through a rejection and I was able to keep going. I continued to make calls throughout the day and was able to make placements in almost half the places I stopped. I placed ten machines on my first day as a salesman. I was proud of myself.

I quit early, worn out from anxiety and excitement. I was ecstatic. Even though I didn't enjoy making the sales calls, the satisfaction I got from realizing that I could place the rest of my machines myself and no longer had to depend on Chuck took a load off my mind. I turned the car radio on full blast, tuned it to my favorite station and boisterously sang with Glen Miller's orchestra all the way back to Brillion.

It was a month since Chuck placed our first machines and according to how often Hermy serviced his regular locations it was time to service mine. I was anxious about what the sales would be.

I took the backseat out of the Chrysler to make room for the two 30-pound boxes of peanuts, one Spanish and one Virginias, and headed for Joe's place in Elkhart Lake. The smell of peanuts in the back of the car made me feel I was in a good business—making fresh peanuts available to people for only a penny.

"Hi," I greeted the man behind the bar. "Are you Joe?"

"That's me," he said.

"I'm Lyle Becker. I'm here to service your peanut machine," I said with a smile.

Joe was washing beer glasses and polishing them with a towel. A couple guys were at the bar drinking beer.

My heart sank. The machine was down only about a quarter of the way. I had hoped it would be nearly empty.

I poured the pennies from the machine on to the end of the bar and counted them as I slid them into my hand. Sixty-eight cents, a little over two cents a day in sales. How devastating. Since most of the machines were in taverns I wouldn't have much of a business if they were all as bad as this.

"The machine took in 70 cents. Your commission is 20 percent. Here's 15 cents," I told Joe as I handed him the pennies. I thought 70 cents sounded better than 68, and 15 cents commission better than 14. I was afraid Joe might be displeased with the sales and tell me to take the machine out. But he didn't, thank God!

Joe looked at the few pennies in his hand and said, "Okay, thanks." He was a nice guy.

"I put in a different kind of peanuts. They're nice and fresh. See you in a few weeks," I said.

"Okay, take it easy," Joe said as I walked out the door.

When I got out to the car, I had a big decision to make. I started out with 60 pounds of fresh peanuts. I now had about 3 pounds that had been in Joe's machine for a month. I tasted them. They still tasted pretty good but, not as good as the fresh ones. Since I took home 53 cents, and the 3 pounds of peanuts I took back cost me about 36 cents, I would make only 17 cents profit if I threw away the old peanuts, a pittance for my time and car expense. I decided I had to mix the old peanuts with fresh ones and use the mix for the next machine I serviced. Mixing stale peanuts with fresh ones probably would reduce sales, but I felt I had no other choice. Hermy said to always fill the machines to the top, because a full machine will sell better than a half-empty one, as the people will think the peanuts are fresher.

I was anxious to get to the other locations where Chuck placed machines that first day, in hopes they sold better. No such luck. One took in almost a dollar, another about 50 cents. The nine machines I serviced that day averaged about 75 cents a month per machine, not nearly as much as Hermy was taking in from his gas stations and a far cry from the $3 a week he took in at his ice cream stores.

With the old adage that one rotten apple spoils the barrel, I didn't have too much hope for the quality of the peanuts I would be vending.

When I got back that day I stopped at Rudy's Lunch in Brillion for a bowl of chili. Rudy, about ten years older than me, opened his own roadside stand selling 5-cent hamburgers and plate lunches two years before I started in business. Rudy became a good friend. I helped him peel potatoes once in awhile when he was shorthanded. I told Rudy about my problem of having to sell stale peanuts in my new business.

Don't worry," Rudy said. "About a third of the people who come in here appreciate my home cooking, the others just eat to fill themselves up. With a beer to wash down the stale peanuts, they won't know the difference anyway," he said with a laugh. I felt a little better.

I hated to go out to place the rest of my machines. I still had more than half of them in the warehouse and they weren't making me any money there. So hate it or not, I forced myself to put them out.

I was more successful in the larger cities of Manitowoc, Appleton, Oshkosh, Fond du Lac and Sheboygan, all in the range of 20,000 to 40,000 people; and within 40 miles of Brillion. I was able to get some larger taverns and gas stations and a few ice cream stores, but even the best of them sold only about $3 a month compared to $3 a week in Hermy's ice cream locations. With somewhat better locations I was able to raise my sales to about a $1 a month per machine.

I was making about $75 a month profit, the same as the salary I was getting from Hermy, however, out of that I had to pay my car expense and the interest on the note to my dad. I was fortunate to have free room and board.

Chapter 4

I had been in business only four months when the Japanese attached Pearl Harbor. Congress declared war on Germany, Italy, and Japan the day after the attack.

It looked like it would be a long war and I knew I would have to go, eventually.

I registered for the draft. A lottery was held to determine the order in which the men would be drafted. I received a relatively high number, so I would not be the first called. My friends, Carl and Jim, were fascinated with flying and were considering enlisting in the air force. Not I. I was willing to be drafted and I would serve, but I wanted to come back alive. I felt the marines and the infantry were the most dangerous places to be in the service. I considered joining the navy, but I couldn't swim and the thought of being dumped into the sea in the event my ship was sunk frightened me. I decided I would wait to be drafted and take my chances; meanwhile I prayed I would not be drafted into the infantry.

A month after Pearl Harbor, tragedy struck our family. My brother Bernard was declared missing in action in the Philippines. He joined the air force as an aerial photographer, because he couldn't find a job after graduating from college with a geology major. I was heartbroken. Even though he was six years older than me, we were close and had lots of good times together. My mother was devastated. Ill with a kidney ailment and worried about whether Bernard was dead or alive, she became bedridden.

Since I was busy with the peanut business only two to three days a week, and not realizing much profit from it, I was looking for opportunities to make extra money. My brother Gene asked me if I wanted to service his cigarette machines, which I agreed to do. He had purchased the machines south of Brillion that Dad had sold to Hermy Plous. Because of the distance and the advent of gas rationing, Hermy was no longer able to service them. After attending trade school to become a machinist, Gene took a job with the Ariens Company in Brillion, which now turned to defense work.

Then Chuck and Ward came up with an idea where I could also make some extra money. They were selling Green Bay Packer football tickets—not tickets to the games, but tickets with game scores on them, where people could win money on the game if they picked tickets with certain scores. You could win $100 if you opened the sealed ticket with the correct final score of the following Sunday's game and $25 if you opened a ticket with the correct score for one of the quarters. The tickets sold for 25 cents apiece. Each week I left a pack of tickets with the taverns and bowling alleys where Gene had his cigarette machines, as well as in some of my better peanut locations. I gave them a 25 percent commission on the tickets they sold. After I was in the ticket business for a couple of weeks, Chuck and Ward told me they had a gimmick to ensure a greater profit for us. They had the ticket manufacturer in Chicago remove the tickets most likely to win—those with three's and seven's—the points scored for a field goal and a touchdown, and multiples of those numbers. Let's say the game ended in a score of 21 to 7 in favor of the Packers. If someone had purchased that ticket, they could turn it in for $100, however, that ticket had been eliminated by the manufacturer and it wouldn't be there as a winner.

I knew it was wrong to sell these tickets. It reduced the odds tremendously for those who hoped to win. I justified it in my mind that I didn't remove the tickets, nor was it my idea to remove them. I also had this feeling that it was difficult to make it in business and maybe one had to be a little dishonest to succeed. I rationalized that everybody does it. Car dealers turn back the mileage on used cars so customers feel they are getting a better car for the money. People cheat on their income tax by not reporting money received in cash. I also had the feeling that you couldn't trust most salesmen; they would lie about their products to make a sale. It was a tough world out there.

I didn't like mixing the stale peanuts with the fresh ones. Mixing them together month after month meant that some of the peanuts that were continually mixed in were probably a year old. I'm sure it hurt business and I know I wasn't building customer confidence. I stuck to the idea Hermy implanted in my mind that people will buy more peanuts out of a full machine, because they will think they are fresh. I just kept plodding along; I wasn't an innovator. Business seemed to be getting worse.

Gas rationing and a 35 m.p.h. speed limit, to save gas and wear on the tires, was the law during the war years. I got some extra gas because I used my car in my business, but I still had to stay out overnight in dingy hotels. I didn't have the money for a nice hotel room and didn't have the gas to make the 60-80 mile round trip to drive home at night and then drive back to the same city to continue my route the next day.

Then there was the roach problem. It seemed that roaches liked my peanuts more than people did. I opened a machine in a tavern in Sheboygan and an army of roaches ran out of the money tray. They were big ones. I don't think they ever got in with the peanuts, as I didn't get any complaints from the owner. The next time I saw Chuck I asked him if he had a roach problem, and if so, what he did about it.

"Back-er, I just fill those machines with the giant redskin peanuts, then the people can't tell the roaches from the peanuts."

Chuck, always the joker.

The low point of the business came at the Corner Tavern in Fond du Lac. I opened the machine, dumped the pennies into my hand, blew out the salt and peanut husks, and counted them—13 cents for one month's sales. It was my last stop of the day. I checked into my usual shabby room at the Retlaw Hotel with the toilet and bath down the hall. Thoroughly depressed, I sat back in the worn overstuffed chair looking at the stained carpeting and faded drapes and wondered how I got into this mess.

I was so anxious to be in business for myself that I never thought through Hermy's statement about there being more money in peanut machines than in his other machines. Undoubtedly what he meant was that in good locations this was true. He probably had less than 30 machines. That's probably all the good locations he could find. I don't know of one tavern location he had. Almost all of mine were in taverns. Most of his machines probably emptied every month and his best locations every week. For the small investment in the machines and the high profit margin his percentage of profit on his investment was undoubtedly better. But dollar volume was small and good locations were hard to find. That's probably why he didn't invest in more peanut machines.

I sat in that ugly room in complete despair, drinking the Coke I brought with me to the room. Chuck and I still owed my dad all the money he loaned us. He was right in questioning why Plous wasn't adding more peanut machines if it was such a good business. We had been stupid for not buying a couple dozen machines, placing them and servicing them on Saturdays. We would have learned in a couple of months that there weren't enough good locations around to support a full-time business.

I sat there looking out the window as the sun was setting. The sunset was unusually beautiful with fluffy pink clouds in interesting patterns against the baby-blue sky. It lifted my spirits a little and I started to think of what else I learned from my year in the business that would help me in a new business when I returned from the army. One thing was sure, I wouldn't continue in the peanut business. The vending business still fascinated me, but no more stale peanuts or other perishable products for me.

While I was sitting there sipping my Coke with the afterglow painting the entire western sky in pastel colors, I thought about a fascinating gumball machine I saw in one of my locations, a gas station in Appleton near a grade school. Mixed in with the multicolored balls of candy-coated gum were some yellow balls with red stripes on them. A sign on the machine stated that you could exchange a striped ball with the merchant for a nickel candy bar. It reminded me of the penny punchboards at Barnard's Drug Store where a lucky punch would entitle you to one or more candy bars. I surmised that all kids liked to try their luck, to win a prize of some kind. I know my sister Anita and I, and other kids at Barnard's, were wild about that punchboard.

I was envious of the guy who had that machine because not only was his machine almost empty, while mine was still half full, but his machine must have taken in at least four times as much as mine. It was a Silver King, like mine, only with a portion wheel that delivered one gumball at a time instead of a portion of peanuts. One gumball took up only about half the volume in the machine as a portion of peanuts, therefore I figured this machine not only sold twice as well, but an empty machine brought in at least twice as much money as mine. I was jealous of this guy's apparent success when my business was a failure. But then I was thankful I saw this competitor's machine; I wouldn't have seen it if I wasn't out servicing my peanut machines. These winner ball machines could be a possible business for me when I returned from service, and candy-coated gumballs were not perishable, they would last for months and they wouldn't smear the glass domes like the greasy peanuts did.

As the afterglow of the sunset was fading I started to think of other machines for my new vending business after the war. I thought about the claw machine at the Firemen's picnic in Brillion when I was a kid and wheedled nickels from my mother so I could try to win some of the prizes in the machine. The machine, about 2-foot square by 5-foot high was filled with toys and novelty items like miniature metal cars, pocketknives, whistles, and what looked like an expensive pocket watch. I maneuvered the claw, that opened and closed like an overhead crane, with the two cranks, one to move it vertically and one horizontally. I wanted that pocket watch so badly. It was near the window, off to the side, but I think it was a come-on because there was no way, as many times as I or other kids tried, that we could get that claw even near that watch.

The other machine that fascinated me, as a kid, I saw when I went with my brothers on the Saturday cigarette route. It was in a restaurant where we always stopped to eat. It was filled with brown candy-coated peanuts called Boston Beans. Mixed in, next to the inside of the glass, were several miniature pocketknives. Those little pocketknives fascinated me and I begged pennies from my brother every time we stopped there. Finally, I got a knife. It was very well made; the blade opened and closed just like a big pocketknife, which my dad would never let me carry, even if I owned one. I prized that knife and carried it in my pocket for months.

The sunset was over, my Coke was long gone, but my spirits were high. Of the three vending machines I was considering for my future business I figured the crane machine would be too expensive, candy-coated peanuts were perishable and more expensive than salted peanuts, so it looked like the winner ball machines would be the best bet.

I could buy parts to convert my 100 Silver King machines to gumball machines and, of course, I would have to find new locations for them, possibly grocery stores where kids went with their mothers. My greatest benefit from my failure in the peanut business is that I learned how to locate my own machines. Even though I didn't like to do it, I proved to myself that I could, and did it.

There wasn't much I could do about changing to winner ball machines before I left for service, as sugar rationing had started and gumballs, being nonessential to the war effort, would be hard to get. I decided I would try to get enough gum to test several machines before I left for service. Then I would know how well they would sell and could estimate how much profit I'd make in the business when I returned—another lesson I learned from my failed peanut machine venture.

Over the next couple of months I was able to get some gumballs to test the winner-ball concept. I was pleased to find that gumballs cost only a little more per pound than peanuts and a machine full of gumballs did bring back $6 compared to $3 for peanuts.

I bought conversion parts from the Silver King Company and changed a dozen of my peanut machines to gum machines. I filled them with gumballs and took 25 striped balls and strategically placed them around the gum next to the glass and put a sticker on the machines about exchanging them for candy bars. I placed them in Mom and Pop neighborhood grocery stores figuring that's where kids would go to buy their candy and gum.

I was anxious to see how well they sold, so I checked on the machines in two weeks. Most of them were about half empty, some more than that, and the one near a grade school was almost empty. Over the next few months, until I could no longer get gum, these machines averaged $5 per month, per machine; I was elated. My profit margin was about 50 percent, like the peanut machines. Gumballs cost less than a portion of peanuts and that saving paid for the free candy bars the kids won.

How I wished I could have changed all my peanut machines to winner balls immediately and start making big money, but my new business would have to wait. There was a war on. But someday I would be rich!

Chapter 5

One Sunday evening in August, with nothing going on in Brillion, as usual, I decided to drive the 20 miles to Appleton to go to a dance at Waverly Beach. Jim and Carl weren't interested, so I went alone. I was surprised to see Dolores Jacobs there, the only person at the dance I knew. I met Dolores the previous month at the Brillion Fourth of July picnic and dance. My friend Jim had taken her to the dance. Jim introduced her to me and we had a couple of enjoyable dances together. Nice looking with an easy laugh, I was fascinated with her long brown hair that curled inward, about six inches below her shoulders. Partial to brunettes, I was interested in dating her, but didn't because Jim was going with her.

Dolores seemed happy to see me again. She introduced me to her friend Lucy. A local band played a pretty good rendition of Big Band music. I had a nice time dancing with each of them, especially Dolores. They didn't know anyone else at the dance either, and had come on the bus, so I offered them a ride home to Appleton at the end of the evening.

Lucy lived down the street from Dolores. I dropped her off first, as I was interested in seeing Dolores again and wanted to talk with her. We talked for a while in the car, in front of her home.

"I was really happy to see you at Waverly tonight," Dolores said as she sat there smiling at me in the moonlight. Music was playing softly on the car radio.

"And I was pleased to see you; it was fun dancing with you. I wanted to give you a call after meeting you at the Fourth of July picnic, but since you were going with Jim, and he's my friend, I didn't want to interfere."

"I've only gone out with Jim a couple of times and he hasn't asked me out since the dance at Brillion. I was so pleased you took Lucy home first. I was sure you were going to drop me off first," she said, looking me in the eye with a smile.

"Never a doubt in my mind," I said, smiling. "I remember seeing you and Lucy at the Catholic Youth Organization tennis meet in Green Bay this summer. You were always laughing. You looked like fun; I wondered who you were then."

"The first time I saw you was at the C.Y.O. basketball tournament in De Pere. You were selling tickets at the door and doing a trick with pennies. There were a lot of kids around you. You'd bend your arm back, put a stack of pennies on it and then try to catch them," she said.

"That's my claim to fame," I said. "I got to where I could catch a stack of 20 pennies and not drop one—sometimes," I said, laughing.

"Next month is the C.Y.O. semiformal here in Appleton at the Riverview Country Club."

"Yes, I know."

"I'm on the ticket committee. Would you like to buy a ticket?" She seemed a little embarrassed to ask me.

"I'll buy one if you'll go with me," I said.

"I'd love to." She answered so fast I could tell it was part of her plan, but I didn't want to embarrass her anymore to let on that I knew.

Two weeks later I picked her up at nine o'clock. The white gardenia corsage I gave her looked nice on her long, bright-flowered dress. She looked beautiful in her full-length black cloak with a rabbit-fur collar.

It was a festive occasion with colorful balloons and streamers decorating the hall and Tom Temple's band playing our favorite Big Band tunes. We exchanged partners with a few couples we knew, but mostly danced the night away together. We especially enjoyed the waltzes in which we twirled until we were both dizzy. We stayed until the end.

I took her for a snack to the Diana, where we danced to a few numbers on the jukebox, then took her home. I did some pretty heavy necking with other girls I dated, but I didn't want to goof up this relationship by being too forward with Dolores. She was quality; I liked her a lot.

We talked awhile in the car in front of her house. She had been sitting close to me and I put my arm around her. She snuggled up. *That Old Black Magic* was playing softly on the radio.

"Tell me more about yourself," I said. "I hardly know you. When did you graduate from high school?"

"In 1938, I spent the last two years of high school at a boarding school, Saint Mary's Springs Academy in Fond du Lac."

"How come you went there?" I asked.

"I was going to Appleton High School, but I wasn't able to get the secretarial courses I needed there. I was expected to take subjects in high school that would qualify me for a job when I graduated. I knew Saint Mary's Springs Academy offered these courses because my sister Leona had graduated from there, and my aunt, Sister Miriam, was a math and German teacher at the school. I wanted very badly to finish high school at the Academy. I wrote the principal, Mother Angeline, and pleaded with her to find a way that I could finish high school there. I wanted a good education and I knew I could get it there. I told her I would be glad to work for my room and board if that would help. I was so happy when she said I could come. It was an all-girls' school. I scrubbed toilets, pots and pans, cleaned the library, and worked in the laundry. I received a good education, Sister Miriam made sure of that. Other kids had a choice of whether to do the extra credit work; with Sister Miriam it was part of my assignment. But I loved it and had a wonderful two years. I wanted to go to Rosary College in Chicago to study drama and journalism, but it was just a dream, we didn't have the money," she continued.

"I'm sorry you weren't able to go to college, I wasn't either," I said.

"My father owned a grocery store next to our home. He had a big heart and he fed everyone in the neighborhood, but most people charged their groceries and many didn't pay their bills. My dad went bankrupt. My sister Leona took over running the house and paying the mortgage after she graduated from high school. She had a job in Madison with the company that had the mortgage on our home and she took the responsibility to make the payments so we wouldn't lose the house. My brothers and I were expected to find jobs and pay half of what we earned to help pay the expenses at home."

"Sounds like you had a tougher time during the Depression than I did."

"About the only jobs for a girl out of high school were to clerk in a store or do secretarial work, so I took commercial courses, and they were good ones. I learned shorthand and got my typing skills up to 60 words a minute. My first full-time job was with Ray LeVee, an architect, who had just been commissioned to draw the plans for a new Outagamie County courthouse. I had to transcribe and type all the specifications for his jobs. I earned $10 a week as his secretary. The government took 10 cents for social security, so I got $9.90. Of that I paid $5 to Leona to help run the house."

"Is that where you work now?" I asked.

"No. I'm a clerk at the Appleton draft board."

"Too bad you don't work at the Chilton draft board; maybe you could lose my records or something," I said with a laugh.

"I wish I could do that for you," she said, smiling.

"You wanted to study drama in college?" I asked.

"I love movies and I love to act. Bette Davis is my favorite. Sometimes I'd stay all day when she was in a movie and see it over, and over, again. Then I'd memorize her lines in a movie, and go home and act them out in front of a mirror. When I was in grade school, I went to the radio station on Saturday mornings and read poetry on the air. I've so much wanted to be an actress. I acted in our church plays and the C.Y.O. plays, but there's no way I can see that I can follow an acting career, as much as I'd love to."

"Now tell me about you," she said. "When did you graduate?"

"In 1940. I wanted to go to college too, but my dad sold his cigarette vending business about the time I graduated and he suggested I work in Green Bay for the fellow who bought his machines. I spent a year working for him, then Chuck, another fellow who worked there, and I went into partnership in the peanut vending business. So, I'm a peanut vendor," I said, with a chuckle. "Can't you smell the stale peanuts in the car? Some of them get under the front seat and I can't get them out."

"It does smell like peanuts. How old were you when you started in business?" she asked.

"Eighteen. My dad financed us. I took in a partner because I was too scared to solicit the locations for the machines myself. I depended on Chuck, but then he had to get his own machines out, so I finally had to force myself to learn how to put them out."

"Wow, that's pretty young to go into your own business. Where do you have your machines?"

"In Manitowoc, Sheboygan, and here in Appleton, and the cities around Lake Winnebago. They're mostly in taverns and they aren't doing too well. But I just got an idea for a gum machine business. Because of the sugar shortage I'll have to wait until I get back from the service before I can change over my machines and start it, though. Say, it's getting late and I don't want to get you in trouble with your parents on our first date. Maybe I should see you to your door."

She agreed, so I got out of the car, went around and opened her door and we went up to the house. She opened the door, held it, inviting me in.

"I really had a nice time," she said, facing me, lifting her head, smiling. "Thanks."

"Thank you for selling me that ticket. It was fun," I said, returning her smile. "How about getting together next Thursday for a movie?"

"I'd like that."

I put my arms around her. She looked up at me. I bent over and kissed her lightly. Her lips moved in response to mine. It was a kiss of deep communication between us, a most precious kiss I shall never forget. I think I was in love.

"That was nice," I said. "Thanks for a wonderful evening."

She was beaming. I opened the door to leave, told her I'd pick her up at seven on Thursday.

"See you Thursday," she said.

As I was driving back to Brillion, I thought about how lucky I was to have found her. I felt more at ease with her than with other girls I had taken out. She kept the conversation going. There weren't those embarrassing periods of silence.

I then started comparing Dolores with other girls I had dated. I liked Eleanor, the cute cheerleader from Denmark High School, but she was so reserved. I don't think I ever kissed her. Then there was the other Dolores, another cheerleader, this one from Hortonville, that I met at a basketball tournament. I met most of these girls because I was a cheerleader—one of the few guys in our conference. I was a little embarrassed about that. All the Brillion girls seemed to be chasing the basketball players, so I looked to girls in other towns. Being a cheerleader and getting to these out-of-town games had its benefits.

The Dolores from Hortonville, a brunette beauty, liked to

neck and so did I, so that's pretty much how we spent our time on occasional dates over the previous two years. I didn't feel good about it, lots of deep kissing and body contact that brought about sexual pleasure. I felt guilty, like I had to go to confession after our dates. I was a passionate guy and I knew marriage was the only moral way I could satisfy this passion, but future marriage was out of the question with her; she wasn't Catholic. When I heard the verbal beating my dad gave my brother Harold when he wanted to marry Sylvia, a Protestant, I decided I would look for a Catholic girl to marry. I would also be looking for a girl I could respect. Even though I was as much to blame as the girls I dated for these heavy necking parties, I guess I blamed them for the encouragement they gave me. Intercourse before marriage was out of the question for me, due to my strict Catholic upbringing, and these necking parties had been too close for comfort.

I was glad my new Dolores was Catholic, I respected her and I wanted to keep it that way. I don't think she would want me to do anything on a date I would feel guilty about. This was a girl worth pursuing. It had been a good evening.

We had fun the following Thursday at the movie. We continued dating twice a week, Thursday and Sunday nights. My sister Anita kidded me, saying I had to switch Doloreses to save gas, because of gas rationing. Appleton was several miles closer than Hortonville.

Besides movies, we'd go bowling or have the Thursday night sauerbraten special plate at the Moose Hall. We'd dance to our favorite Big Band tunes and waltzes on the jukebox at the West End Tavern or, at the edge of town, at the Flagstone. The Flagstone was our favorite necking place, sometimes never getting inside to dance. But I never went home with the guilt feelings from dates with this Dolores as I did with other girls I had dated.

Dolores had a class ring with her school insignia on it. I didn't have a class ring, couldn't afford it; so after going with her for a while, I bought a signet ring with the idea of asking her to exchange rings with me. One evening after attending a piano concert together at Lawrence College I suggested we exchange rings to seal our commitment to go steady with each other. We had been going together for seven months. It was difficult for her to give up her ring as she treasured it. The filigree insignia was quite delicate and she was concerned it would get damaged if I wore it all the time, but she agreed. It was a real act of love, and I loved her more for it.

It was about a year since the United States entered the war and my brother Bernard was declared missing in action. We had heard nothing further. My mother was still confined to her bed, her health failing, worrying whether Bernard was alive or dead. The Calumet County draft board held up drafting any more of her sons as she was not expected to live much longer. She died that December. She was only 62. The doctor said it was kidney failure. I think her body just wore out, raising 11 children, nursing my father back to health after his T.B., and worrying for the past year about Bernard. She was a saint. I was sorry Dolores didn't get to know her better, but I was happy that she did meet and talk with her in our downstairs bedroom, shortly before she died. I was 19. I felt badly about her death, but it was a blessing after her confinement to her bed for more than a year. I knew I would miss her, but living in Green Bay after I got out of high school made it a little easier, since I had a chance to live by myself for a while before she was gone. She was a wonderful lady, always so kind and gentle. Dolores attended her funeral. I didn't realize until then how much I needed Dolores to lean on.

Four months after my mother died, I received my draft notice for the army. I had arranged with my sister, Anita, that she would service my machines while I was gone and she could keep the profit the machines earned. If for some reason she couldn't take care of the machines at a later date, she could bring them back to Brillion and store them in the old cigar factory. So that was taken care of. The day before I was inducted into the army was April 25, Easter Sunday, and my 20th birthday. Anita had a combination Easter and birthday party. Dolores was there, of course; it would be the last day we would see each other for a while. She gave me a Parker fountain pen and a clever foldout birthday card which she signed "Love, Dolores". I set it up on the library table with the other cards I had received.

"Lyle, what's this old birthday card doing here?" Anita pointed to the card I received from Dolores.

"This is the card Dolores gave me with her gift, why do you ask?" I said as I picked up the card and looked at it again.

"Oh, my gosh," Anita said laughing. "Do you realize this is exactly the same card that the Dolores from Hortonville sent you last year?"

What a coincidence. She, of course, had also signed it "Dolores". The cards were identical. Dolores was a little embarrassed, but we all had a good laugh over it.

Later in the afternoon, after the party, Dolores and I went to the Brillion quarry. We sat on the grass on the hill above the pond. We had the area to ourselves; there were no bathers, it was too cool. The following day I would be leaving for the army. We knew it might be months before we would see each other again, if and when I got a furlough.

"I sure hate to see you leave. I'm going to miss you terribly," she said, turning toward me.

"I'm just happy we found each other when we did. It would be a lonely life in the army without your letters and you to think about. Do you realize it's only eight months since our first date? It seems like I've known you forever," I said as I snuggled up to her.

"And what a wonderful first date it was," she said.

"I'm sure glad you asked me to buy that ticket, best money I ever spent," I said with a chuckle, kissing her on the cheek.

"How I remember that night. I was involved in planning the dance and was on the ticket committee. It was two weeks before the dance and I didn't even have a date. I hoped you would ask me, and you did," she said with love in her eyes.

"When you asked me to buy the ticket I figured you might be available. I was pleased you were. I already had a date with Lois, a friend from high school. I broke the date using the excuse that I needed to bring a Catholic girl even though that wasn't true. I really wanted to go with you."

"I've been praying for years that I'd find the right man in my life. I always thought I'd meet him on the church steps; I didn't know it would be through the C.Y.O.," she said, kissing me on the cheek.

"I'm glad you found me," I said as I drew her closer. "I'm going to miss you terribly."

"I want you to come back to me. I've been praying that they won't put you into the infantry. I was so excited a few weeks ago when John Lappen said he could get you an appointment to West Point, if you wanted it. I was disappointed when you said you weren't interested."

"As I said, I have no desire to make the army a career and I don't want to take the place of someone who does. I just want to get back to you when this war is over and start my gumball machine business. Who is this John Lappen? He must be a pretty important guy to be able to get someone into West Point."

"He's an old family friend. He likes me. He even came to my high school graduation. He was county sheriff and he and my dad worked together, since my dad is a county supervisor. Now he's a state senator and a member of the draft board."

"I've been praying too that I don't get into the infantry. It's very dangerous and I can't imagine myself living outdoors in the cold, sleeping in a foxhole. I never was a Boy Scout or even a camper. The only gun I ever shot was a BB gun."

"We'll just have to pray you into some other part of the army, where you'll be safe and be sure to come back to me," she said with tears in her eyes. "I love you so much."

She put her arms around me and we laid back on the grass. I held her tightly, my body pressing against hers. We lay there a long time kissing passionately, I respected Dolores and wanted her to respect me. Sexual intercourse never entered my mind and I'm sure not her's. We both believed it to be a serious sin outside of marriage.

When I took Dolores back to Appleton that evening we sat in the car in front of her home for hours talking about our future together, hugging and kissing each other's tears away.

"It's getting late and you have to catch the bus to Fort Sheridan in the morning. I better go in," she said.

We went into the house and stood inside the door where we had experienced our first kiss.

"I'll write you every day," she promised, smiling, tears running down her cheeks.

"I will too," I said, wiping away her tears with my kisses. "I'll miss you."

"I'll miss you, too. I'll pray for you every day until this war is over and you come back safely to me," she said, tears streaming down her face. "Take care of yourself," she said as she stood on the porch waving good-bye.

Chapter 6

The next morning I arrived in Fort Sheridan, Illinois, and was inducted into the army. I received a battery of tests and a series of personal interviews to determine my schooling, skills, aptitude, and intelligence.

Dolores's and my prayers were answered. The following day I was assigned to the air force ground force. There couldn't be a safer place in the army.

We boarded a troop train for an air force training camp in Greensboro, North Carolina. Basic training consisted of calisthenics, learning to march in step while singing air force songs, and hiking, to get our flabby bodies in shape. We got none of the hand-to-hand combat training or crawling on the ground with live ammunition whizzing over our heads that we heard the infantry recruits were getting. We weren't even issued a gun.

After completing eight weeks of basic training, my name appeared on the bulletin board, along with several others, stating that I was eligible to apply for the Army Specialized Training Program. Under the A.S.T.P. I could go to college at government expense while receiving a private's pay, which had just been increased from $21 to $50 a month. I was elated. Disappointed that I couldn't go to college when I got out of high school, now I would have a chance to do so in the army. I signed up and found I would be taking a basic engineering course. We understood the government was concerned about a shortage of engineers after the war, as very few men would be going to college during the war.

I was accepted into the program and spent the next eight months at North Carolina State College in Raleigh. Our courses in English, math, physics, and chemistry were accelerated, covering a full semester's work in 12 weeks. It was a tough schedule, but I loved it.

We lived in dorms, two to a room and ate in the college cafeteria. The only resemblance to army life was our army uniform. I found the courses relatively easy and got good grades. I made some good friends and we had lively philosophical discussions in our rooms in the evenings. We played touch football in the quadrangle and swam in the college pool. On weekends we went into Raleigh for movies and U.S.O. dances.

At the end of each 12-week term we received a 7-day furlough which gave me five days at home, due to travel time. To make the most of my time, Dolores would take the train to Chicago from Appleton, so we would have an extra evening together. On my first furlough we splurged for dinner and dancing at the Stevens Hotel, dancing to the Big Band orchestra and laughing ourselves silly at the zany piano antics of Victor Borga. Then we took the midnight train to Appleton.

On my second furlough I asked Dolores to marry me. It wasn't a very romantic setting. Dolores drove with me to Green Bay one evening to pick up cigarettes for my brother Gene's vending machines. I popped the question while we were sitting in the car waiting for the fellow to come open the warehouse. She was thrilled and said yes. We had written each other daily since I entered the army and our love for each other grew.

Then the bottom dropped out of our lives. When we were almost finished with the third 12-week session, all the A.S.T. programs across the country were abruptly closed and most of the fellows, including me, were thrown into the infantry! My greatest fear, and that of Dolores, came to pass. I felt like I carried a rock in my stomach and it stayed there continually. I felt that God had been watching over me until now. Why had He abandoned me!

Italy had been defeated by the Allies and they were preparing for the invasion of Europe. This would require huge infantry forces. I was now in a very dangerous spot—a private in E Company of the 346th Regiment of the 87th Infantry Division in Fort Jackson, South Carolina—a foot soldier in the coming battle to take back Europe yard-by-yard from the German army.

Training was a lot tougher in the infantry. I was issued an M-1 rifle, learned how to take it apart, clean it and assemble it again. On the rifle range, I learned how to shoot it, as well as a Browning automatic rifle. Five-and ten-mile hikes with daily calisthenics strengthened our muscles and increased our endurance. They were whipping us into shape. But I hadn't had infantry basic training which was necessary for a hope of survival on the battlefield.

I was drawn even closer to Dolores. I needed her strength to face the future. I surprised her with a ring on Valentine's Day, to seal our engagement. From an ad in the *Wall Street Journal* for estate jewelry my dad had sent me, I had several sets of engagement and wedding rings sent to me on approval by Railway Express. The express agent at camp let me take all the rings to my barracks for a couple of days so I could choose the set I liked and could best afford. My buddy Don Charles helped me make the decision.

"Becker, aren't you afraid someone will steal these rings from under your pillow?" Don couldn't believe that's where I kept them.

"I put them under the pillow when none of the guys were around. Nobody knows about them other than you. I guess I can trust you," I said with a smile.

I had met Don at the A.S.T. program at North Carolina State. I went into the bathroom in the dorm one day and noticed this guy reading the *Green Bay Press Gazette* in one of the stalls. I told him I was from Brillion. We talked about the Green Bay Packer football team and became good friends.

The engagement ring Don helped me select had a quarter-karat center diamond with three small diamonds on each side. There were five tiny diamonds in the wedding ring. I had saved most of my army pay every month and had enough money to pay for them. They were beautiful. I had them expressed to Dolores. She loved them. I didn't tell her they were from an estate, or maybe were even pawned rings. I wondered about the life of the previous owners.

With the love of my life waiting for me and a business idea that could make our fortune, I had a lot to live for. The infantry with its high percentage of casualties was the last place I wanted to be.

I decided my only recourse was prayer. Dolores was also very concerned about my being in the infantry so we both got down to some heavy-duty praying. Most Catholics didn't pray directly to God like Protestants did. We thought God too awesome to approach directly. We thought we had to go through an intermediary, and who better than Mary, the mother of Jesus who we believe to be God. I started saying the rosary daily as well as the 30-day novena to the Blessed Virgin Mary from the little prayer book my mother had given me when I left home for Green Bay. With the novena was a promise that if I said the prayer for 30 consecutive days, my petition, which was to get out of the infantry, would be granted. Dolores said she would also say the novena and a daily rosary for the same intention. I didn't know how I could possibly get out of the infantry, short of a miracle, but after a couple of months and two 30-day novenas and daily rosaries I tried to garner enough faith that God would somehow answer our prayers.

Then a miracle happened! Colonel Cartwright was transferred into my regiment, the 346th, one of the three regiments in the 9,000 man 87th Division, as my commanding officer. This didn't mean a thing to me at the time. I didn't know him, but my sister-in-law did! Esther, who was married to my brother

Richard, grew up in the same little town of Bloomer, Wisconsin, and Colonel Cartwright was a friend of hers! She had been corresponding with him as well as with me. All women on the home front were encouraged to write their friends and relatives in the service, to boost their morale. When Colonel Cartwright was transferred to command the 346th Regiment, Esther noticed our addresses were the same and that Colonel Cartwright must be in the same regiment I was, and she mentioned this to me in her letter. I wrote her that not only was he in my regiment, but he was the commanding officer of our regiment. This had to be a miracle; of the millions of men in the service, this man, whom I had never known or met, was transferred to the 87th Division. Not only that, he was transferred to the 346th Regiment, not the 345th or the 347th, as my commanding officer. I wrote the exciting news to Dolores, telling her that somehow this is how God was answering our prayers.

I also wrote Esther that I wanted to get out of the infantry and into officer's training school and suggested that possibly the Colonel could help me. Without my commanding officer's recommendation there wasn't a chance for a private to go to officer's training school. I didn't particularly want to be an officer, but I was willing to do anything to help my chances of getting out of the infantry.

Within a week of hearing that Esther was a friend of the Colonel's I landed in the army hospital with a broken collarbone. We were learning how to protect ourselves in hand-to-hand combat when one of the guys flipped me over. I wasn't very agile and I landed on my shoulder instead of my feet. I never played tackle football; I was afraid of getting hurt. If I had, I might have learned how to fall without being hurt.

Other patients with fractured collarbones were walking around my ward with a shoulder cast to immobilize the bones until they healed. But my doctor put me in traction—in bed, flat on my back with no pillow, with boards under my mattress, with one weight pulling at my elbow to straighten out my collarbone and another weight attached to my hand to hold my forearm up straight. This must have been a new procedure, as the guy next to me and I were on display and the topic of conversation for visiting doctors. Our doctor would tell them how easy it was to take care of a fractured collarbone; he didn't have to do a thing, the orderlies set up the traction apparatus. He forgot to consider us poor guys who had to lie flat on our backs for six weeks. I was able to raise my head a little to eat. I was lucky it was my left shoulder; I could write letters, using a clipboard, but I wasn't able to get out of bed to go to the bathroom. I felt sorry for the orderlies who had to empty all those bedpans.

My stay in the hospital had to be part of the miracle, because while I was there my name was posted to go overseas as a replacement for infantrymen killed or wounded in action. I thanked God I didn't have to go.

While I was in the hospital, Colonel Cartwright came to visit me! I was floored. This man, my commanding officer with 3,000 men under his command, took the time to visit this lowly private, which I doubt he would have done if he wasn't a friend of Esther's. He said Esther told him that I was her brother-in-law and that I was interested in a transfer to officer's training school. He asked me how I got my broken collarbone and how I was doing. I told him how it happened and that it would probably be a couple of months before I would be released from the hospital. He said there was a possibility of my applying for officer's candidate school, that he would check my qualifications and I should contact him when I was released from the hospital. I thanked him and almost hit the ceiling with excitement. I wrote Dolores immediately with the good news, telling her I was sure God was answering our prayers. God wouldn't go through all the trouble of getting Colonel Cartwright to be my commanding officer unless it was for a reason.

Dolores was also convinced that a miracle had occurred. She

said she still had faith that somehow the Colonel would help us.

In our daily letters, we discussed our future after I returned, our marriage and the kids we would have. We talked about our dream home we both liked, the one with the pillars in front. We would build it with the profits from our new business. I told her we could live where we wanted since I should be able to place my machines anywhere. She said she had a beautiful area in De Pere, near Green Bay, picked out. Of course, in the beginning, we would have to rent a place to live because we would need the money we saved until then to convert the peanut machines to gum machines and get going with the winner gumball machine business. We talked about the fun we would have with our friends and how we would invite them to dinner parties. It was all very exciting, this dreaming about our future together.

But as the six weeks wore on, I became despondent and couldn't wait to get out of traction and out of that hard bed.

From the hospital I went to a rehabilitation center to build up my atrophied muscles after six weeks of inactivity. I would have to stay there for another four weeks. It was pleasant enough, living in cabins in the woods, but I was anxious to get out of there so I could talk to Colonel Cartwright about my future.

Don Charles visited me a few times while I was in the hospital and rehab center. "You mean you're a personal friend of Colonel Cartwright and he's the commander of the 346th and came to visit you in the hospital?" he said when I told him about the letter I received from Esther.

"He's not my personal friend, he's Esther's friend." I told him. "He said he'd try to help me get into O.C.S."

"You're a lucky son of a gun Becker. I envy you. I'd like to get out of my antitank outfit. Why don't you ask him to get your buddy Don into O.C.S. too," he said with a chuckle. "You know the latest rumor is that the 87th Division is in training to enter combat in Europe."

"At least you have had some training. I never had infantry basic training and now I'm missing ten weeks of combat training. I'd be a sitting duck for the Nazis if I went over there with E Company. I wish I could get out of this place. The Colonel said I should come and talk to him as soon as I get out."

I shared my thoughts with Don about Dolores's and my dreams of married life and having kids and that I even thought maybe we should get married before I went overseas.

"Why do you want to take on all that responsibility, Becker, with all of the uncertainty in your life?"

"I guess I like the feeling of security and warmness of having a wife to be loving and caring for me if I do end up in combat," I told him.

With Don's questioning whether or not I should get married, I became confused. I worried whether the Colonel would really be able to help me. Then the financial pressures of supporting a wife and family began to worry me. I was living at home, not paying any room and board, when the peanut business bombed. What if the gumball business was a failure and I'd be saddled with a wife and kids to support?

My letters to Dolores changed. Instead of sentiments of love I told her I longed for normal times again, wondered what another year would bring and that I'd give anything for this damnable war to be over. I told her of my worries and that I couldn't think straight anymore. My letters turned cold.

Dolores kept reassuring me of her love and said it was probably the monotonous life in the hospital that was getting to me. She said she was praying that God would help me through these difficult times.

In my next letter, I let it all hang out. I questioned whether I really loved her, or if I was like some of the other guys in the service who were just looking for someone to write to them and be there for them when they returned. I also told her about my doubts and that maybe I asked her to marry me because I was lonely and was overcome by the excitement of being together on my last furlough. I even wrote that maybe it wasn't love at all, but my sexual attraction for her. This was heavy stuff.

As I was lying on my bunk in the rehab center listening to the radio, they announced the Allied invasion of Europe. It was D-Day, June 6, 1944. I thanked God I was in the hospital when my name came up to go overseas as a replacement, or I might have been one of those infantrymen storming the beaches of Normandy.

The day after I mailed that doomsday letter to Dolores, I stopped to pick up my mail as I was walking to church to attend Mass. There were two letters from Dolores. I opened one and she said something about her being a worrywart too, but after we were married the most she would have to worry about would be one of our kids skinning their knee. I crumpled up the letter, only to straighten it and read on. I began to think of how much she meant to me and how foolish I was to think of letting her go. Instantly I snapped out of my depression and my intense love for her returned.

I immediately sent her a telegram not to read the last letters I had sent. It was too late, the damage had been done. I learned later that she had already read them. She told me how devastated she was, stayed home from work, couldn't eat and spent the next two days in bed totally depressed. She said she lost six pounds and almost wore out the crystal rosary I gave her, praying that somehow God would help us out of this predicament.

I sent an airmail letter immediately following my telegram. I told her how I snapped out of my depression while reading her letter about our future kids and how at that moment all my horrible thoughts and fears vanished, and I now loved her more than ever. I hoped she could forgive me. I told her I didn't sleep the previous night thinking about our future and that maybe we should get married before I went overseas. I said we could talk about it when I came home on furlough in four weeks.

She wrote how elated she was when she received my telegram and airmail letter. She said she was excited about the prospect of our getting married before I went overseas, but her father wasn't.

He said, "What's the matter with that guy? First he doesn't want to marry you, and now he can't get married fast enough."

But she said she wasn't concerned about what he thought.

I was finally released from the rehab center to rejoin E Company, only to learn that Colonel Cartwright had been transferred to Fort Mead, Maryland, a few days before! What a shock! I was devastated.

The Colonel had suggested I contact him when I got out of the hospital and now he was gone! What was God doing to me? I thought this was a miracle in the making, and now the Colonel was no longer there to help me. But I didn't give up. I sent him a letter and asked if there was anyway he could still help me. When I told Dolores the news, she said not to give up; she would keep praying. The current rumor was that the 87th Division was expected to be sent to Europe within the next few months for combat duty. In a couple of weeks I would see Dolores. It had been eight months since my last furlough. We would make a decision whether or not to be married before I went overseas. I was excited about seeing her again, but still shook up about the Colonel's departure.

Dolores again met me in Chicago. We had so much fun at the Stevens Hotel on my last furlough, we went there again. The dinner and dancing was wonderful. It was a warm July evening so we walked to the park overlooking Lake Michigan.

"It sure was disturbing news about Colonel Cartwright's transfer. I'm glad you wrote him, but I'm wondering why you haven't heard from him yet," Dolores said as we sat on a hill on the cool grass, under the stars, with our arms around each other.

"I imagine he's busy getting settled in his new job. We'll hear from him, I'm sure. Honey, I'm really sorry for all I put you through a few weeks ago when I sent you those horrible letters. I know they really hurt you." I drew her closer to me.

"I realize you were under a lot of strain laying flat on your back for six weeks, and then in rehab for another four weeks. I was relieved when it was over and you were your old self again," she said, turning her head so she could kiss me. "I'm excited about the possibility of getting married before you go overseas. I like the idea," she said, smiling, snuggling into me.

"I do too," I said as we lay back on the hill. "There's a rumor the 87th Division might have to stay on as occupation troops when the war is over. We could be in Germany as long as three years. If we were married, maybe you could come over to live with me, possibly in government housing."

"If we weren't married, my dad would never let me go," she said.

"Nor would my dad approve of your coming," I said. "And now with the Colonel's help up in the air, there's so much uncertainty in our lives. The only thing we are certain of is our love for each other. I think we should be married on this furlough and enjoy the couple of months I expect we'll have together before I go overseas."

"Darling, I think that's a great idea," she said. I kissed her passionately. "We'll have to make our wedding plans and hopefully find time for a honeymoon within the next 13 days, but we can do it."

We took the late night train to Appleton and arrived there early in the morning and took a cab to Dolores' home. We had a lot to do. Dolores and I went to Brillion to talk to my dad about our getting married. He said, "You know what happened to Mildred Kleiber, after they got married, her husband left for overseas and she's at home taking care of their baby." But in the next breath he added, "I suppose you'll need my car to make the arrangements." Dad liked Dolores. He wrote her a beautiful letter when we were engaged. I never told Dad about the doubts I had about my love for her only a month before.

Dolores told her sister Leona we were going to be married, but she didn't think it was a good idea in those unsettled times. When Dolores asked her mother—a meek, loving, lady who was intimidated by Leona—about our getting married, she didn't want to say anything to upset Leona. All she said to Dolores was, "I like Lyle."

We had to wait until Monday night to talk to her dad. Dolores said he usually slept most of the day—until it was time to listen to the baseball game on the radio—and was up most of the night. We were a little apprehensive after his remark about my not being able to make up my mind whether I wanted to marry Dolores. It was midnight when we went to talk to him. Her dad, not much taller than five feet, in his sixties with a large nose and heavy black hair, was in the kitchen smoking a cigarette—down to the usual half-inch. He was glad to see me; we always got along okay. He started talking about the upcoming presidential election and said I should be sure to vote for Dewey. He didn't think much of the Democrats, which is the way I leaned. He saw how happy Dolores was when I told him we wanted to get married before I went back to the army camp and he didn't object. We later joked with people, telling them I had to promise her dad I'd vote for Dewey to get his daughter's hand in marriage.

We got our marriage license and blood tests the first week I was home and set the wedding date for the following Tuesday. Dolores kept working at the draft board most of the week and bought her wedding dress during her lunch hour. Dolores's mother suggested Dolores ask Leona to be her maid of honor. Leona was pleased, her opposition to the marriage had softened.

We should have planned the wedding ceremony thirty minutes later, because at ten o'clock, when the ceremony was to have started, I was still at the tailor picking up my khaki army shirt which he was altering around the chest so it wouldn't look so baggy. Dolores's cousin Father James, who performed the ceremony, told me later that at ten o'clock Dolores's Uncle Peter, an accomplished organist, started the wedding march. When we didn't walk down the aisle—we had decided to walk down together—Peter improvised variation after variation of the wedding march "enough to make J. S. Bach green with envy," he said, until I appeared at ten-thirty. Dolores told me she didn't panic, she was sure of my love and knew I was at the tailor and hadn't deserted her.

Dolores looked beautiful in her white wedding gown and veil. The reception was at Dolores' home. Her brother Bob bought the wedding cake and a barrel of beer, which he set up in the garage. Dolores's two brothers and my three brothers could not attend, since they were in the service. (We still had no word about my brother Bernard). The wedding was perfect.

My friend Chuck Buckman's gift was a room at the Stevens Hotel in Chicago on our wedding night. We boarded a Greyhound bus for Chicago and didn't arrive there until one o'clock in the morning. The hotel had given away our room with a double bed and put us in a twin bedded room. We, of course, used only one of the beds. But the naive kids we were, we mussed up the other bed before we left as we didn't want to scandalize the maid.

My oldest sister Mary, was concerned that Dolores might become pregnant before I went overseas, and so were we, so she gave us a booklet on the rhythm method of birth control, which we followed. In the few hours we had before our early morning train to New York, we had plenty of excitement exploring each other's bodies as that's all the calendar said we could do that night. It was so much fun I couldn't believe it wasn't sinful.

We had a glorious three-day honeymoon in New York City, staying at my sister Lillian's home in Springfield, New Jersey, where she and Bill gave us the queen bedroom over the garage. It was the first time I had slept in a queen-sized bed. It was glorious, especially on our honeymoon. My sister set up breakfast for two each morning on the back porch overlooking the flower garden. We saw the Rockettes do their precision dance at Radio City Music Hall, the Ice Capades at the City Center, did the Circle Boat Tour around Manhattan, and experienced lunch at the Automat where we had to put nickels into a slot for each selection of food we wanted. The roasting chestnuts and the hot dog carts on the street corners provided smells and tastes we shall always remember. The highlight had to be Times Square, at night, with its thousands of blinking lights.

We hopped a train out of New York on Saturday for Columbia, South Carolina, and checked into the Wade Hampton Hotel so I could report for duty at Fort Jackson on Monday morning. It had been a whirlwind couple of weeks.

Chapter 7

Awaiting me at camp on Monday was a letter from Colonel Cartwright. It was dated July 25, 1944—our wedding day. Hopefully, it would turn into a wedding present for us.

My dear Becker:

As to your request, I know that as your commanding officer, I could have done something for you. Unfortunately, I was transferred because I was too old for the position I held. However, I suggest you go to Captain Menashie (the personnel officer of the 346th Regiment) and tell him I told you to do so. He can acquaint you with all current requirements for Officer's Candidate School. I believe you have the qualifications for O.C.S. I do hope you can get a break. I don't know anything else I can do. I don't even know your new commanding officer. If Captain Menashie says there is anything I can do for you, let me know and I'll be only too happy to do so.

I hope you have a pleasant furlough, and let's hope we may soon each take two furloughs a year—each of six-months duration.

Very Sincerely Yours,
(signed)
C. J. Cartwright
Lt. Colonel, Infantry

There was hope. God was answering our prayers. Something was happening. I was anxious to share the news with Dolores. I hurried back to the hotel as soon as I could that afternoon. I burst into the room and threw my arms around her. "We got a letter from the Colonel!" I blurted.

"What did he say?" She was so excited.

"Here, read it," I said as I handed it to her.

She opened it hurriedly. I noticed her sadness when she read the part where he said he could have done something for me when he was my commanding officer. Then she brightened when he suggested I go to see Captain Menashie.

"It gives us hope," she said, always the optimist.

"I'm going to see the Captain tomorrow, first chance I get," I said, holding her tight.

The next afternoon, as soon as I was off duty, I went to see the Captain. Regimental Headquarters was in a large barracks-type building with various areas of desks and wooden chairs—no upholstered ones in the army—for the officers and enlisted men in the various departments.

Captain Menashie, probably in his early thirties, was tall and thin with the usual army crew cut. He seemed like a nice guy, not pompous like so many of the regular army guys. I presume he was a draftee like me. He asked me to take the chair at his desk.

"This is a letter from Colonel Cartwright. I had talked to him about getting into O.C.S. after I landed in the hospital with a broken collarbone. He said to come to see him when I got out of the hospital, but he was transferred before I got out. I wrote to him and this is his reply. Would you like to read his letter?" I asked as I handed it to him.

He took the letter and read it. "Let me get your file and take a look at it," he said as he got up from his desk.

"I notice you were drafted into the air corps and then you transferred to A.S.T.P. You never had infantry basic training."

"I also missed the last ten weeks of combat training being in the hospital."

"Why were you in the hospital?"

"I broke my collarbone in hand-to-hand combat training. A guy flipped me over and I landed on my shoulder instead of my feet. Not too agile," I added with a smile.

"Why do you want to go to O.C.S.?" he asked as he continued to look over my file card. "The only O.C.S. schools open are the infantry and artillery."

That would be like jumping from the frying pan into the fire, I thought to myself. Second Lieutenants, which is the rank I would graduate with from O.C.S., usually led their men into combat.

"I wouldn't care much about either of those," I said, hoping he might have some alternative to offer.

I see you went to North Carolina State for eight months in the A.S.T.P., you play a musical instrument, and you can type."

"Yes, I played baritone horn in our city band and got up to 40 w.p.m. in my typing class in high school."

"One of the departments is shorthanded. They might be able to use a clerk-typist," he said.

"That would be great," I responded, a big smile on my face. "I had an office job before I was drafted."

"I'll look into it and let you know." He stood up, indicating the interview was over.

"Thank you, sir," I said as I stood up, saluted him, and left.

I jumped for joy when I got outside. Regimental Headquarters had to be at least a mile or two behind the front lines. God wasn't getting me out of the infantry, but I was happy about the alternative. I would be in a much safer and more comfortable place than fighting the enemy from a front-line foxhole. Again, I couldn't wait to get back to the hotel to share my excitement with Dolores.

I took the bus into town and burst into the room with the

good news. "I saw the Captain today and there's a chance I may get a typing job in regimental headquarters," I said as I threw my arms around her, hugging her tightly.

"Oh, that's wonderful," she said as tears came to her eyes. "See, God is taking care of us. Our prayers are being answered."

"It isn't for sure, but he said he'd let me know as soon as he could check it out."

"I'm so happy I could cry," she said as the tears started to roll down her cheeks. "I'm sure it will happen," she added. "God wouldn't go through all the trouble of moving the Colonel in and out of your regiment and then not answer our prayers in some way."

"I think God was testing our faith when He moved him out," I said, "showing us He still had the power to help us."

A few days later E Company was on a three-day bivouac to train us for survival in the field. Everything we needed for survival for the three-day exercise was carried on our backs in a field pack. Each of us carried half of a two-man tent, a raincoat, and a small shovel for digging foxholes in combat. K-rations were packed in a Cracker Jack type box. Each box held a small can of beef, pork loaf, or cheese, crackers, instant coffee, sugar, fruit bar, four cigarettes, and some toilet tissue. In addition to our field pack we carried our M-1 rifle and bayonet, with clips of bullets on our belt along with a mess kit and water bottle. This was serious business.

I was there only a few hours, when a jeep pulled up to the area. The driver talked to the Sergeant-Major, showing him his orders. I soon found that the orders were from Captain Menashie to take me to 346th Headquarters. The guys in my platoon razzed me, asking me what I'd done wrong. I just smiled as I packed up my gear, got in the jeep, and left them in the field.

"We've got a job for you in Plans and Training as a clerk-typist," Captain Menashie said with a smile when I reported to him. I think he knew I would be pleased.

"Great," I said. "When do I start?"

"You can move your gear over to Service Company today. Report to Major Shields and Captain Schuh in S-2, S-3. That's the Plans and Training section."

"Thanks," I said with a big smile. "I really appreciate this."

I went to E Company barracks, packed my duffel bag, carried it on my shoulder to Service Company where I was assigned a bunk and rushed home to share the great news with Dolores. I felt so good, I was walking on air, confident that now I would survive the war.

We had moved from the hotel to a small furnished one-bedroom apartment with a 4 x 6-foot kitchen and a 5 x 8-foot living room, that Dolores found for us to rent. I burst into the living room with a big grin, took her in my arms, kissed her and told her the great news. She was so happy, tears came to her eyes.

We decided to celebrate by going out to dinner. We shared a bottle of red wine with our candlelight dinner at a little Italian restaurant with red-checkered tablecloths. We talked about the gift God had given us in each other and the miracle He had performed in answer to our prayers.

Great news made a great evening. We topped it off dancing at the U.S.O. I knelt down that night by the bed and thanked God for the great gift He had given us. I told Dolores I was anxious to write the Colonel and Esther, thanking them and sharing the good news with them.

I liked my job. Captain Schuh and Major Shields were pleasant to work with, as were Heath and Higgins, the two regular clerks who worked in the Plans and Training department. The Table of Organization called for only two clerks, but I was added as they expected to be overloaded with work when we were overseas in combat. The S-2, S-3 Department then would be responsible for battle plans and enemy intelligence. On stateside my job was typing and mimeographing various training plans. This would be a breeze compared to training in E Company.

Service Company was a picnic compared to E Company, not nearly as much discipline and the food was great, probably because there were more officers attached to Service Company. Don Charles would walk a couple miles on weekends, from his anti-tank unit in the 345th Regiment, to get a good meal at our mess hall. He said he never had steak before in the army; I hadn't, either. I traded my heavy M-1 rifle for the lighter Carbine. This suggested to me that my rifle was more for my protection, than to be used as an offensive weapon.

Dolores and I had 13 glorious weeks together before our division went overseas. Heath and Higgins came to dinner and Don joined us a few times. It was great for the guys to have a home, small as it was, to visit. I'm sure it reminded them of their own homes they missed. With hot dogs, hamburgers, and Dolores' great apple pie and a bottle of wartime gin, that tasted more like paint thinner, we had some great times.

Then my orders came through. The 87th would be leaving immediately for overseas. We were glad our destination was Europe and not the Far East. We could see an eventual end to the war in Europe, but the kamikaze attitude of the Japanese war machine made the end of that war more unpredictable.

Dolores stayed with me in the guest house on the base the night before we left. Parting was very painful. Even though my chance for survival had improved greatly, I would be in danger and there was still a possibility of my being killed or injured. For some unknown reason, we were scheduled to leave at three in the morning. We shared lots of tears, holding each other, lying in bed, in the guest house. It was one of the most difficult times of my life and of hers too, I'm sure. We finally tore ourselves apart before the three o'clock deadline, only to find that our departure had been delayed for two more hours. I went back to the guest house and two hours later we had the same wrenching separation to go through a second time, but the extra time together was worth it.

The 87th sailed to Europe on the *Queen Mary*, the British luxury liner converted to a troopship. At 30 knots, it was fast enough to outrun the German submarines, so we sailed alone, without escort ships and arrived in Scotland five days later. As I lay in my hammock in the hold of the ship, I kept up my spirits thinking of my future life with Dolores, the 300 winner gumball machines I was going to have, and the dream home we would build some day. I was transferred back to E Company for the trip overseas as I was not officially a member of Service Company.

The British people welcomed the American soldiers with open arms. They held dances for us. We danced with their daughters in the town near the estate where we camped and waited to be transported to France. It was a nice three-week vacation before going into combat. Several of us had a chance to visit London for an evening before we left for France.

Six months after the Allies successfully conducted the D-Day operation, securing the beachheads at Normandy, we were transported by ship across the English Channel to the French port of Le Harve. The city had been bombed so heavily, it was nothing but huge piles of rocks. When I got off the ship and walked into the city it reminded me of walking down the roads during our Wisconsin winters after a heavy snowstorm. After the snowplow had gone through, the snow on either side was higher than my head. Only at Le Harve, it was huge chunks of concrete instead of snow, and bulldozers cleared the way.

By the time we arrived, Paris and most of France had been liberated. The Russians had defeated the Germans at Stalingrad and were advancing into Germany from the east while the Allied forces were advancing toward Germany from the west. The 87th took up positions in the Saarland. Due to its extensive coal deposits, the area was very valuable to both France and Germany. They fought several times for control of the coal deposits, which also meant oil for Germany, since they learned how to produce oil from coal.

The day prior to going into combat, our regiment was in a staging area near the front and I was concerned because my transfer from E Company back to Service Company had not come through. I decided to take things into my own hands and started walking back to Regimental Headquarters. When I got there I found the orders had already been issued. I was relieved.

The next day, our regiment was transported to the front lines in trucks and took up our positions there. The fellow in E Company, with whom I shared a pup tent two nights before, was killed in action the first day. I barely knew him and I don't even remember his name. His death confirmed my fears of how dangerous it was to be a frontline infantryman. I had some guilt feelings. If I had gone into battle with E Company, would I possibly have been killed instead of this young man? Did he die instead of me?

And yet I did no wrong, committed no crime, just followed my instincts for self-preservation in the only way I knew how. Dolores and I prayed for my survival. Then a miracle happened.

I knew some people would think me cowardly or unpatriotic. My Brillion friends Carl and Jim had volunteered for the Air Force. (Jim spent the war years as a flight instructor in Lincoln, Nebraska. Carl became a bomber pilot and survived the air war in Europe.) Other men volunteered for the Marines and stormed the beaches of the islands of the Pacific. I admired the courage of those volunteers and wondered if some of them realized how dangerous the assignments were when they enlisted.

I felt that I would rush into a burning building and risk my life, probably without thinking, to save Dolores or my children, but I really admired the real heros of the war, who knowingly, risked their lives. I feel they were real Christ-figures, who gave their lives for their friends, even for men they didn't know.

Our headquarters was in the basement of a bombed-out farmhouse. I heard Captain Schuh and Major Shields discussing, in hushed voices, the number of casualties in our outfit that first day. I didn't hear how many were killed or wounded and I didn't want to know, but from their sullen spirits I knew it had been a bad day for the 346th. The Germans were fighting furiously to keep this important coal-mining region.

Artillery shells screamed overhead on their way to the front line, then exploded. At night I would hear machine-gun fire in the distance from my sleeping bag in the hay in some farmer's barn. I thanked God I wasn't one of those guys out there in a foxhole worrying whether I'd live through it.

Sergeant Mansfield, in charge of the S-2, S-3 office, moved us from the basement of one bombed-out building to another as our regiment advanced. We moved our office equipment and supplies in a trailer behind our jeep. This was a 24-hour, 7-day-a-week job. We kept around-the-clock contact with the troops at the front. With three of us to man the phones, and log the calls, we staggered our hours so that two of us were always on duty, but even that made 16-hour days and 7-day weeks.

A few weeks after our outfit went into action in the Saarland, the Germans broke through the Allied lines near Bastogne for one final offensive in what came to be know as the Battle of the Bulge. We spent New Year's Day heading north in army trucks to the bottom of the bulge, created by the break in the Allied lines. Our 87th Division, part of General Patton's Third Army group, was sent to exert pressure at the bottom, near the start of the bulge, so as to encircle the German troops.

After the German army was defeated in the bulge, our division advanced toward Germany through the Maginot Line, the French line of fortification thought to be impregnable when the Germans invaded France five years before. (Instead of attacking it head-on, the Germans had made an end run around the line, through Belgium.)

Resistance in the Maginot Line was light as we advanced east and all the French gun emplacements faced west, toward

Germany. Resistance stiffened on the Siegfried Line, on the western border of Germany, which the Germans built to counter the Maginot Line. After our division broke through the Siegfried Line we were using the German bunkers for our S-2, S-3 headquarters.

We were in combat steadily for several months, advancing toward the heart of Germany, while the Russians continued their advance from the east. I followed the destruction of the German army in my *Time* magazine; my subscription was mailed to me weekly.

In spring, the German resistance collapsed and their troops surrendered by the thousands, mostly young boys in their early teens and old men. Germany was running out of a first rate fighting force. From our interrogation of prisoners, we found out that food was very scarce, one report stating some German soldiers were even eating their shoe polish. I wondered how that tasted, and what nourishment they got from shoe polish.

By April our division advanced to Koblenz, where the Rhine and Moselle Rivers joined, and there we waited for the Russians—due to the Yalta Agreement between Roosevelt, Churchill and Stalin—to take Berlin. Huge fields were filled with surrendered German prisoners.

In Koblenz, Sergeant Mansfield housed our S-2, S-3 unit in a beautiful spacious contemporary home with formal flower gardens near the Moselle River. We slept in beds for the first time in months, under feather comforters. We "liberated" a stash of Holland gin, Five Star Hennessey brandy, and numerous bottles of Moselle and Rhine wines hidden under a large pile of sand in the basement. This was the life. We sat out the rest of the war until Russia took Berlin and the war in Europe ended.

V-E Day,—Victory in Europe—was a happy day. I thanked God the war had ended, but it was not over for the 87th. Since we were one of the last divisions to be sent to Europe, we were also one of the first to be sent back to the States. We heard we were slated for the invasion and later possibly the occupation of Japan.

Before we left Germany for the States I had a chance to visit one of the German death camps. We did not know until the war ended that these camps existed. When I heard what the G.I.'s saw there, I chose not to go; I didn't feel I could stomach the horrors of it all.

In July our regiment boarded a troopship for the States. I boarded the ship with the guys from E Company. They were almost all new faces; E Company had suffered nearly 100 percent casualties in men killed or wounded during our six months in combat! Our ship was much smaller than the *Queen Mary* that took us there, and the orchestra on board playing Les Brown tunes helped pass the time on the ten-day trip home.

We were pleasantly surprised when we arrived in the U.S.; the entire division got a 60-day furlough. The bad news was that when the furlough was over we would be sent to the Far East.

"Guess what?" Dolores said to me, excitedly, as she woke me with a kiss. We were staying at her parents home on my furlough. "They just dropped an atom bomb on Japan and one bomb destroyed a huge city! I just heard it on the radio." She hugged me with all her might.

"Really? An atom bomb? What's an atom bomb?" I asked as I tried to wake up and absorb what she was saying.

"I don't know. It causes some sort of an atomic explosion. It must be very powerful if one bomb can destroy an entire city. Do you still think you'll have to go to Japan?" she asked with hope in her eyes. "They are speculating that the war could be over in days."

"If Japan surrenders I don't see why they would send our division over as occupation troops. They have plenty of men over there now." I got up, dressed quickly and went downstairs to listen to the radio.

The atomic bomb had been dropped on Hiroshima. It was

entirely different from conventional bombs; it derived its enormous destructive power from the release of nuclear energy.

Three days later the U.S. dropped a second atomic bomb on Nagasaki, and on August 15, 1945, the Allies announced the unconditional surrender of Japan. World War II was over!

I thanked God that I had come through the war safely. If we were sent to Japan as occupation troops, I would still be safe. Eventually, Dolores and I could start living our dreams.

Dolores and I were deliriously happy. We celebrated V-J Day with our friend Don and Chuck Stimpson, a friend of Don's from the 87th, in a bar in Green Bay. The place, filled with ecstatic servicemen, was one mass of uncontrolled excitement with beer mugs sloshing as we toasted each other's good fortune at surviving the war and being home in the good old U.S.A. to celebrate its end.

After my furlough, the 87th was assigned to Fort Benning, Georgia. I was happy to learn upon my arrival that our outfit wouldn't be going to Japan. Dolores and I were relieved. She joined me in Georgia.

Now that the war was over, all the G.I.'s wanted to get out of the service at once, so a point system had to be set up for discharges, based on the number of months in service and the number of months spent overseas. I was fortunate to be in the U.S. when the war ended. Our division had been overseas only eight months, while other G.I.'s had been in Europe or the Far East as long as four years. If we had been in Europe when the war ended most of the other guys there would have come back before us because they had more points than we did. We also might have been assigned to occupation duty in Germany. Now there was nothing for us to do at Fort Benning but wait for our discharge, so a few weeks later they gave us another furlough, 30 days this time.

Dolores was anxious to have a child. She became pregnant while I was at Fort Benning.

On this latest furlough, I decided to buy my brother Eugene's cigarette machine route. I knew I couldn't start my winner gumball machine business right away because sugar was short and still rationed. The cigarette business would give Dolores and me some income.

Dolores had continued her job at the draft board while I was overseas and between us we saved about $900. I used several hundred dollars for a down payment on the machines, and Gene let me pay off the balance in monthly installments. I still owed my dad for my half of the peanut machines. Anita had placed them in storage after she left Brillion. She took a defense job in Milwaukee during the war. My dad said there was no hurry in my paying off my note and he would not charge me interest while the machines were in storage. Chuck did not have to go into the service because he was married and had a child. Chuck sold his half of the machines during the war and paid my dad what he owed him. That ended our partnership.

After 33 months of service, I was discharged. I let out all my pent-up venom on the Sergeant at the end of the line when I picked up my discharge papers. He was looking for recruits for the Army Reserves. "Hell, no." I told him along with a few other choice words. It was great to be able to speak my mind again. I thoroughly disliked army life, especially the discipline and the system of ranks and privileges. I felt like I had been released from prison and was free again!

Chapter 8

Dolores and I rented an upstairs apartment with a small living room, bedroom, kitchen, and bath from Joe and Maggie Pritzl, elderly distant cousins of mine. The price was right, $15 a month including utilities, plus half the cost of the telephone and the kerosene to heat the water for the washing machine. Art Heimke came clump-clumping up the stairs twice a week with a block of ice in his tongs, dripping water, for our icebox. The only furniture we bought was a davenport and chair from Sears for $100. All the other furniture and appliances were cast-offs from our families.

We enjoyed our little apartment. It was home. We had friends over to play cards and Monopoly, drank Edelweiss beer we could buy for 10 cents a can, and mixed a Tom Collins in a jar for the girls.

Servicing my cigarette machine route took only a couple days a week. I decided to take my 100 Silver King machines out of storage and try vending Spanish salted peanuts, mixing in miniature pocketknives—like the one I got out of the Boston Bean machine and cherished as a child—along with any other inexpensive small toys I could locate. Gumballs or candy-coated peanuts still were not available due to the sugar shortage, and even though Spanish peanuts didn't sell well to adults in taverns, I felt that children would buy them if I mixed in the little knives and other small toys. I would place them in drug stores, ice cream shops, and grocery stores, where kids would go with their mothers. It was worth a try.

I hired Ken, a friend who was going to the University of Wisconsin, to place the machines in Madison, Wisconsin. The peanuts mixed with the prizes, sold well; there was no problem with stale peanuts. This time the problem was having broken glass in the peanuts. The kids picked up the machines and turned them upside down, trying to manipulate the toys into the hole in the portion wheel so they would vend with the next penny they inserted. Some of the kids dropped the machines in the process and broke the glass domes. Not only did I have to buy new domes, but I had to throw away the peanuts from these machines for fear they might have glass mixed in with them. I struck out again on the peanut machine business and had to remove the machines because the business wasn't profitable.

I found another use for the Silver King machines. The nut company I had been dealing with suggested I vend cashews in them at a nickel a handful. Cashews were quite expensive, but vending them for a nickel gave me a good margin of profit. I bought the parts to change the machines to vend for a nickel and placed them in taverns in Milwaukee.

After servicing the cashew machines for several months I wasn't happy with the results. Although the profit margin was over 50 percent, the money I was taking in each month didn't add up to a reasonable profit.

I asked Chuck Buckman if he would sell my route of cashew machines for a percentage of the proceeds. After Chuck sold his peanut machines he made a business of putting out routes of machines and selling them to people interested in going into the vending business. He agreed to try to sell mine for me and we placed an ad in the business opportunities column of the *Milwaukee Journal* for a vending route for sale. We got several replies. We rented a room at the Schroeder Hotel. Chuck called our prospects and made appointments to interview them in our hotel room.

Although I usually serviced the machines once a month, I hadn't serviced them for two months because I was trying to sell them; I knew there would be plenty of cashews to last. But how do you interest someone in buying a business that isn't profitable enough to keep yourself? Chuck and I decided we would sell the route on approval. I would take the buyer around to all the machines and I would give him all the money that was in the machines. We would ask for a down payment, and if the prospect was satisfied with the money he took in as we went around on the route, he would pay us the balance of our agreed price in cash.

Of the several people Chuck interviewed, we found one fellow, a relative of a Milwaukee industrialist, that was interested in buying the business. He went around the route with me and was satisfied with the money he took in from the machines. I told him I usually serviced the machines on a monthly basis, but I didn't tell him that this time it was two months since I had serviced them, and that the money we took out was for two months sales instead of one. My desire to sell the machines was greater than my concern about not being honest with him. We accepted his check for the balance agreed on; I gave Chuck his commission on the sale, then I tried to live with my conscience.

I tried to sell myself on the idea that I hadn't really lied to him. I didn't tell him the money he took out of the machines was only from one month's sales; I just didn't tell him I hadn't been around for two months. But my dishonesty gnawed at me. My dad's words haunted me, "People who lie, steal." I was taking this fellow's money under false pretenses. That was stealing.

I feared I would hear from him the following month when he serviced the machines again, but I didn't. That familiar rock was back in my stomach. I didn't tell Dolores what I had done; I was too ashamed. I knew I needed to go to confession and tell the priest and try to get rid of my guilt. I finally went. The priest gave me conditional absolution and told me my sin wouldn't be fully forgiven until I made restitution, which meant that I must make good for the loss or damage I caused this man.

I needed to contact him, but what would I say? I struggled with it for days and finally got up the courage to call him. I was very nervous. It was a rather short conversation. I asked him how the route was doing and if he was satisfied with it. He said he was and thanked me for my interest. I couldn't believe it; I was off the hook. Evidently his expectations for the amount of profit the machines should generate was not as high as mine.

I was anxious to start my route of winner gumball machines that I had dreamed about since before the war, but gum was still in short supply. I received a quota of 100 pounds a month from Leaf Gum Company in Chicago. I didn't need to mix in the striped balls that entitled the kids to a candy bar to make it sell; they were willing to pay a penny apiece for just a gumball, and happy to get them. The few machines I put out emptied every couple of weeks and I was making $80 profit per month on the amount Leaf was sending me. I wanted to get more gumballs as they sold like the proverbial hotcakes.

I drove to Chicago to talk to Pete Trent, sales manager for Leaf Gum. He was a big, burley, friendly sort. I told him I needed a lot more than 100 pounds of gum a month and thought I was entitled to a larger quota than people just starting in the business because I was an old customer; having purchased gum from Leaf before the war. He wouldn't budge. I offered him some money under the table—a bribe I guess you'd call it—if he would raise my allocation of gum. He told me he had all the money he needed and was doing well with it in the stock market. I was humiliated. On the drive home I felt guilty and embarrassed. I hadn't made a good impression on Mr. Trent.

An ad appeared in *Billboard*, the trade magazine for the vending industry. A distributor was advertising Leaf gum for 80 cents a pound, 50 cents over Leaf's price. I wondered how this guy was getting it. At 80 cents I could only make 30 cents a pound profit and it wasn't worth the effort. In a few weeks the price dropped to 60 cents. I bought some. Then in a couple of months, sugar became plentiful and I could get all the gumballs I wanted directly from the factory at 30 cents a pound. But with the increase in supply, down went the sales in the machines. The market was flooded.

The next step would have been to go into winner gumball machines, but it was lucky I didn't get started with them. Wisconsin passed anti-gambling laws to prohibit slot machines and other gambling devices. The winner ball machines were considered gambling devices because you had a chance to win a nickel candy bar for a penny. They slapped a $50 yearly tax on them, effectively outlawing them. There went my dream, while I was in the service, of eventually owning 300 winner gumball machines.

We had lived in our little apartment about six months when our first child was born. We named him Michael Peter, the names Dolores and I had agreed on in our letters when I was in service. Our birth announcement read, *Michael Peter Becker and Michael Peter Jacobs announce the birth of their grandson Michael Peter Becker.* (Both Dolores's and my father's given names were the same, so it seemed the natural name for our son.)

Having a baby and caring for it was a traumatic experience for Dolores. She had never held a tiny baby, much less bathed one. I wasn't any help, as I knew even less about babies. She yearned for her mother, someone to teach her what to do, but she lived in Appleton and was unable to come.

Michael's continual crying bothered Maggie, the elderly landlady living downstairs, and she continually yelled up the stairs for Dolores to keep the baby quiet. Dolores held Michael and walked him up and down the hallway; then the noise of her continued walking bothered Maggie as well.

Dolores was nursing Michael and she told the doctor that he seemed to be continually hungry and she was worn out because of the tension. The doctor's reply was that he was just a little pig—always hungry.

Finally, after a couple of months, the doctor agreed with Dolores that Michael wasn't getting enough nourishment and put him on a bottle. That helped, but didn't fully solve the problem. Michael was used to being held and cried if she didn't hold him. Maggie asked us to move. We looked, but because all of the married returning servicemen looking for places to live, places just weren't available.

After a couple of months, with Maggie now complaining to my dad, who was her cousin, I came up with the idea of remodeling the electrical shop we were using for a warehouse, into a home for us. My dad offered to let us live in the upstairs apartment of the small house he lived in with Margaret, the lady he married after my mother died, until the carpenters could finish remodeling the electric shop. Dolores wanted to buy the home that was for sale down the street from Maggies, but I felt we could save money by remodeling the electric shop instead. My friend Rudy, who made a big success operating his little restaurant during the war, said he would loan us the money for the remodeling.

Grandma, as we called Margaret, was like a second mother to Dolores. A kind gentle soul, she felt Michael was spoiled from being held so much and had Dolores stay downstairs with her when Michael wouldn't stop crying, so as to "let him cry it out," as she put it. It was hard for Dolores to hear Michael cry so long, but he finally stopped and things got better after that. I was of no help to Dolores in the crises over Michael's crying. I thought it was the woman's responsibility to take care of the children and that she should know how to do it. This caused a strain on our marriage.

Our new quarters were not as nice as we had at Maggies. We

lived in the dining room; the living room was filled with furniture my dad was storing for my brother Richard. There was a bedroom for us and one for Michael along with a bathroom, but Dolores didn't complain. She looked forward to the new house.

Chuck's brother Ward stopped to see me at my warehouse, Heunefeld's two-car garage I rented, down the street from the electrical shop that was being remodeled.

Chuck and Ward were putting out routes of winner ball machines and selling the routes to people who wanted to go into the vending machine business. Ward was looking for new ideas for machines they could sell now that the winner ball machines had been taxed out of existence.

I told him my gumball machines had slowed down to almost nothing and I was looking for a new idea, too. "Kids can now buy kiss-wrapped Fleer's bubble gum over the counter for a penny. It's a much bigger piece than we can offer in our machines," I said.

"What are you going to do to stay in business?" Ward asked.

"I don't know," I said. "I've got an idea I've been thinking about. I've got some of the little knives, rings, and plastic charms we mixed in with the salted peanuts in the Silver King machines. If we could mix these toys with gumballs and vend them in a machine I think they would sell. Kids like gum a lot better than peanuts. A gumball is a lot cheaper than a handful of peanuts, so we could put a lot more toys in a machine and the domes of the machine wouldn't get so messy, like they do with the greasy peanuts. I'd still have to find a way to keep the kids from breaking the glass domes, though."

"But how can you vend a mixture of gum and toys without them plugging up the round hole in the merchandise wheel? Couldn't a gumball and toy get wedged together in the hole?"

"I've got this new Victor Model V machine that vends

peanuts or gumballs. It has three adjustable V-shaped openings in the portion wheel, and the wheel revolves instead of going back and forth like it does in the Silver King. I think there might be room in the V- shaped opening to allow a toy to sometimes get into the hole with the gumball without plugging it up," I said.

"Sounds like a good idea," Ward said. "Why don't we try it?"

"Why not," I said.

We opened the adjustable V-shaped portion wheel so almost two gumballs could get into the opening. That left some room for a toy. We mixed a healthy portion of toys with the gum, figuring the more toys, the more chance of it plugging. We wanted to give it the ultimate test. We started putting pennies in the machine. I held my breath.

"It works Becker!" Ward said, after we had put in about a dozen pennies.

"Just what I hoped. Sometimes you get a gumball, sometimes a toy, and sometimes you get both; but you always get something for your penny," I said as we continued to play the machine.

"How much do these toys cost?" Ward asked.

"A couple of cents each for the Czech knives and rings, and a half-cent each for the plastic charms like the Scottie dogs. I think we'd be able to average about a penny apiece for the toys we'd mix together," I replied. "At a penny apiece we'd be able to use five times as many toys as the number of 5-cent winner balls we could use in a machine. I think it would sell better than the winner ball machines, as the kids would win a prize more often. Kids like to win," I added.

Ward got up from the desk where we were working. With his hands on his hips and a grin on his face he declared, "Becker, I really think you've got something here!"

"It's remarkable," I said. "I don't know of another machine on the market besides this Victor Model V that would vend a mixture of gumballs and toys without plugging."

I was excited about the prospects of this new business. I had about a dozen Model V machines on hand so I displayed the toys around the outside of the gum next to the glass domes of the machines and placed them in grocery stores for a test. I wanted to attract the kids who came into the stores with their mothers. A week later I checked the machines; the sales were unbelievable. From what was sold in a week, I could see that some of the machines would empty in a month—at least the amount of sales I had expected from the winner ball machines.

From that test, a new idea was born and eventually a new industry—the selling of a mixture of gumballs and toys in a vending machine!

I was able to purchase about 300 Model V machines and the gum and toys to fill them, with the money I received from the sale of the cashew machines, plus the proceeds from the sale of my cigarette machine route, which I decided to sell. I knew the penny gum and toy machines would make more money per dollar invested than I was making on the cigarette machines. Hermy had been right about penny machines being more profitable than cigarette machines. I just had to find the right one!

The gum and toy machines were easy to place in Milwaukee and the smaller cities in Wisconsin. I had no competition. There was nothing like them in grocery stores, which I found to be the best locations for the machines. I was doing as well with them as I had expected to do with the 300 winner ball machines I dreamed of having while I was in the service.

Now I wanted to have more machines, thousands of them, because I figured if there wasn't any competition in the grocery stores in Wisconsin, the same would be true in other states.

I tried to borrow money for additional machines from the Calumet County Bank in Brillion, but found that banks don't loan you money unless you have collateral for security. I offered Mr. Schroeder, the bank president, a mortgage on the 300 machines I had out on location, but he didn't like the machines backing the loan, being spread all over the state.

"How would I ever collect all the machines and to whom would I sell them if you couldn't make your payments and I had to foreclose?" he asked. I could have asked my dad for more money, but I still owed him for my original peanut machines, and although he wasn't pressing me for payment, I guess I wanted to do it on my own after his initial investment in me. I could have asked my friend Rudy, but he had already agreed to hold the mortgage on the house we were building.

After several months, the sales in my machines were falling and I knew it was because of the lack of new toys. Kids liked to collect the different charms and toys they got from our machines, and they weren't going to keep putting in their pennies if we didn't continually present them with new toys. I went to the library and searched the *Thomas Register* for categories of small toys that would vend through our machines. I contacted Standard Specialty Co., in California, who was listed for imported toys, but I hit the jackpot with a company named Dowst Manufacturing Company. They manufactured miniature die-cast charms here in the U.S. I drove to Chicago to see them and found they made the silver colored die-cast metal markers for Monopoly, like the top hat, thimble, iron, race car, and rocking horse. They were small enough, and inexpensive enough, to vend in our machines. If we could use large enough quantities they would make new dies for casting a variety of other charms and toys for us. It was a big breakthrough and now our business really started to take off.

It took almost a year to remodel the electrical shop into our home on Dewey Street. The carpenters had to move the wooden building back from the street, so we would have a front yard. They jacked it up on beams and built a concrete-block basement wall under it. They made the mistake of filling in the dirt on the outside of the wall before they lowered the structure onto it to give it support, and the wall collapsed in a freak snow and rainstorm in May. It was a mess of mud and concrete block and this delayed the construction. We were fortunate the entire structure didn't fall into the hole they dug for the basement.

Dolores was especially happy to move out of our cramped quarters above my dad's. But this house was also very small, measuring only 18 x 26-feet, less than 500 square feet on each floor. It had two stories with a fair-sized living room and a small kitchen and bath on the first floor. An open stairway at the center of the house led to our bedroom on the left and a small children's bedroom on the right. There was also a small nursery accessible from our bedroom. I used the basement, other than the space for the laundry room, for my office. I should have followed Dolores's intuition and bought the house she wanted down the street that was for sale for $9,000. This one, instead of the $6,000 the carpenters though they could build it for, cost us $10,000.

But it was our own home and it was new and fresh with a large picture window in the living room and one in the kitchen to let in the southern sun. We would soon have need for the nursery, as Dolores was four-months pregnant with our second child.

I could plod along with my 300 machines and buy 50 or 100 machines a year with the money I made over and above our living expenses, but it would take forever to make some real money. I figured I needed a $10,000 loan, then I could expand as fast as I could locate machines, using the profits from the machines I put out to provide funds to buy more machines. But I didn't want to give up any part of the ownership of the company to get the money for expansion.

Prayer had worked for me in the army, so I asked God to help me get the money I needed for expansion of my business.

I asked a wealthy farmer friend of mine for a $10,000 loan at 10 percent interest, almost double the going rate. He turned me down. Then I got up my nerve and asked the president of the Brillion Iron Works, the largest company in the city. I met Butch Peters when I joined the Lions Club and became friendly with the "movers and shakers" in our little town. He turned me down.

My friend Chuck had an idea. "Why not ask Hermy Plous? He's more of a moneylender than a vending machine operator these days," Chuck said. "Hermy is in the second mortgage business. With all the guys coming back from service and buying homes on the G.I. Bill (a low interest loan program guaranteed by the U.S. Government) he supplies all or part of the down payment—at a high rate of interest, of course—to those who can't come up with the money. I think Hermy likes you. He asks about you when I see him. I told him how well you were doing with your gum and toy machines."

Chuck and I went to see Hermy. He was glad to see me, happy I survived the peanut business. I told him I was doing well in the toy and gum machine business, but I needed $10,000 for expansion. I told him how well my machines were doing, so I would have no trouble paying back the loan. He said he would see what he could do; he'd let me know.

He called me a couple of days later and said he could arrange a loan for me through his friend Charley Abrams, so I went to Green Bay and Herman and I went to see Charley. He was a dealer in pelts for the fur trade. The floor of his warehouse, which also doubled as his office, was covered with piles of mink and fox pelts. The odor was oppressive, but I didn't care. Hermy told me Charley would loan the money to me at 10 percent interest—about 4 percent over the going rate—and there would be a finder's fee of $1,000 which would be deducted up front from the $10,000—Hermy's commission for guaranteeing the loan. I received $9,000. I didn't care. The finance charge didn't bother me. I knew I could easily pay back the loan with the profits of the business. I was in "seventh heaven!"

I then drove to Chicago to see Harold Schaef, the owner of Victor Vending Company to see if I could get some credit and time payments on machines. It had been "cash on the barrelhead" for all the machines I had purchased so far.

Harold, a big burly guy, whom I had met before on trips to his company, was in the back room of his office working on some improvements in his machine. Between sentences he would spit tobacco juice from the cud in his cheek, missing the spittoon almost as often as he hit it. A big friendly teddy bear sort, he showed me the improvements he had made in the Model V machine to solve the problems of the broken domes I complained about when the kids tried to manipulate the toys into the delivery holes in the merchandise wheel. It was great. He had come up with a square cabinet, metal on three sides with an unbreakable Plexiglas front. Not only would it eliminate broken domes, but it had more capacity and would allow me to place most of the toys next to the Plexiglas, so they would be more inviting to the kids.

I told Harold how well my machines were doing, and how I planned to place them in other states, because the stores there were evidently as free of competition as those in Wisconsin. I told him I needed some extended terms for payment; it would mean I could place more machines, which meant I would buy a lot more of them. I was elated. He agreed to sell his new cabinet machine to me at $10 each with $5 down and $1 a month for five months, without interest. I was so happy, I almost got up and hugged that teddy bear. This meant with the $9,000 I got from Hermy I could buy about 1,500 machines and the gum and toys to fill them. The machines should pay for themselves quickly and allow me to buy not only the 1,500, but as many as I wanted to put out in the future. My goal was to place thousands of them. Prayer worked again for me. I thanked God for the loan Hermy arranged and the time payments from Victor Vending.

Eppy and Company from New York, who molded the black and white Scottie dogs for Black & White scotch whiskey, started molding many of the Dowst metal toys out of plastic at a fraction of their cost; then they vacuum plated them in a gold-or silver-metallic finish. You couldn't tell a plastic gold-plated football from a solid metal one plated with real gold, that sold for $5 or more in the jewelry store—unless you weighed it in your hand and saw how light it was. Paul Price Company molded plastic rings, plated them, and sold them to us for as little as a penny apiece, a fraction of the cost of a die-cast metal ring. Kids loved key-chain fobs, like the skull-head rings molded out of glow-in-the-dark plastic, and especially the gold-and silver-plated skull rings with Czech cut-glass stone eyes in them.

Then two-color plastic charms came into being. Eppy molded a miniature two-piece dental plate and glued the pink and white pieces together to make miniature false teeth charms. Kids loved them and emptied machines to get them. These were followed by a two-color toilet bowl with seat, a black frying pan with a yellow and white fried egg inside, a yellow baby chick coming out of a white egg, and many other interesting colorful toys we could buy for an average of a penny apiece. Continual new toys kept the kids interested in playing our machines. Business was good and profitable.

I hired a young man from Brillion, just out of high school, to service my 300 machines in Wisconsin. Then I purchased more machines and spent my time placing them in Iowa and Minnesota.

Chapter 9

I was gone frequently, sometimes overnight, many times for several nights at a time, even a week or two, when trips were out of state. When I was working around Wisconsin and did come home evenings, many times it was after the dinner hour. Dolores would keep the food hot for me, never complaining. But one stormy night, I came in very late and never called to let her know I was okay. When I came in the door she was hysterical. She told me she was so worried that something had happened to me because of the rain storm. I admonished her for worrying about me.

I guess I was a workaholic. I worked six days a week, taking Sundays off. The Catholic Church forbade work on Sundays or I would have spent even less time with Dolores and the children. Besides running myself ragged all day long, I seemed to have a compulsion to keep busy every night when I wasn't out of town. I ran for the city council and was elected. I played in the Brillion City Band, rehearsing one night each week and playing concerts on the Fourth of July, Memorial Day, and every Labor Day weekend, plus several Sundays throughout the summer at picnics. Then there were Lions Club meetings and Chamber of Commerce meetings and Calumet County Hospital board meetings. I was a joiner.

About a year into my expansion program, I formed a partnership with my brother-in-law Al Leonard, Anita's husband, a likeable hardworking guy, raised on a farm, in the merchant marine during the war. Al was anxious to "chuck" his welding job at Chain Belt Company in Milwaukee and he moved to Indianapolis with his wife and children to run the Indiana territory. Afraid of his shadow like I was when I started, with no sales experience, he had enough drive and confidence in himself to give it a try. I told him I would loan the partnership the money for the machines and merchandise and help him place the machines. We would share the profits 50-50, over the salary he would receive for running the business. We would start with 500 machines and as they paid for themselves, we would buy more.

I suggested to Dolores that she and Michael come with me to Indianapolis for the three-week trip to help get Al's route started. She was six-months pregnant with our second child. Indianapolis, about 300 miles from Brillion, was too far for me to commute on weekends and I didn't want to leave her alone that long.

We checked into a cabin on the outskirts of Indianapolis. (Groups of small one-room cabins preceded the advent of the motel.) We were really cramped in the small room with cartons of machines and boxes of gumballs stacked high wherever we could find room, even between the bed and the wall, so both of us had to get in and out of one side of the bed. Dolores said she dreamt about the boxes falling on her at night, as she was nearest the wall. The baby bed the management furnished for Michael crowded the room even more.

Dolores spent her time taking care of Michael and filling the 20 or so machines I would need each day for my next days placements, displaying the toys next to the Plexiglas fronts in our new Victor cabinet machines. The days were long for her and she passed the time handstitching a lace baptismal gown for the new baby.

I was successful in averaging about 20 placements a day, but I hated every call I made. I was still not comfortable talking to people. It was hard work in the hot, humid, July climate of Indianapolis. After working at it about ten days, with no air-conditioning in my car, I had finally had it. It was mid-afternoon. Without much luck in placing machines that day, my shirt soaking wet, perspiration rolling off my forehead, the salt burning my eyes, tired from not getting much sleep in a hot room, and not liking what I was doing, I was depressed. I quit for the day and went back to the cabin. It seemed all I did was travel around the country doing work I didn't like. I was taking Dolores and the baby along so we would have some time together, but it was tough on her, too. Having all our meals in restaurants with an unruly two-year-old is not what we called fun.

I kept expanding my business out of Brillion and wanted to place some machines in Minneapolis, about 300 miles from home. I couldn't bring Dolores and Michael with me as Dolores was due to deliver our second child within a few weeks. She told her doctor I would be gone on a trip for two weeks. He cautioned her not to stay alone, as she might go into labor and the Appleton hospital and doctor were 20 miles away. So Dolores packed up Michael and stayed with her mother in Appleton while I was away. Kristine was born five days after I returned.

Kristine was a beautiful child. Dolores and I were both happy it was a girl. Dolores was already thinking about the pretty dresses she would buy for her.

After Kristine was born, I stayed on the same busy schedule, placing machines during the day and going to meetings almost every night of the week when I was home. When I did have a night at home, I'd lay on the living room floor after dinner and fall asleep. She would do the dishes and put the children to bed. About 9:30, when she went to bed, I would usually wake up and be ready to spend the evening with her; but by then she was tired and needed her rest for her next big day.

Dolores held down the home front. I was a workaholic out of an intense desire to be financially successful. She was a workaholic out of necessity, keeping house, preparing meals, shopping, taking full responsibility in caring for our children—as well as having them. Besides being a mother to them she was also a stand-in father, both when I was away placing machines, and when I was home managing the business and being involved in community activities.

I felt she was a partner in the success of the business, taking on these responsibilities was her duty as wife and mother. She reminded me of the frontier women in movies who shouldered the burdens of the women as well as those of the men they married, when it was required of them.

Dolores didn't have much to say in the direction of our lives. I usually set the course. She told me that she married a peanut vendor and would have been happy with the simple life I was living when we were going together. I told her, I was then living with my parents, didn't have any financial responsibilities, and didn't have a business that was making any money.

The beautiful white house with the pillars, that we both dreamed of having some day, was not to be attained in the peanut vending business, nor was the college education we both wanted for our kids.

I couldn't relate to the children. To me children were not necessarily to be enjoyed, they were to be raised, educated, and prepared for life. Being raised in the Depression, like we both were, I wanted more for our children, and for us, than we had when we were young.

I don't think Dolores was unhappy those days even though she thought I worked too much and didn't spend enough time with her and the kids. She seemed happy and enjoyed visiting with our friends. She spent time visiting with Elaine, who lived across the street from us and had kids about the age of ours. Sometimes when I was free for a night I'd suggest going out to dinner or a movie. She'd get a sitter in a flash, and out we'd go.

We also had great parties in our little house, with our friends sitting on the open stairway because we didn't have enough chairs. They'd sometimes have to go out the front door, around the house, and in the back door to go to our only bathroom, because our dining area in the kitchen blocked their way.

Dolores sometimes would go with me on business trips to Chicago when I went to see Leaf Gum or Victor Vending and we'd stay overnight at the Palmer House. We shopped for clothes for her in the afternoon and had dinner at Agostino's or George Diamond's and we'd top the night off with some loving in our hotel room.

Dolores sometimes would go with me to New York City when I went to hunt for new toys for our machines. Our favorite places for dinner were Elaine's on the east side, and Peter's Back Yard in Greenwich Village, stopping later in the Village at our favorite piano bar and asking Lenny Bruce to play and sing our favorite tune, *A Foggy Day in London Town.* On our first trip there together we saw our first Broadway show, *Annie Get Your Gun.* I thought this would be the highlight of our trip, but it was a disappointment. The only seats we could get were in the last row in the balcony. The stage props were worn and in need of paint, and I hated Ethel Merman's raspy voice. Stopping at Lindy's for a piece of their famous cheesecake and seeing Walter Winchel enthroned in his booth talking to celebrities, none of whom we recognized, made the evening.

When we didn't go on a business trip together for a while, I would plan a getaway trip to a Milwaukee motel for a few days during the week. We were fortunate for our wonderful grandmotherly baby-sitter Mrs. Riechert. The kids loved her and she loved them. I would plan these trips around the safe periods in the rhythm cycle until Dolores caught on to me and finally said, "No more trips to Milwaukee; all you want is sex and you spend the rest of the time berating me about how I'm being critical of people."

She was right about the sex and I know we got into some

discussions, she called them arguments, about who among our personal and business friends she didn't like. She didn't let on to them she didn't like them, but sometimes it showed and it embarrassed me.

I had to find a solution to the problem of finding locations for our machines. I hated doing it, and it took me away from home a great deal. I had my own routes to build, and I had promised my partner Al I would help him find locations for our partnership machines. Dolores and I talked about it one night at dinner, and I told her I felt we needed a full-time person to locate the machines for us, someone who would like doing it. She suggested I talk to her brother, Fabian. About my age, unmarried, he couldn't seem to find a job he liked since he returned from service. Dolores said he loved driving around the country in his car and he might enjoy a job like this. I approached him, telling him he could work at his own speed and we would pay him on a commission basis for the number of machines he placed. He would be responsible for his own travel expenses. Fabian liked the idea. He didn't mind staying out weekends when it was too far for him to drive home. He said he liked talking to people, so he took the job of placing machines for us. He started the following week in Al's territory. I was relieved.

The Indianapolis business was very successful so I formed another partnership with my brother Harold. Now a high school band director in a small Wisconsin school, he wanted to make more money and have the freedom of being his own boss. After checking various areas of the country for competitive activity, we decided on Northern Ohio. With his wife Sylvia, and their two children, they rented a house in Akron, Ohio, and he and Fabe started to place machines in that area.

I then expanded my own business, headquartered in Brillion, hiring Dolores' cousin Roger Jacobs, who was working for a photographer in Brillion, as a branch manager for a new Nebraska territory. He, his wife Toni, and their two kids, moved to Omaha to develop that territory. Roger had a good gift of gab. I knew he would have no trouble placing his machines.

Then my army buddy, Don Charles, said he was interested in going into a partnership with me. Don had finished college on the G.I.Bill, a government program for veterans. Using the credits he accumulated in the army at North Carolina State where I met Don, he was able to get his degree in a couple of years. Working as an accountant at Charmin Paper Company in Green Bay, he and his wife Jackie decided that new England was the place for them, so they moved to Hartford, Connecticut, to start our partnership business there.

Fabe now had to divide his services among several territories and he fulfilled his wish to see the country. Our machines were now being spread throughout a 16-state area from Wisconsin, west to Nebraska, east to Connecticut, and south to Indiana.

For the next two years we were plagued with serious problems around the country and my employees and partners looked to me for solutions. It seemed like every couple of months someone would call me with a health department or gambling problem regarding our machines.

First it was Milwaukee. A picture of our penny toy and gum machine appeared on the front page of the *Milwaukee Sentinel*, claiming it was a gambling machine. That familiar knot was back in my stomach as my body filled with anxiety. Would I get arrested? Would I have to remove the 200 machines I had in that area? I could see why winner ball machines could be considered a gamble as the kids could win a nickel candy bar for a penny, but we were vending a mixture of gumballs and toys and the kids got a portion of the mixture every time for their penny. None of the toys in the mixture cost us more than 2 cents each, and the average cost was less than a penny.

Besides, there were real gambling devices around the city,

like quarter ticket jars—five nickel tickets stapled together with numbers on them—and if you drew a lucky number on a ticket you could win as much as $5 or $10 in cash.

I was worried. What should I do? Then I thought of my brother-in-law Les O'Hearn who was working for Milwaukee County selling their tax-delinquent lands. I called Les and explained my problem. He said he was friendly with the district attorney and if I would come to Milwaukee he would take me to see him. I told Les about the real gambling devices around Milwaukee and wondered why they were picking on our penny machines. Les said there was an election coming up, and it was probably political and that some of the politicians were probably trying to make points with the public by cleaning up gambling. Les said it wouldn't hurt if I brought along $50 in cash we could give the D.A., as a campaign contribution. That sounded like a bribe to me, but when they were singling out our machines while letting genuine gambling devices go untouched, I figured I was justified in doing so. I drove to Milwaukee and Les and I had a friendly chat with the D.A. in his office, explaining the situation. He seemed sympathetic. He couldn't see that this was gambling. On the way out Les handed him the "campaign contribution" and I never heard another word about it.

Most of our problems developed in Harold's territory in Ohio. First he called me because the Cleveland health department was concerned about kids swallowing a toy, even though the kids could plainly see the toys and that's what they hoped to get when they played the machines. Little kids would be with their mothers. They would caution them about not putting a toy in their mouth, as they would about paper clips or thumbtacks at home. Harold argued with them, stating that Cracker Jack toys were mixed in the box with the Cracker Jacks. (It wasn't until later that the toys were packed in a separate compartment at the end of the box.) Harold also told them our company had about 2,000 machines out in the field, and we never received a complaint of a child swallowing or choking on a toy. But they still insisted he remove the machines. The closest large city was Cincinnati, in southern Ohio, so Harold and Fabe had to relocate the Cleveland machines there. But then, besides the cost of relocating them, it was also more costly to service them as Cleveland was 200 miles from his home.

A couple months later, Harold called and said we had a court date in Youngstown, Ohio. He said they considered our machines a gambling device, the same problem as in Milwaukee. Now, again, would we be arrested? Would we have to remove the Youngstown machines also? The problem gnawed at me. Was this going to happen in other parts of the country, too? It could put us all out of business. I drove to Akron, then Harold and I drove to Youngstown for the court date. The judge was pleasant, but firm. He wanted the machines out—more machines for Cincinnati—Harold was getting discouraged and I was becoming a nervous wreck.

One thing that was good about the vending business, compared to owning a restaurant or hotel, was that we could always move the machines to another city. If someone opened a nicer hotel or restaurant across the street from yours, you'd be stuck there if you owned the building.

Then there were lesser problems like my serviceman in Brillion who had an accident, fell asleep at the wheel and turned over our delivery truck. Besides, he was off duty and wasn't supposed to be using the truck, so I had to deal with that. Lucky he wasn't seriously hurt.

Then Don called me from Hartford. He said he thought his serviceman was stealing from him. When Don had serviced the route, the store managers occasionally would buy back some of the pennies the machines took in, for change, and would give Don paper money for them. Since he turned the route over to a serviceman, the man never brought back any paper money and Don figured he was pocketing it. Don confronted him about it and he denied he was taking any money, but Don decided to let him go and hoped he could find another man that he could trust. That was one of the big problems with the bulk vending business. There is no way of determining how much money should be returned from the routes. The gum and toys are put into the machines in bulk rather than in packages like in a candy or cigarette machine, and it is impossible to know whether employees are stealing from you. That is one of the main reasons I expanded our routes through friends and relatives I could trust.

Then after a couple of months of peace, Roger Jacobs called from Omaha. Another court date with a judge. He didn't like the mixing of toys and gum in our machines. He thought it was unsanitary.

I was less anxious this time, because I had already done the court scene and I didn't land in jail. Roger and I went to see the judge. He insisted that we either vend all gum, or all toys, but not both in one machine. I asked him whether it would be okay to mix the toys with glass marbles and then we would have all toys. He had no objection to that. It showed how silly the ruling was. Kids could mistake marbles for gum and break their teeth on them. We tested a few machines, replacing the gumballs with marbles. The mixture didn't sell well enough to be profitable and some of the merchants, as well as Roger and I, thought the marbles were hazardous. We had to remove our machines and since there were no other large cities in Nebraska, we had to take out the machines and close the Omaha branch. Roger moved to Milwaukee. I was happy he found a good job there. But now we had more machines to locate elsewhere at additional cost.

I was getting a phobia about answering the phone. I'd get a sick feeling in my stomach when I heard it ring, afraid of what new problem might be on the other end of the line.

The business was driving me batty. It was December; I hated the thought of struggling with the ice and snow and blistering cold of Wisconsin in January and February. I suggested to Dolores we take the two kids and drive to California.

I had Jeannette taking care of my office in Brillion and Jim working out of there to service the gum and toy machines in the midwest. I had an idea, maybe I could run my business from California. Contact with my partners by phone and mail could be done as well from California as from Wisconsin. I still had that burning desire to go to college. Maybe I could run the business and go to college in sunny California. The thought intrigued me and I discussed it with Dolores. She went along with the idea. It sounded like a vacation to her.

We drove to my brother Richard and Esther's in Corona and stayed with them for a couple of weeks. Richard suggested Pomona College at Claremont, about 25 miles from Corona. He said it was a great college with an Ivy League reputation.

We rented a small house in Pomona and I started college in January. I thought it would be as easy for me as I found North Carolina State College when I was in the service, but that was almost seven years ago and coming back to college to second year literature, math and physics, between semesters, was more than I could handle. Living at home, I missed having other students to consult with in the evenings when I didn't understand something. I was dreaming when I thought I could take a full college course, be a father and husband, and run my business from several thousand miles away. I quit at midterm and returned to Brillion. I finally got the college bug out of my system.

Then the big one hit. The one that could put my partners and me out of business.

I opened the weekly *Billboard* magazine to the vending section and the lead article stated that the Federal Food and Drug Administration had brought a lawsuit against a Virginia company that vended gumballs and toys in the same machine! The FDA claimed the toys in the machine "contaminated" the gum. The court had ruled for the FDA and against the vending company. The Virginia company was taking their case to the court of appeals. If the ruling was upheld by that court, my partners and I would be out of business, and out of money as well, since the higher court ruling would be the law of the land. My partners and I would be stuck with 5,000 machines, on which we owed money!

I couldn't stand the pressure. I lost my appetite. I was totally preoccupied with the possible failure of the entire business. With chest pains from the anxiety I was ready for a heart attack or the "booby hatch."

I checked with an engineering firm to see if our machines could be modified to vend a one-inch gumball, without toys, which Cramer Gum Company was successfully doing, using an all-plastic machine they manufactured. They said it wouldn't be possible because the diameter of the machine was too small to vend gum larger than the gum we were now mixing with the toys. It would "bridge" in the machine and not drop down into the holes in the merchandise wheel.

I called Chuck Buckman to see if he had any ideas. He heard about the court ruling, but said it wouldn't hurt his business. He was setting up, then selling, routes of gum machines, but his were strictly gum machines on a charity program to benefit an organization for the blind.

"Why don't you sell the machines now before the court hearing on the appeal?" he asked. "There's no law against that."

"But what if the lower court ruling stands after the appeal and all the people who buy our routes lose their money? They'll come after me."

"It's legal, Back-er. Didn't you ever hear the phrase 'let the buyer beware'? Even the Catholic Church preaches that."

"It does? It doesn't seem honest to me—selling routes of machines that later could be worthless. I'll have to think about that." I said.

If I could salve my conscience, knowing that it wasn't against the law of the church, I could consider it. I knew a priest, who I met through my friend Rudy, in a neighboring town, so I went to see him the next day. I didn't want my parish priest to know what I was considering.

"Yes," he said. "*Caveat Emptor*, Latin for 'let the buyer beware.'" He quoted the saying from the law of the church. He felt what I would be doing wasn't against church law and therefore not a sin. Since I religiously followed the church laws—or confessed it when I didn't—I decided that if the church didn't consider it a sin and my partners went along with me, I would have Chuck sell our routes for us.

I called each of them and told them we would probably go broke if the higher court upheld the present ruling, as we'd have to remove all the machines we had in the stores. Since they were all Catholic, I told them what the priest told me, and they said I should do what I thought best and they would go along with it.

I decided to let Chuck sell the machines. I told him I would be happy to sell them to him at $10 each, which is what the machines cost us, and we would absorb the cost of the $3.50 in merchandise in each machine and the costs of setting up the routes. I told him these were "fire sale" prices, and he could add whatever he wanted to his cost for his profit. I was surprised when he said he would offer the machines at double his cost, $20 each. He would ask half down and my partners and I would get our $10 in cash.

I figured it was a roll of the dice for Chuck. We were selling the machines to him. He stood to make $50,000 if he was able to sell them all at $20, but his profit would probably be in notes receivable from the people who purchased the machines. If the court ruling was upheld he'd have a tough time collecting from them. They might even sue him for the down payment he would be turning over to us.

It was quite a gamble. If the lawsuit was settled in our favor, we would be able to continue our businesses and no longer be bothered by judges or health departments around the country forcing us to remove our machines. But if the suit went against us, I and my partners would be broke, or nearly so, and have warehouses filled with 5,000 practically worthless machines.

Then if I didn't have enough problems, Don Charles called me. He had been called back into service for the Korean War. Don and his friend Chuck Stimpson joined the reserves when they were discharged after World War II, never believing they might be called back some day. They thought it would be fun playing poker with the guys after the reserve meetings and they could earn a little extra money. I was surprised when Don joined. I remembered how I gave the Sergeant a piece of my mind when he asked me to join the reserves when I was being released from the army.

Don was devastated, and so was I. He had to leave in a few weeks, and we saw no alternative but to take in the 500 machines from his territory and place them in storage. This was one more reason I'd had enough of this damn gum and toy business!

Chuck and I got together at his office in Green Bay to talk about his strategy for selling our machines.

"How do you plan to sell them?" I asked Chuck as he was leaning back in his chair, behind his desk, his hands clasped behind his head.

"Got it all figured out Back-er. I'm going to divide the 4,500 machines into three routes, one based in Wisconsin, one in Indiana, and one in Ohio, with about 1,500 machines in each area, and then find three buyers. Do you know who I'm going to offer the first route to?"

"I have no idea."

"Hermy Plous," he said, laughing.

"Herman Plous," I exclaimed. "The guy who got the loan for me, and trusted me with the $10,000 I needed to expand my business? Now you're going to stick him with one of the routes?"

"Why not," Chuck said. "He's loaded with money."

I couldn't believe the nerve of the guy.

"Well, I'll be darned. Hermy will be pretty angry with both of us if the lawsuit goes against him and his route becomes worthless." I said.

"He's a smart businessman and a gambler. He's been gambling for years that people will pay all those second mortgages that he has been investing in. If he doesn't have the smarts to look into this business before he buys it, it's his funeral."

"Think he would be interested?" I asked.

"Back-er I already approached him," Chuck said with a smug look on his face. "He said he'd like to talk to you about it, says he hasn't seen you in years. That's why I asked you to Green Bay today. I've got an appointment with him this afternoon. I thought you'd like to come along."

"You son of a gun. You had this thing all cooked up, before you told me you wanted to sell my machines for me."

"Not really, Back-er, but I had a hunch Hermy might be interested."

We went to Hermy's storefront office on South Washington Street, walked in the door, and there on the counter dividing the waiting area from his desk, staring Chuck and me in the face was the *Northwesterner*, the newsletter published by the Northwestern Corporation where Hermy, Chuck, and I had purchased some of our peanut machines. The headline read, "FDA Rules Toys Contaminate Gum!"

"You see that," I whispered to Chuck. Evidently Hermy was back in the warehouse area where he stored the candy bars for the candy machines he still operated.

"Either it just came or Hermy doesn't read his junk mail," Chuck said quietly. "Just ignore it. Don't worry about it."

Hermy came to the front office and greeted us, telling me he was happy to see me and glad I made a success of the gumball business. I hadn't seen him since he arranged the $10,000 loan for me, four years before.

"Chuck tells me you want to sell your routes. How come?" Hermy asked.

"I'm a nervous wreck trying to manage these routes all around the country with partners and managers. I'm about ready for the "booby hatch," I told him. That part was honest anyway.

"Chuck says you've got three routes for sale. Which is the best one?" he asked me.

"Indiana," I said. "That route does more business and makes more money than either of the other two."

"Can you send your books from the Indiana business to my accountant so he can look them over?" he asked. I was excited that he was interested.

"Be happy to," I said. "I'm sure you'll be pleased with the sales and profits this route is making."

When we got out on the street we both agreed we probably had a sale, providing Hermy didn't read the *Northwesterner*.

I had Al send the books to Hermy's accounting firm and in a few weeks Chuck had the sale. I guess Hermy didn't read his junk mail or his *Billboard* magazine, either.

"Who are you going to sell the other routes to smarty?" I asked Chuck when I came to pick up the check for $15,000 for the Indiana route.

"I was thinking of selling one of the other routes to Hermy's accountants. They've got money to invest and one of the guys has a son who could manage the business. I figure if the accountants thought the business was good enough for Hermy to buy they would see no reason why they shouldn't get in on the deal themselves."

And that's what happened. The accountants bought the Ohio machines, and one of the accountant's sons went to Cincinnati to manage their route. Hermy sent his Green Bay serviceman, Mike Raleigh to Indianapolis to manage his route there.

Then Chuck sold the Wisconsin based route to a fellow in Green Bay, to whom he had previously sold a route of machines on a charity machine program to aid the Wisconsin Association of the Blind. My partners and I got the other $30,000 in cash as Chuck promised. He also paid $5 to Don and me for each of the machines Don had in storage.

I carried a lot of guilt for selling the machines without disclosing the possible FDA problem. In a way this was a repeat of the sale of the cashew machines in Milwaukee when I didn't tell the buyer the whole truth about the business, only this was on a much larger scale. There was a possibility the buyers would be buying worthless businesses. If the superior court did not reverse the lower court ruling, Chuck and I would have fleeced the buyers out of $90,000. It would almost be like stealing $90,000. Although it bothered my conscience, I didn't feel I had to confess it because the priest told me it didn't violate church law. But I still felt I was violating God's law.

Al and I paid off what we owed on the Indianapolis business and split what was left. Al moved back to Milwaukee, and with his share of the profits and the money from the sale of his Indiana home was able to buy an older Milwaukee home mortgage free. He found a metalworking job in maintenance, for the Milwaukee school system. Harold, because of the disruptions in his business and the relocation expenses, ended up with about enough for his moving expenses to Corona, California, where my brother Richard, a school administrator there, told him about an opening for a high school band director. I came out with about $15,000 for my share on Al's machines and the sale of my Wisconsin routes. This wasn't too bad, it was one-and one-half times as much as I paid for the small home we had built out of the electrical shop four years before. The rest of the money was used to pay what we owed on the machines and merchandise.

I worried for weeks, awaiting the results of the case in the court of appeals. What kind of a mess would I be in if the machines we sold would turn out to be worthless? Would I be involved in a lawsuit? Would I be able to live with my guilt? Even if church law absolved me I knew deep down, what I did was morally wrong. What about my faith when I was in the army that resulted in a miracle? I didn't even think of trying to garner enough faith in God, that my partners and I could have stayed in the business and things would have worked out for us. I had been too busy, too confused, and mentally disturbed with health and gambling problems, to think much about God in my life the past few years.

It was one happy day when I got the news the court of appeals had reversed the lower court ruling and settled the FDA case in our favor. Chuck and I were off the hook. The ruling stated the toys could not contaminate the gum in the machines, because the gum did not "contain" the toys! The industry was finally free of the health departments going to judges and trying to stop us from mixing gumballs and toys in the same machines. Chuck and I were greatly relieved. We took our wives out to dinner that night to celebrate the victory.

I learned it's tough to be a pioneer. The problems fall on the ones breaking new ground. Those who follow have an easier path. It didn't bother me that we had sold businesses worth $90,000 for a fraction of that price. I just couldn't stomach the business any longer. In addition to the sick feeling I got every time the phone rang, I couldn't even look at a grocery store. I'd had it. I needed a rest. I was glad that phase of my life was over—or so I thought at the time.

Chapter 10

Chuck told me he had started going to church every morning before going to work. He said his dad got after him for not going to Mass on Sundays; his dad wanted to fulfill the pledge he made to his wife, before she died, to bring the boys up Catholic. It was considered a mortal sin for Catholics to miss Mass on Sundays.

"I showed him," Chuck told me. "I not only started going on Sundays, I started going every day of the week. It got me up in the morning and it was a peaceful way to start the day."

I thought, if Chuck could go to Mass every morning, so could I, even if I had to drag myself there with half-opened eyes. I had a lot to be thankful for with the favorable outcome of the court case.

My mother had given me a gift of a small prayer book the day I left home, years ago, when I moved to Green Bay. I carried it with me during the war. I took this prayer book and a little booklet called *Confidence of God* with me to church in the mornings. These two prayer books changed my spiritual life. The novena I prayed in the service to the Blessed Virgin to get me out of the infantry was in that prayer book.

The *Confidence in God* booklet changed, forever, my concept of God. Up to then I feared God, especially the God of the Old Testament, who seemed to rule like a tyrant. The New Testament talked about a loving God, but I had a hard time believing in a loving God when the nuns at St. Mary School told me that if we did not confess mortal sins, like eating meat on Friday, or missing Mass on Sunday, we would burn in hell for all eternity. I couldn't imagine what punishment awaited me in hell for sins I thought were much worse, like the sexual sin of masturbation. To me God was a ruthless dictator sitting up in heaven cracking the whip over us, expecting us to be perfect, and if we denied ourselves and prayed hard enough for something, we might get it.

In the *Confidence in God* booklet it said that most people viewed God in this way, but it went on to convince me of God's love for me, stating that if God had ever shown me any love He must always love me. I thought of the miracle that happened in the service and through it how God showed His love for Dolores and me.

The booklet went on to say, "God does not care for us one day and hate us the next. He is not capricious or inconstant like man, and above everything God wants our love." The rest of the booklet reinforced the thought that God is like a loving father who only wants good for us. I began to believe that God is not to be feared—as I feared my father—and that He understands and forgives our weaknesses, our sins. I began to realize that as a loving father He may let us suffer the consequences of bad choices we make in life—to teach us a lesson—as my own father sometimes did.

I thought about the outcome of the FDA lawsuit. If it had not been settled to the benefit of the people who bought the routes of machines, Chuck, and most likely I as well, would probably have been in deep trouble. Besides the guilt we would have had to live with, Hermy and the others would very likely have brought lawsuits against us to recover their money, which they would try to prove we took under false pretenses. That would have been the punishment we would have brought upon ourselves and which we would have deserved.

I needed a vacation, and so did Dolores, after putting up

with me through this terrible ordeal. I also needed to figure out my future and talk it over with her. We heard about a beautiful vacation area on the peninsula in Door County north of Green Bay. We took a sitter along so Dolores and I could spend some time by ourselves. Michael was five, Kristine three. Dolores was pregnant with our third child.

We rented a cabin in Sister Bay and had a glorious time exploring the peninsula. Dolores and I discovered Schmitz Gazebo, a fine German restaurant, where the yachts docked in Baileys Harbor. Before dinner we sat at the bar for a drink and watched the raccoons, through a picture window over the back bar, eat corn from a feeder they set up for them. We relaxed and I talked about my ideas for the future.

I knew I wanted to be in business, I didn't feel I would be happy working for someone, and I liked the income possibilities of a business of my own.

Anything to do with gumball vending machines was out of the question.

As a kid I was fascinated with magic tricks. My dad was, too. I guess I got interested in them when he showed us kids how he could put out a burning cigarette stub in a handkerchief he put over his fist, pushing it down into the space he made in the handkerchief with his index finger. Not only did the cigarette not burn the handkerchief but the cigarette also disappeared. Then he showed us the metal flesh colored cap that fit over the end of his finger which he placed in the handkerchief. He had extinguished the cigarette stub in the metal cap and made the cap disappear by slipping it with the cigarette inside, over the end of his finger.

My dad even helped me organize a magic show I put on in a tent, at our church picnic, when I was about 12 years old. I bought the magic tricks from ads I saw in kid's magazines, the only place I knew to get them other than in magic stores, which were usually located in the larger cities.

When I scoured the market in New York City for small toys for our gumball machines I noticed that some of the importers handled trick and joke items made in Japan and Hong Kong. I was fascinated with them and picked up samples even though they were too large to vend in our gum and toy machines. There were joke items like a real fly molded inside a plastic ice cube to drop into somebody's drink, a horrible looking rubber bloody finger bleeding through the bandage which you could slip over your thumb, and squirt rings, flowers, and cameras you could use to surprise your friends by squirting water at them. I thought about ways I could market these trick and joke items to kids and their dads when they didn't have access to a magic store.

By the time we returned from our vacation I had the idea pretty well worked out. I would package trick and joke items, display them on wire racks and sell them in taverns for fathers to take home to their kids. I figured other fathers would be fascinated with them as my father was.

When I got back from our weekend vacation I tested the idea by placing a dozen racks in taverns on consignment. The taverns would pay only for the items they sold. They sold quite well, but not well enough to afford to send someone to go around and service the racks. The other problem was the items were in cellophane bags and the people could choose the items they wanted and I had to pick up the items that didn't sell. That would eat into the profit.

So, I bought some cardboard boxes about the size of a Cracker Jack box, had them printed with "Tavern Fun Tricks and Jokes, 25¢ each" and wrapped the tricks and jokes in joke sheets I had printed with jokes I selected from joke books in the library. They sold well and I didn't have any items to take back to eat into my profits. But to send someone around to the taverns to sell just one item at a time would not be profitable.

I recalled how my dad sold candy and tobacco to taverns and grocery stores years ago as a wholesaler. I decided I wanted to sell my Tavern Fun to wholesalers throughout the U.S. I went to the library and found a publication that listed trade associations, and learned there was a trade group called the National Candy Wholesalers Association. I called them for a list of their members.

I looked in the Appleton Yellow Pages for a commercial artist and found Ray Hudson who designed a four-color box for the individual Tavern Fun items and a colorful display box to hold 24 of the individual boxes. I had a small quantity of boxes printed for a test and purchased enough trick and joke items from my New York importer to fill them.

Rather than hiring people to do the packaging for me I looked for a contractor who could package the Tavern Fun item. In the Milwaukee Yellow Pages I found a contract packager called the Workshop for the Blind. They were happy to package and ship the Tavern Fun item for me. The blind workers were able to wrap the items in a joke sheet and insert them in the folding boxes, then one person would put one each of the 24 assorted small boxes in a display box and pack 12 displays to a corrugated case. I had them make up 10 cases and hold them until I could get some orders.

I designed a brochure with a picture of the display box on it and the information about taking the jokes to the jokesters, sending it to 100 wholesalers on the list as a test. I offered the item on a guaranteed sale, and told them I would take back any unopened display boxes they couldn't sell.

I watched the mail daily, wondering whether or not I would receive any orders. A week after the mailing I received my first order. It was from Bur-Bee Company in Walla Walla, Washington. I was excited. Then a few more orders started to trickle in. It looked like I had a new business.

New business, new baby. Susan was born—beautiful, healthy and strong. Dolores and I were pleased the baby was healthy, because Dolores had hemorrhaged during her pregnancy and had to spend part of the time in bed to prevent a miscarriage.

Tavern Fun
NOVELTIES
25¢
Willie Whistle's
BUBBLE GUM
SURPRISE
THIS BOX MAKES A WHISTLE
SEE OTHER SIDE OF PACKAGE
© L.M.B. & CO.
SURPRISE INSIDE
GR. WT. 23½ LBS.
CU. FT. 0' 8"
CARE
UNITED STATES OF AMERICA
5¢
LARRY
MOE
CURLY
ROCKET RINGS
5¢

We put Michael and Kristine in the children's bedroom and Susan in the nursery. We didn't have room for any more children in that house. I hoped our new business would prosper so we could build a larger home. If we spent the money from selling the gumball machines to make a down payment on a new home, we wouldn't have money to build our business.

On a trip to Milwaukee to see the contractor I stopped for lunch at the Port Silver Diner and ran into Vern Vechart, a friend a few years younger than me, that I had known at Brillion High School. A short red-headed outgoing bundle of energy, Vern was selling medical supplies to doctors. I told him about Tavern Fun and how I wanted to market it nationally through candy and tobacco wholesalers, and that I needed a sales manager. Vern smiled and laughed a lot and seemed to find humor in everything. I suggested he'd have a lot more fun selling tricks and jokes than medical supplies. He said he'd think about it and a couple of weeks later took the job. I still was not comfortable in the salesman's role.

Vern started calling on the candy wholesalers in Wisconsin and came back with an excellent idea on how we could expand our business. In talking with one of the wholesalers he learned that self-employed salesmen, called candy brokers, came to call on him regularly, each representing several different candy companies. If we could get these brokers to show our Tavern Fun item in various territories across the country along with their candy items, we could get national coverage on our item. He said candy brokers work on a commission of 5 percent on the wholesale selling price, make the territory regularly, and pay their own expenses. They would take the orders and send them to us, we would ship the merchandise to the wholesaler who would pay us for what they purchased. The broker would also get a commission on any repeat orders the wholesaler might send us from their territory. The wholesaler suggested a broker, Bob Morgan, to represent us in Wisconsin. Vern was excited and the idea sounded great to me.

I knew it would involve a lot of travel for Vern to build a national sales organization of brokers for us, so I gave him a 20 percent partnership interest in the company. Vern was a hard worker and I knew he would do a good job.

Vern talked to Bob Morgan and Bob agreed to show our Tavern Fun along with the candy items he carried for other companies. Vern rode with Bob for a week calling on the wholesalers in Wisconsin.

"That was a week from hell," Vern said when he got back. "Bob not only drove like a maniac, but he held a fifth of Jack Daniels between his knees and took a swig whenever he felt the urge. I'm glad to be back alive, but we wrote some orders and Bob recommended his broker friend, Ralph Lee, in Chicago for that area. I plan to go to see Ralph and talk to him about representing us. I hope he isn't a crazy driver like Bob." Vern said with a laugh.

Vern drove to Chicago to talk to Ralph Lee and he agreed to represent us in Chicago and the rest of Illinois. Vern asked him if he could recommend any other brokers, and he suggested Bernie Leonard, a friend of his in St. Louis. Ralph also suggested we rent a booth and exhibit our Tavern Fun at the National Candy Wholesalers Convention at the end of July. He said it would be in Washington, D.C. that year and that brokers from all over the country attend the show. We could put up a "brokers wanted" sign in our booth. Ralph also suggested we try to add more items to our line so the brokers had more than Tavern Fun to offer from our company.

We were successful with our 25-cent Tavern Fun, so why not add a 5-cent prize package for the grocery store trade for the little kids.

As a kid I learned I could take a Juji Fruit box, punch a hole in the side, open both folded ends a little, blow into the side of the box and the box became a whistle. After talking to our artist, Ray Hudson, we made a similar box, with instructions on it, calling it Willie Whistle, filled it with five individually wrapped gumballs and a prize, like a plastic animal or a toy ring. Ray came up with a drawing of a bird on the front of the box. We worked like mad to have it ready to show at the candy convention only a couple of months away.

We rented an empty grocery store building on Main Street in Brillion and hired housewives to do the packaging for us. The Workshop for the Blind was 100 miles from Brillion and not very convenient for us. With our new nickel prize package we felt we could save money by packaging the prize packages ourselves.

We checked into the Shoreham Hotel in Washington, D.C., where the convention was being held, and set up our booth the afternoon before the convention opened. Vern brought along a giant 2 x 4-foot wooden Willie Whistle box and set it up on our display table. I was glad Vern was there to talk to the prospective brokers and the wholesalers who stopped by our booth. I did not feel comfortable or knowledgeable enough to talk to them.

We rented a small suite, stocked it with a couple bottles of booze, beer and soda, and Vern invited prospective brokers to stop at our suite in the evening after the convention closed for the day to have a drink with us and talk about our line of merchandise. Vern's outgoing personality won them over and with the help of Ralph Lee we added Bernie Leonard in St. Louis, Jack Stanley in Cleveland, Ted Brierley in Boston, and several other brokers from various parts of the country.

After the convention, Vern and I knew that if we could come up with items that sold well in grocery and candy stores we could continue the growth of our business, adding new brokers, and eventually cover the entire country. We noticed that other companies were using the convention as an opportunity to hold meetings with their brokers, individually and as a group, saving them the time and money it would take to see them in their home territories. We would do that at future conventions.

The additional brokers gave our sales a boost and by the end of our first year we had sold more than $100,000 worth of our products, mostly Tavern Fun. Even though candy was the mainstay of the candy wholesalers' purchases, they also sold a lot of novel items that kids would buy in a grocery store. Baseball card packages with a slab of gum inside were big sellers. This type of item, like our prize packages, were called specialty items in the candy trade.

Over the next several years we tried many other specialty items. Like most novelty items, some sold well for a while then slowed down, so we dropped them and added others.

We bought men's black pocket combs at a penny apiece and retailed them at a dime. Packed in a six-dozen, round, transparent, plastic container, they sold slowly, but the store owners bought them because we had enough profit in the item to give them a premium like a free flashlight or glass fishing rod with each container of combs.

We did the same thing with 29-cent, name-brand toothbrushes that we bought on a closeout at a nickel apiece. With each two dozen, packed in a Libby glass juice shaker, the retailer received a premium like a six-piece German made set of screwdrivers or a German handsaw with five interchangeable blades. The empty juice container became an added premium for the retailer. This item was so successful that we contracted with Mel Koch who started Rent-A-Truck in Brillion, about that time. On his back hauls from New York City, delivering Brillion Iron Works farm machinery there, he picked up the toothbrushes, screwdrivers, and handsaws in New York, and stopped in Ohio to pick up the juice shakers at the Libby plant. When the deal, as we called it, was first introduced it sold exceptionally well. He would bring in a semi load for us as often as every month or two.

Three years after Susan was born, James arrived. With Kristine and Susan in twin beds in the small children's bedroom and Michael occupying the tiny nursery, the only place left for James' baby bed was the walk-in closet between our bedroom and the nursery. We moved the clothes out and the new baby in, another beautiful child, healthy and smiling, he didn't know he should have a larger room.

During the three years between Susan and James' birth, Dolores had a miscarriage when she was four and one-half months pregnant. She told me she suffered from extreme guilt, after it happened, feeling guilty because she didn't want to have a fourth child in that small house.

The miscarriage was a traumatic experience for both of us, Dolores going through labor that resulted in a stillborn baby, thinking that God was punishing her for her thoughts. With me it was the task of taking the baby in a small cardboard box to my dad's family cemetery plot, where my brother Joseph, who died at birth, was buried, and burying the baby all by myself at the side of the lot. Dolores told me the nun at St. Vincent's Hospital had baptized him, which pleased us.

After the guilt of the miscarriage, Dolores told me she made sure she allowed no similar thoughts in her mind about not having another baby in that small house.

It's fortunate the business was doing well, so we started plans for building a new, larger home in Brillion. It took more than a year to plan and build, as we hired an architect to design it for us.

I don't know what became of our dream home idea with the white pillars, as we didn't even consider it. We built a four-bedroom ranch home, with a contemporary look on a corner lot, in a new subdivision in the city. It had two and one-half baths, a large family room, a large combination living-dining room, with a large fieldstone fireplace in the living room, and a red brick, floor to ceiling barbecue grill in the family room. There was a separate laundry room and a kitchen with a large dining area, a small screened porch plus a two-car detached garage.

It was the second largest of the new homes in Brillion. Only

Butch Peters, the president of the Brillion Iron Works, had a larger one. I felt inferior to the professional and business people in town because I didn't have a college education. Maybe this would help my self-image. I could show everyone that I was a success in business.

The house was beautiful and Dolores and I loved it. The living-dining room area had about the same square footage as our entire Dewey Street home. But again I should have listened to Dolores. She wanted to face the family room toward the rear of the lot with the sunny southern exposure and put the living room on the north side. I told her I didn't want people driving by at night looking in our living room. Dolores said that's what draperies are for, but I won, as usual. It would have been so nice to have the winter sun warm the family room when the children were playing there and we could have had doors opening onto a patio for outdoor living in the summer months.

We were especially happy to have some nice-sized bedrooms and a separate bathroom for the kids. Michael, being the eldest, got the smaller bedroom for himself, the two girls occupied twin beds in the largest room and we used the third bedroom for a nursery for James. He was just one-year old when we moved in. Dolores was pregnant with our fifth child. It looked like we would fill up the house in a hurry.

We had a big housewarming party, inviting Butch Peters, the other Iron Works executives, and the other "important" people in town for an open house on a Sunday afternoon, and our close friends for the evening. Dolores had hired a couple of ladies to help with the buffet. We served champagne punch, made with white wine instead of champagne. We had a great time showing off our new home.

The only problem with our new home was Dolores wished it were in Appleton. Now that we had a dining room that would seat ten people, Dolores and our friends formed a couples' dinner group with the Thiessens, Frisbys, Hoeltkes, and the Ariens.

We met once a month at each other's homes. It was fun, I really enjoyed their company and Dolores did, too. When she had talked about moving to Appleton I told her it wouldn't be convenient for me, because I had my business in Brillion. I also told her I wouldn't feel comfortable anywhere but Brillion as I knew the people there, most of our friends were there, and I even knew where the cracks were in the sidewalks.

Chapter 11

Our broker Ralph Lee had a great idea. Why not find a way to package cotton candy so we could sell it in the grocery stores through candy wholesalers. Ordinarily children could get it only at fairs and carnivals.

We found a cellophane that was airtight to bag it in, and started to manufacture it in the Chicago area, spinning it in a machine like they use in carnivals. It sold well when we could get it to the kids nice and fluffy in an airtight bag, but if there was one pin hole in the bag, all the delicious colorful fluffy stuff ended up a glob of sugar the size of a dime, which is what the kids paid for it. The freight companies soon put us out of the cotton candy business. We shipped it by truck under the candy rate, but we were filling their trucks with air. They petitioned the Federal Commerce Commission to triple the candy rate, which they did, and that did us in.

Another innovative item was a 10-cent package of Wisconsin Cheddar cheese with two soda crackers; there were a dozen packages stapled to a card for the tavern trade. Wispride Cheese Company made it for us, so that it didn't need refrigeration. We put so much importance on making sure the cheese wouldn't spoil; we didn't think about the cellophane not keeping the crackers from breaking and going limp in the hot, humid Wisconsin summers. (Don't know if that's where Kraft got their idea, but they have sold a package of unrefrigerated cheese and crackers for years in a plastic container that protects both the cheese and the crackers from spoiling.)

We also tried other specialty items that failed, such as caramel corn and G-Nuts. The caramel corn and G-Nuts were made for us by the Bowlby Candy Company in Appleton. Bowlby was an innovative guy, but we found the caramel corn stuck together in the hot, humid Wisconsin summers and the G-Nuts, various flavors of sugared peanuts with cinnamon or—believe it or not—garlic, did not sell well enough to continue with them.

All at once it dawned on me. All these items that failed were perishable. From then on I imagined a large sign in my office above the door, "No More Perishable Products", I was afraid I might get the bright idea to try another one.

Vern seemed to be getting restless. He enjoyed the building process of setting up our broker organization. Now that he had that accomplished, he wanted new, fast-selling products to increase sales.

Sales of our prize packages, combs and toothbrushes with premiums had fallen off. We tried some new items, like the perishable ones that failed, but our business wasn't growing.

Vern felt he was as far as he could go with our company, so he decided to take a sales management job with Katherine Beich, a manufacturer of quality candies for the fund-raising business. We came to a mutual agreement on the value of Vern's 20 percent partnership interest and I bought him out.

After several years of working with Vern I had gained confidence in my sales and marketing ability, so I took over the job myself. I still didn't like face-to-face selling, but that wasn't necessary in our business; our candy brokers did that. All I had to do was manage them properly and motivate them to take more time selling our products.

Another item we came up with for the candy wholesalers was two silver metal-plated plastic space rings on a six-inch candy stick, all for 5 cents. We called them Rocket Rings. It was fairly successful, but then we hit the jackpot.

The Three Stooges became very popular again when their old movies were re-released. At the same time flicker-action pictures were invented, so we made a deal with the Stooges' agents to pay them a 5 percent royalty for the rights to sell a Three Stooge picture action ring, on a stick of candy for a nickel. The picture would change from one of the Stooges to another as you moved the ring. We called the item Ring Ding and the kids went wild for it; we sold millions of them.

One day we received a handwritten letter from Moe, one of the Stooges. He had seen the Stooge rings and wanted a few hundred to pass out to the kids. He said they would be performing at the Wisconsin State Fair in a few weeks and if we were coming to the fair maybe we could bring the rings, and if we had any kids to bring them too, meet the Stooges, and see their show. We were to meet them at their motel before the show.

Not only was it a thrill for our kids, but even I couldn't sleep the night before because of the excitement. We drove to Milwaukee in our Volkswagen Beetle and went to their motel. Moe said it reminded him of the circus clown car when all of us kept coming out of that little car. They goofed around with the kids, doing some of their funny antics. We took some pictures of them with the kids, went to see them perform at the fair, and then drove home. It was a great day, a memorable one for our family.

It had been many years since we sold our routes of penny gum and toy machines. I still had a yearning for the vending business. We had a successful business selling our specialty items nationally through candy brokers. Why not figure out some way to sell gum and toy machines nationally through our present distribution system?

We got a sitter for the weekend and Chuck and his wife

Bernie (Chuck's first wife Caroline had passed away) and Dolores and I shared a cottage on a summer weekend at the Alpine Resort in Door County. On Sunday afternoon while Chuck and I were playing gin rummy together I told him I wanted to manufacture a 5-cent gum and toy machine to sell nationally through the candy wholesalers, but a metal machine would be too expensive to sell to the candy trade. He said he could also use a cheaper machine to place on the routes he was selling.

About five o'clock Chuck decided to take a shower. A few minutes later he came out of the shower, hair disheveled, bath towel around his waste, dripping wet, walked into the living room and proclaimed, "Back-er, I've got it. We'll build a plastic vending machine like the Jaw Teaser machine!"

"That's it," I said immediately. I don't know why I didn't think of that. Jaw Teaser had been selling their plastic 1-cent jumbo gumball machines through the candy wholesalers for years. All we'd have to do is change it to vend 5-cent capsules.

"We could design the machine together," Chuck said, "and each of us could buy the machines we need from the molder."

"Gee, Chuck, we'll be partners again," I said. "Put it there." I put my hand out and we shook on it.

"That's great. Let's get working on the design right away," he said, looking me in the eye with a big grin on his face.

The penny toy and gum vending business was changing to a nickel business due to inflation. The vending operators now were using larger action toys with moving parts and vending them inside a clear plastic capsule. The kids were willing to spend a nickel for a nicer toy. Chuck and I decided we would share the expense of the tools and dies necessary to mold our own plastic machines. We would prorate the tooling costs according to the number of machines we each used from the molds. We would contract with a molding company to mold the parts for us.

"Let's celebrate," I said, "I'll pop for dinner tonight at Schmitz Gazebos."

"Great idea Back-er. I'll tell the girls to get their duds on."

When I got to Brillion and thought about what I would be undertaking, it overwhelmed me. Designing a plastic machine to vend plastic capsules was a tremendous undertaking. I was glad I had Chuck to help me with it.

In addition I decided I needed to have dies built to mold the capsules as well as the toys that went into them to sell to the candy trade. To insure the capsules would sell well, I wanted to give something extra to the kids so they would buy ours rather than our competitors' capsules. I decided to add four or five pieces of Chicklet-style gum, only a smaller size made by Leaf Gum Company, to each capsule with the toy, so I needed a larger capsule than the standard one used in the trade. I had to sell the capsules filled with gum and a toy, including the labor to assemble, pack and ship them all over the country at 3 cents, as this was the standard price in the candy trade for a 5-cent item. It was a tremendous challenge.

It would mean that in addition to designing the machine that Chuck would be involved in, I would also have to design a larger capsule and an assortment of toys to go in it.

We would not do the actual molding of the various parts for the machines, capsules and toys. This would be contracted out to factories that did injection molding of plastics. But I would have to design these parts and find competent tool and die makers to also make the molds for the capsules and toys.

The tens of thousands of dollars all of this would cost could break a fledgling company like ours if we failed to come up with a workable machine, or if we figured the costs wrong.

I prayed and asked God to guide me and the answer seemed to come as I mulled it all over in my mind, "Don't let all these plastic molds scare you, just look at them one at a time and they won't seem so overwhelming." And that's what I did and it seemed easier.

Chuck and I drove to Milwaukee and checked the Yellow Pages for tool and die makers. After driving around and talking to a few of them we decided on Fred Kroenert, a delightful German-born fellow who owned a small tool and die shop. He seemed to be creative and would be able to help us with the design of the machine.

Several times a week for about a month, Chuck would board the Chicago Northwestern train in the morning in Green Bay and Dolores would drive me 20 miles to Neenah to get on the same train when it stopped there, and we would go to Milwaukee to Kroenert's shop for the day to work on the machine. We would return on the evening train.

We used the plastic Jaw Teaser gum machine and a Victor capsule machine for ideas and worked on it until we finished a working model of the 5-cent plastic capsule machine we envisioned. Then Kroenert started working on the molds for the various parts, cutting them out of blocks of steel.

Then I concentrated on the capsule mold. I found a plastics molder in Chicago, the Mallory Company, whose claim to fame was molding Melmac dinnerware, unbreakable colorful plastic dishes to use instead of breakable china. Mallory gave me a price of $10,000 for two 30-cavity molds, one for the capsule top and one for the bottom. Our cost of the capsule would be a penny apiece.

Then I went to see Mac Mansfield of Ben-Art Company, a plastic button manufacturer in New York City who also made small toys for the vending trade. He recommended the Mercorelli brothers, John and Pat, to design toy charms for us. These guys were artists in metal. I watched how they carved various shapes into small blocks of steel. The top and bottom block would then be clamped together in the molding machine and out would come several three-dimensional toys. In one block I had them carve a football, arrowhead, rocking horse, cowboy hat and a bullet. In another block they carved an assortment of 24 different western figures. In another 24 military figures along with army tanks, trucks and guns. Yet another had a train engine and all the different railcars all made to hook together. After Ben-Art molded them, they also vacuum plated them in gold or silver, an inexpensive process giving them a metallic look.

It took months to have the various molds made for the machine, capsules, and the toys, and then have the parts molded and shipped to us for assembly.

Chuck and I were pleased with the machines produced from the molds. I paid for the molds as I used the lion's share of the machines. Chuck paid me for the machines he needed.

The sales of the nickel gum and toy capsules through the machines were fantastic. We immediately got calls and telegrams from our candy wholesaler customers for additional refills.

We couldn't assemble enough capsules for the refill orders we were receiving, and in the haste to get them sent out, we sent machines that broke down and capsules that didn't stay closed in the machines. I realized later that I should have released machines to test territories first to make sure we could maintain satisfactory quality.

We added 30 women to our production lines and struggled to satisfy our customers as best we could. In spite of our production problems, we had more than $1 million in sales our first year with the 5-cent machine. The value was there and the kids liked it. It was a shame I hadn't been more experienced in manufacturing and been able to produce better quality machines and refills, but over the years we sold over 150,000 machines and over 75 million 5-cent capsules with gum and toys inside.

I decided to build another plastic machine and do it right this time. Ray Hudson, who was very creative, designed a machine in the shape of a clown face. It would be a penny machine and vend a mixture of gumballs and toys, the same merchandise we vended several years before through the 5,000

Victor machines my partners and I placed and then sold. Since the favorable superior court ruling, some years before, there were no more health or gambling problems with penny toy and gum machines.

Ray designed a machine in the shape of a clown's head with a hat on top. The kids would insert a penny in the machine, grab the big red clown nose, move it to the right, then back again, and out of the clown's mouth would come a toy or a gumball, a little gross for adults, but the kids loved it.

Learning from my last mistake, I tested a couple of territories to make sure the machines worked well before we went national with it. It sold well, but not nearly as well as the capsule machine, because, the toys we were able to vend in the penny machines no longer attracted the kids. But, it proved to be a good addition to our line and helped keep our sales steady over the next few years.

Even though I had been successful in selling our plastic machines nationally, I knew we could not build a stable national vending business through candy wholesalers in this way. The wholesalers were unable to repair the machines if they malfunctioned and plastic machines did not hold up nearly as well as metal machines.

Chapter 12

After James was born I told Dolores that following the rhythm method for eight years was enough and I would like to go off rhythm. With my extensive travel as sales manager as well as trips to Chicago and New York City to design toys and buy premiums for our candy wholesaler business, it was sex by the calendar, in the mood or not. I was frustrated. I said I thought it took a lot of loving pleasure out of it for both of us, for me especially when I happened to be home and in the mood, but it was the wrong time, for Dolores when I came home and there were only a few days left in the safe period, and it was do it now whether or not we were in the mood, or wait another ten days and I might then be gone again.

I didn't realize how much I was gone until Dolores showed me the calendar where she had marked the days I had dinner with the family, eleven times over a nine-week period. Although, some of those nights Dolores said she and I went out to dinner.

Dolores said the kids get confused as to when I'm around home. She said one time one of them took a phone call for me and called out, "It's for Dad." Another one of the children answered, "He's in Hong Kong." "No he isn't, I think he's in the basement," the other replied. I was in Hong Kong.

Dolores also pointed out that I spent very little time with the kids. About the only time I spent with them was a few of the evenings when I was home, helping them with their homework. Then sometimes at five o'clock, when I came home from the office, I took the older kids, along with a couple cans of beer and my *Time* magazine, and went to Horn Park so they could play in the sandbox and on the swings. I didn't enjoy playing cards or board games with them, or even playing catch. The little ones enjoyed sitting on my lap in my big, black, leather chair when I listened to their reading or helped them with their spelling. Dolores was very appreciative of any time I spent with them.

It really hit me hard how little time I spent with the kids when Patrice, about two years old, sat on my lap one day by the kitchen table, looked up at me and said, "So your my daddy, you're not the oil man." In the winter she saw the oil man at least every ten days, when he would sit in the kitchen and wait for the oil to be pumped from his truck into the 300 gallon tank in our basement. He had to come that often to keep our large house heated in the really cold winter.

Dolores reluctantly agreed to go off rhythm. That meant no birth control at all, as with our Catholic upbringing we wouldn't consider using any birth control devices. (The pill hadn't yet been discovered.)

Dolores said she felt having children was expected of her as a wife and mother, and that the rule of the church was you never said "no" to your husband.

But she asked me one day why I wanted to have so many children. I said I didn't think about it, they just came. I told her I liked children, but had a hard time with their early years. Their crying grated on my nerves; I couldn't wait until they were past the crying stage.

Patrice was born on January 2nd, another beautiful, healthy baby. She was the first baby of the New Year in Brillion, as well as Calumet County and entitled to gifts offered by merchants in the area.

One gift was 50 pounds of flour, so Dolores, being frugal, felt she had to learn to bake bread. Then there were gifts like baby food, a bottle of wine, photos of the baby, but it embarrassed Dolores to go around and collect them.

Paul's birth, 15 months later, was traumatic. He was premature by one month. I was in New York City when I got a call from the office that Dolores was in labor at the Appleton hospital. Our friends, the Frisbys, had taken her there. I called the hospital and asked them to tell Dolores I would get the next plane home and I'd try to get there before the baby was born. I called again from the Detroit airport to have them let her know how far I had gotten. I arrived a half-hour after he was born. Although he was a month premature and quite small, he was a good-looking baby, content to be kept in an isolette. Dolores was doing fine and was pleased I had tried to make it in time. She said the nurses were so excited following my progress home. Dolores was released from the hospital a few days later, Doctor Young telling her our five children at home needed her. Paul would have to stay awhile in the isolette. Believe it or not, I was also out of town on business when she was released from the hospital, so our friends Howard and Hattie Thiessen brought her home. Howard never ceased to kid me about having Ray and Joan bring Dolores there and he and Hattie taking her home, saying he had to pay the bill, too. Dolores drove the 40-mile round-trip to the hospital every day to feed Paul his formula and hold him for an hour or so.

Ten days later Paul turned blue. Luckily he was still in the hospital. The doctor didn't know what caused it, only indicating there seemed to be some problem with his blood. Dolores and I were worried that being premature he might not be able to fight off whatever was causing his illness. When we received the call from the hospital that Paul was ill, I prayed continually all the way there, that he would survive. His color came back a couple days later after being treated with an antibiotic. We thanked God. Dolores didn't miss a day going to the hospital in the seven weeks Paul was there.

With three children under the age of three, Dolores needed full-time help. She hired a high school girl to stay after school and overnight during the week. When Dolores had to leave for the hospital for Paul's birth, the girl's mother came each day to stay with the small children. During summer vacation Dolores hired another young girl, but she didn't stay long. When school started again in the fall, Dolores hired a full-time girl, Cica, a young Hungarian refugee. Communication was a little difficult with Cica as her knowledge of the English language was minimal. She would give the baby a bathtub and iron the floor, and she'd swing her long ponytail around and stomp away when she became angry.

Dolores held up well. She didn't complain about all the work she had to do. She spent Mondays doing the laundry for our family of eight, all day Tuesdays doing the ironing; she loved to see her three girls in dresses, starched and ironed to perfection. She cooked great meals, many times with one or more children hanging on her legs as she worked in the kitchen.

Every summer we would rent a cottage for two weeks at Sand Bay Beach, south of Sturgeon Bay. It was one of the nicest sand beaches in Door County. The kids loved to play in the water, build sand castles, and have me take them out in the rowboat once in awhile.

Dolores and I were not able to attend Mass together on Sundays. One of us would have to go to an early Mass and the other a later one so there would be someone with the little kids.

Every year between Christmas and New Year's we spent the week skiing with the family at the Porcupine Mountains in upper Michigan, a couple hundred miles north of Brillion. We went to ski swaps to buy skis and boots for ourselves and the kids. Everyone not old enough to ski stayed home with dear Mrs. Reichart. I bought the boots a little large for the children as their feet were growing, but one pair of boots I bought a little too large. I picked up one of the kids, and the kid came with me but the boots stayed attached to the skis. We and the kids took ski lessons and skied on the bunny hill until we had confidence to master the bigger slopes. Sitting around the huge fireplace in the chalet with a hot chocolate or hot cider after a cold ski run was glorious. Our family slept dormitory style at Hokan's Motel in Ontanagan, buying cereal, milk, and sweet rolls from the store for breakfast, making sandwiches for lunch and going out to dinner at night.

Eighteen months after Paul was born Dolores again became pregnant. This time she hemorrhaged a great deal, having to stay in bed as much as two weeks at a time. We no longer had full-time help, only a lady who came in once a week to clean. Kristine, almost 11, was attending summer school at the local public school, taking classes in typing and German. Dolores had to ask her to quit because she needed her help at home. Kris was disappointed; she was enjoying her classes, but she also was concerned about her mother.

Kristine took care of the children in the morning. In the afternoon Dolores required all the younger children to take a nap and Susan, who was 8, stayed with them. Kristine could play, but needed to be back to make dinner for the family. She followed Dolores' cooking instructions by telephone between the bedroom and the kitchen. Dolores stayed in bed at least half of the time all summer, but she decided to come with me to the candy convention in Chicago as she needed to get away.

When we were checking into the hotel in Chicago, our Minneapolis candy broker Bob Edvartsen was also checking in with a huge set of golf clubs and his luggage. He had known Dolores from other candy conventions, and when he saw us he said, "What's new?"

I said, "Well, Dolores is pregnant."

"It would be news if she weren't pregnant," he said, laughing heartily.

Dolores happened to bump against his bag of clubs and they fell over.

"Hey, be careful of my clubs." He seemed a little irritated.

I asked Dolores later, "Did you bump them accidentally—on purpose?"

"You bet I did," she said, smiling.

After the convention we asked Ted and Edie Brierley to join us at Schmitz Gazebos in Door County for a few days of rest and relaxation. Ted was our Boston broker and they were a lot of fun. The four of us drove there from Chicago. We rented cabins overlooking Baileys Harbor and enjoyed one of their fine German dinners. That evening Dolores started to hemorrhage again, so I called the doctor and he said she should stay in bed with her feet elevated and not get out of bed until the bleeding stopped. I went out to shop for a bedpan.

"How stupid of me," Dolores said when she got into bed. "This could have happened in Chicago and I'd be stuck in a Chicago hotel."

I brought Dolores her meals, but she had to eat them flat on her back. It sort of dampened our vacation with Ted and Edie, but they were understanding and sympathetic. They were just happy to relax in the beauty of the area. I gave them a tour of the peninsula. Ted said it reminded him of Cape Cod. We played shuffleboard and gin rummy and sat around and talked with Dolores. They could only stay a few days. Ted said he had to get back and sell some more Becker products. That was okay with me. I took them to the bus for Green Bay so they could catch their plane back to Boston.

Dolores was in bed for ten days before the hemorrhaging stopped and I could drive her back to Brillion. Thank God, Mrs. Reichart could stay with the kids that long. George Schmitz, the owner of the resort whom we had gotten to know over the years, felt sorry for Dolores, and after a few days of my picking up meals for her at the restaurant he stopped to see her and brought her some reading material—Elk's Club magazines—I guess that was all he had. I took the hint and went out and bought Dolores some magazines she enjoyed a little more.

The bleeding started again after we got home, and Doctor Young said I should bring her to the hospital in Appleton; she was six and one-half months into her pregnancy. Dolores was in the hospital for 13 days when labor pains started. I asked the doctor how serious this was as Dolores was pretty weak. He said, "We'll do all we can to save her!"

I was stunned, I had no idea it was that serious. The baby was born the next morning. It was a boy. We had planned to call him John. She told me she heard the doctor tell me, the night before, he would do all he could to save her, and she worried about it all night. "I had a very spiritual experience last night while I lay there worrying," she told me as I was sitting near her bed. "I was awake all night praying and looking at the picture of Christ on the wall. I finally totally surrendered myself to God. I was ready to accept whatever God wanted of me. If I had to leave my children, I knew God would take care of them. It was a real commitment of faith."

I hugged, and held, her close.

The next day the hospital Chaplain, Monsignor Kersten, came to see Dolores, as he had done each day while she was in the hospital, but this time to tell her that our baby had died! He tried to comfort her. "He was so tiny," he said. "Whatever his mission was in life, he accomplished it in 28 hours; he didn't have to stay any longer. I baptized and confirmed him John Michael. You now have a little angel in heaven."

That night when I came home from the hospital and went to bed I felt badly about John's death, but so happy that Dolores was all right. I told the children the baby had died. Kristine came into my bedroom crying. She was shaking. I had her come into bed with me so I could hold her. I talked to her and held her tightly until she relaxed.

Doctor Young told us later that he feared the baby would have been mentally disabled if he had lived because the blood Dolores was losing was from the placenta and the baby wasn't getting enough oxygen.

The funeral was a couple days later at St. Mary's Church in Brillion. The school children were there as usual for morning Mass, and Michael, Kristine, and Susan were sitting with their various classes. I missed Dolores. She told me later she felt she should have been there, as she was released the afternoon of the funeral. She could have attended the funeral if it had been postponed for a day. I'm sure the children were sad. I wish I had thought to ask the nuns to have the children sit with me. They went with me to the cemetery, and baby John was buried in a new plot we bought for our family.

Dolores told Doctor Young how disturbed Kristine was about the baby's death. She had also fainted in church during the funeral. He recommended she see a psychiatrist since it was the second time she was fearful concerning Dolores' problems with her pregnancies. The other time was the problems Paul had at his birth. He recommended two doctors, one in Sheboygan and one in Green Bay.

Doctor Young also told Dolores her six children needed her, that she couldn't handle more than the children she already had, and that her body couldn't handle any more pregnancies. He suggested that she take the birth control pill. Even with the church's prohibition of the pill, which recently had become available, Dolores and I felt with the doctors strong warning and suggestion that she take the pill, it would be wrong not for her to do so. Dolores reminded me that if John had lived, we would have had four children under the age of five. She started taking the pill immediately.

A few weeks later, Dolores and Kristine visited Doctor Kalina, the psychiatrist in Green Bay. He talked to Dolores, then to Kristine. He then told Dolores he would be happy to see

Kristine on a regular basis, but thought she was okay. He remarked about her exceptional beauty and how impeccably she was dressed. Then he suggested that perhaps Dolores and I might like to see him individually on a regular basis.

Dolores and I talked about it when she came home. I said I would like to go, so I started with a one-hour session on a weekly basis. I wanted to see if I could overcome some of the inhibitions I had with strangers, even friends. It seemed to help; after a few months I started to feel more self-confident in my relationship with others. At first, I didn't tell any of my friends or relatives I was seeing a therapist, as they would think I had severe mental problems, but I continued for two years and felt it was the best money I had ever spent.

Dolores either saw some changes in me or decided she needed some help. She started going six months after I started, and continued for eighteen months. She told me although her sessions were difficult for her, she was making progress. Then a couple months later, she let it all hang out one day when I asked her how things were going.

"Doctor Kalina helps me feel that I'm a person, that I have rights, that I'm okay. He helped me to know there is nothing good or bad about feelings, they just are. He asked me why I didn't like myself. I was shocked; I didn't know I didn't like myself. But I think he's right. I told him you always tell me what's wrong with me and I guess I believe it. He also told me he thought I had too much work with six children under thirteen, and a big house to keep."

We were sitting in the living room, she on the davenport and I on a chair. I got up and sat beside her and put my arm around her. "I agree that you have too much work and I guess I do find fault with you and let you know about it, but I'm usually critical of you when you're telling me what you don't like about some of our friends. This bothers me because you don't seem to be very tolerant of their faults. I guess I want you to be perfect."

"Well, I'm not perfect and I don't pretend to be." She sounded angry. "Doctor Kalina's the first person who ever gave me a feeling of self-worth. My sister Leona dominated me all my life, telling me what I should or shouldn't do; now you do. He said I let it happen to myself. I need to be more assertive."

"I guess I'm the controller in the family," I said.

"He says I have to take the responsibility if people don't treat me as I would like to be treated."

"How does he expect you to do that?"

"He said I've got to tell you and Leona how that makes me feel inside, but that's hard to do. I shy away from confrontations, as you know. You always say I don't argue enough. Dr. Kalina says I'm entitled to my feelings no matter what they are. Everybody is."

"I'm sorry, honey, that I'm critical of you. I guess I want you to overlook the faults in our friends. We all have our faults. I know I do," I said.

"I don't feel your love. It seems the only time you show any affection toward me is when you want to have sex. I wish you'd first learn to love me standing up. I'd just like you to hold me and hug me like you did before we were married. I need the security of feeling your arms around me. I have so many responsibilities with the children and the house. I need your help to feel secure in the decisions that I'm starting to make."

"I love you darling," I said as I held her tightly and kissed her.

"Besides criticizing me, you never listen to me. You make all the decisions. I wanted to buy the house down the street, instead of remodeling the electric shop. We would have had a lot more room in that house. Then in this house I told you I thought we should put the family room in the back, but you did it your way."

"Yes, and I told you, you were right in both cases. You need to be more assertive when you tell me those things; you need to argue your point," I said.

"I don't like to argue. That's all Leona, Fabian, and Bernard did at home. They told me I didn't know anything. They called me 'the prune.' Why would I think my opinion is worth anything now?"

"I'm sorry, honey. I'll try to listen to you more in the future, but I wish you'd be more assertive, make more decisions yourself. It seems I have to make them all." I said.

"I know, you decide where we're going to eat, what movie we're going to see, and I go along with it because I don't want to make you unhappy."

I knew she was right. I liked to make the decisions because I liked things to go my way. I had my favorite restaurants and I was easily bored in some movies.

"And sometimes you're not very nice; you yell at me. You don't seem to consider my needs and my feelings," she continued.

"I know," I said. "I always have so much on my mind and I don't have much patience."

"I'll bet you don't talk to your employees like you talk to me. They wouldn't stand for it."

"You're right. I think I take out my frustrations on you. I'm sorry, honey, I'll try to do better, I really love you, darling."

"I know you've got a lot on your mind, and I appreciate how hard you work so we can have a nice home, we can take vacations with the kids, and we have everything we need. I love you too, even though it might not seem so sometimes," she said.

"I think these sessions with Doctor Kalina are doing us both some good, if for no other reason than to be able to learn to communicate with each other. I think we need more of these talks together in the future," I said.

"I agree," she said. "But now I've got to start dinner."

The spiritual retreat movement was quite active in the Green Bay Diocese. I made several weekend retreats throughout the years after I returned from service at Monte Alverno Retreat

House in Appleton or one of the other houses in the Diocese.

Most of the retreats at that time required complete silence for the 30 men in attendance except for confession or a conference with the priest giving the retreat. The idea of the silence was to have the retreatants step back from their daily routine and think about who we are, why we are here, and where we are going.

The primary activity on a retreat is listening to a series of talks by the retreat master, then reflect on what these talks mean to us in our daily lives. The library, chapel, the outdoors, or their private rooms are available for meditation.

There was a certain amount of anxiety for me on a retreat, as I didn't always like what I saw in myself, but the retreats helped me to change for the better. I didn't like myself when I thought about how years before I wasn't truthful with the guy in Milwaukee who bought our cashew machines, and the big lie when we sold our 5,000 gum and toy machines, never telling the buyers a lawsuit was pending that might put them out of business.

The meals were good at the retreat and the silence didn't bother me. Usually someone read a spiritual book to us while we were eating. The cost was a bargain for a few days of solitude, probably half the cost of a hotel room, and that price included meals.

Private retreats are also available at some of the retreat houses, usually during the weekdays, where a person of any faith can go to a quiet setting, away from a job or business, to step back from life for a few days to look at where they're going. There are no required conferences, but a priest is available, if desired. Women's or couple's retreats are also available at most retreat houses.

Dolores and I made a couple's retreat at Chambers Island Retreat House, owned by the Diocese, on a secluded island several miles off Fish Creek in Door County. It shouldn't have been a silent retreat as Dolores and I really needed to communicate with each other—we had one of the worst arguments of our marriage when we stopped for dinner on our way home.

Due to my involvement in recruiting others to make retreats for the Diocese, Father Borusky, the Diocesan director, invited me to attend a convention of the National Laymen's Retreat Conference in Detroit. At this convention I was appointed to the National Retreat Board. I was honored to be involved at the national level in helping the 250 men's retreat houses throughout the United States set up recruiting programs to help fill their retreat houses.

I also had a wonderful spiritual experience while making a 30-day retreat under the direction of Father Bill Alcuin at Monte Alverno. He had volunteered to take the time to give me this special retreat, not available at most retreat houses, because Dolores and I had helped with the expenses for him to make a similar retreat in California a few months before, which he said was fantastic. The 30-day retreat consisted of one hour of instruction each day, early in the morning, then a couple hours of private scripture reading and meditation on my own sometime during the day, and then when possible another visit with Father Bill at the end of the day.

My first instruction was on Genesis from the Old Testament, and after I left the retreat house and turned onto Wisconsin Avenue I had a sensory experience. The neon in the daylight was intensified and I was extremely aware of the lights in motion. I noticed the sparrows lined up on the power lines, some coming, some going. The sounds of the automobiles and trucks were also intensified. I parked the car and drank it all in. It lasted possibly a couple of minutes. Maybe I was being taught to be more aware of my surroundings or aware the movement was only there because God was in it all. Without God it would have been only a frozen snapshot.

The retreat was based primarily on the fatherhood of God, that God is a loving father and only wants good for us, a reaffirmation of what I learned from the *Confidence in God* booklet years before.

We lived in our new home in Brillion only six years, then moved to Appleton. Dolores was happy she was moving out of Brillion; she never really liked it there.

Both Dolores and I wanted our children to continue their Catholic education. That was the main reason we moved. The closest Catholic high school was Xavier in Appleton, and while we lived in Brillion we arranged for Michael to commute to Xavier with Florian Pfeffer, a friend of ours, who worked near Appleton.

Michael commuted for two years. Xavier was getting crowded and they decided not to take anymore out-of-town students. Kristine would be ready for high school in another year. That's when we decided to sell our Brillion home and build a new one in Appleton.

Finding a buyer for our high-priced home in Brillion was a problem. There hardly were any prospects. After trying to sell it for several months we finally sold it at a substantial loss. The new manager of the Iron Works would be living in it.

We were fortunate to find a beautiful lot in Appleton on Reid Drive overlooking the Fox River. The former owner had willed the lot to the Green Bay Diocese. We bid on it and were the highest bidder in a sealed bid auction.

While our home was being built, we rented a small three-bedroom house across the street from our Brillion home for 15 months. It was a tough year for Dolores. It was almost as bad as being back on Dewey Street, only now there were eight people and only one bathroom. Dolores went into the bathroom one day to find Patrice sitting on the front of the toilet and Jim standing, relieving himself behind her. "I just couldn't hold it any longer," he told her. Dolores cried in bed one night about having to live in that cramped space. I tried to comfort her, telling her it wouldn't be long before we would be living in our new beautiful home on the river.

The four-bedroom split-level home we built was somewhat smaller, but just as comfortable as our home in Brillion. Michael, being the oldest, got the single room over the garage, and the three girls shared a room, as did the other two boys. The family room, kitchen, and three bedrooms overlooked the river.

When Dolores asked me why we lost money on the houses we built and sold, I said jokingly, "If I knew how to build houses and sell them at a profit I'd be in the real estate business." Dolores dearly loved the river, enjoying the waters constant movement and the sunlight sparkling on it at sunset. Xavier High School was only a block down the street.

Our business had deteriorated for lack of new items to sell to the candy wholesalers. Our plastic machines were being replaced by metal machines owned by the vending machine operators in various parts of the country. Our refill business for the plastic machines was almost nonexistent. We still had some prize-package business, but our assembly crew was down to three or four people working in a small building attached to a barn on the south end of Brillion, where we stored our merchandise.

I rented a small office above a tavern on College Avenue, the main street of Appleton. We didn't need much space. There were two girls in the office, a bookkeeper and one to type my letters and the few orders we received.

I desperately needed a new idea so we could build the business to where it had been a few years earlier. We were fortunate to have had some good years in Brillion to be able to take the loss in the sale of our home and still have enough for a down payment on the new one. The business now was barely making enough money to support our growing family, and in a couple of years Michael would be ready for college with Kristine following shortly thereafter.

Chapter 13

One part of the gumball vending business that always fascinated me was the charity business, where penny gumball machines were sponsored by various service clubs to raise money for their charitable causes. This was big business. Ford Gum Company manufactured their own machines and gumballs and had about 200,000 machines in locations throughout the United States. Ford Mason, the president, even had his own plane to visit his franchises all over the country who placed and serviced the machines. Charity machines were placed in retail stores, the space for them donated by the store owners. Instead of paying the commission on sales to the stores it went to the service clubs, or sponsor, to be used for their charitable causes.

I wanted to get a nationally known charitable organization to sponsor our machines so we could put them anywhere in the United States. I thought of CARE, Inc., the organization that sends CARE packages to needy people throughout the world. I made an appointment with Mr. Leonard who was in charge of fund-raising in their New York City office and went to see him. I explained how we intended to place thousands of machines across the country. We would put a label on the machines stating that part of the proceeds would go to CARE, and we would give CARE $1 (which was then the cost of a CARE package) for each fill of gum sold through the machines. With thousands of machines out there earning money for their cause, they could send thousands of CARE packages to needy people all over the world through the sale of gumballs.

In a couple weeks Mr. Leonard called me saying his people liked the idea and that we had a deal.

We had the molds redesigned that we used to make the plastic clown machine, removing the clown motif and making a standard gum machine out of it that would appeal to adults as well as children. The next problem to solve was how to find people who wanted to go into the gumball vending business. The only way I knew was to place ads in business opportunity columns of newspapers and magazines to attract prospects.

A marketing man in Appleton helped me design a booklet and brochure describing the CARE program which I then sent to the people who answered our ads. I received quite a few replies but found it very difficult to close a sale on machines by mail or telephone. There were several inquiries from the eastern part of the country, so I decided to drive east and combine my business trip with a visit to my sister Lillian and her husband Bill in Wilmington, Delaware. I stopped to see a couple prospects in Ohio on the way, but wasn't impressed with either of them, as they weren't excited about having to place their own machines. I then drove on to see a woman prospect in Pennsylvania.

I should have turned around when I entered her yard. She lived in the country, and the yard was filled with old cars and rusted machinery. But since I had come this far I decided to knock on her door. A young man in his twenties, dressed in jeans and a baseball cap, I presumed her son, opened the door. My prospect, an obese woman in a housedress, sitting at the dining room table in a room as messy as the outdoors, was reading the stock reports in the newspaper.

I told her I had come to see her about the ad she answered about starting a route of CARE gumball machines and went over the program with her that was outlined in the booklet we had sent her. She answered me in a nasal voice telling me she played the stock market and was doing quite well in it. It didn't look like it to me by her surroundings. I got out of there as fast as I could, realizing I had to reassess my marketing strategy.

In Wilmington, I stopped to see Lillian's son-in-law, Dick Hare. Dick had recently married my niece Marlene, but I had never met him. He was another guy that laughed while he was talking, with an exuberant personality. Dick, about 25, worked for his brother supervising a group of women in an office selling magazine subscriptions by phone. He said his brother was quite successful in the business.

Dick and I had lunch together. I asked him how they operated the business. He said the women would call people listed in the city directory to interest them in subscribing to a magazine. If they sounded interested, Dick would go out and try to get their signature on an order. I figured that if he could sell magazine subscriptions he had to be a pretty good salesman, so I told him about the CARE program and how I was trying to sign up people to start their own routes of machines. I told him how the ones I talked to on my way out, were reluctant to go into the business because of having to solicit locations for their machines.

"You mean you have the right to use the CARE name on your machines for a charity program? I'll bet I could place those machines over the phone," Dick said. He was excited.

"It would be a lot easier to talk retailers into donating space for CARE machines than selling magazine subscriptions."

"That's a great idea," I said. "That would solve half my problem. The other half, is finding good prospects that want to go into their own businesses and convincing them to part with their money to buy machines."

"How much do the machines sell for?" he asked.

"The investment is small. We make a plastic machine we can sell for $10 each, including a fill of merchandise. That's $500-$1,000 for 50 or a 100 machines. By the way, I need a sales manager to talk to people about going into the business. Would you be interested?"

"I don't know. It beats pressuring little old ladies into buying magazines they don't need," he said with a chuckle.

I didn't want to be running all over the country trying to sell CARE machines and I certainly didn't enjoy the calls I made so far. Maybe Dick was the answer. "We could target various cities around this area, advertising in the business opportunity columns of their local newspapers, and sending them our literature. You could call on the ones that seemed interested, sell them some machines, and help put them out by phone solicitation." I told Dick.

"You mean I wouldn't have to move?"

"You could try it out around here. If it works we could expand the territory," I said. I talked with him about the salary and expense allowance we could offer him and he seemed excited.

"I'll talk it over with Marlene tonight. I don't feel good about selling magazines to some of these people who don't look like they have enough money for food. I'd feel a lot better about myself if I was working on a program to raise money for CARE."

We met the next day and Dick decided to take the sales manager's job with our company.

In the first three months of the CARE program Dick Hare put 25,000 miles on his Falcon. He started about 20 people in business, but the prospects we were getting from business opportunity ads in newspapers did not necessarily make good business people. Most of them had no business experience whatsoever. With Dick's promise of getting placements for them by phone, some of them expected him not only to make the initial placements but to keep placing machines from locations they had lost, or ones they didn't consider were good enough to keep. Dick ended up placing many of the machines twice. There were also some problems with breakage of the plastic machines, and the low level of sales from the type of locations that would accept the machines did not excite the distributors we put into business.

We gave up the CARE program. It was a failure. I felt badly that we had not come through with the thousands of dollars in royalties we hoped to give CARE. It was a great cause and the CARE people were great to work with. They also felt badly that the program had not succeeded.

In analyzing what went wrong I decided we were attracting the wrong type of people to our program with our promise to do everything for them, and we needed better locations for our machines.

To be really successful in vending we had to get our machines back into the grocery stores throughout the country. That's where our gum and toy machines did the best. In no way did I want to get back to our original business of owning, placing, and servicing our own machines. There were too many headaches in trying to do that nationally, and where would I get the money to buy the thousands of machines I wanted to put out?

Some months after we moved into our new home in Appleton, I had the greatest spiritual experience of my life. Father Bill Alcuin asked me if I wanted to make a Cursillo. I said, "Make a what?"

"A Cursillo. It's something new in the church. It started in Spain. It's a weekend experience like a retreat, except you sleep dormitory-style on cots in a high school gym," he laughed.

"That doesn't sound like fun to me," I said.

"Trust me," he said. "I made one a few weeks ago in Michigan and it was terrific. You'll love it. Jim Asmuth and John Steckert are going to the one being held early next month in Milwaukee."

They were friends of mine and fellows I respected in the retreat movement and I trusted Father Bill so I told him I'd go.

What a great weekend it was. We sat at tables of six, a few priests making the Cursillo with about 30 laymen, and discussed talks given by a team of lay theology students from Marquette University. The talks were very timely, as the Second Vatican Council had taken place a few years before. Pope John XXIII called the cardinals and bishops together from all over the world for a conclave in Rome that resulted in tremendous changes in the Catholic Church.

One change that already occurred is that there would be no more Latin Masses; they would be said in the language of the people in the various countries of the world, with the priests facing the people instead of having their backs to them.

Other changes already implemented were that Catholics were no longer prohibited from eating meat on Fridays, except for some restrictions in Lent, and it was no longer necessary to fast from food and liquids from midnight the previous night before taking Holy Communion in the morning.

One talk given by a speaker at the Cursillo, was on the changes in the role of the layman in the Catholic Church. The speakers said that in the past laypeople looked to the priests and the bishops as to how to interpret the Ten Commandments. Prayer books listed sins under the headings of Mortal and Venial.

Vatican II emphasized that mortal sin is serious, and must be confessed, because it breaks our relationship with God. However, for a person to commit a mortal sin, requires the same three conditions I learned about in Catholic grade school: it must be an important matter, it must be done with full consent of the will, and you must know it's a serious sin and do it anyway. Venial sins need not be confessed, which was also the same as I learned in grade school. Therefore, if you haven't committed a mortal sin there is no requirement that you go to confession.

Confession could now be heard face-to-face with the priest,

instead of going into the confessional box. It was recommended that confession be more like a therapy session, in that problems be discussed, and advice possibly given by the priest. Hopefully, it would make confession easier and more comfortable for the people and the priest.

I got the impression that it was now up to each person to decide which sins were mortal sins, and which were not, instead of the church telling us. This made sense as two people could commit a serious offense against God, one with, and the other without, the full consent of their will. This became more difficult for some people, as they liked to think of sins as black or white. This gray area made them take the responsibility, before God, for their actions.

We were also told we can have our venial sins forgiven by telling God directly in a prayerful way that we are sorry for them, the way the Protestants have always done. This resulted in much shorter lines at the confessionals.

Holy Communion was stressed as being of great benefit and importance to people, and it was suggested they take advantage of receiving Jesus, who Christians believe is God, as often as possible (Catholic belief is in the Real Presence).

Another speaker suggested that we look at the Ten Commandments, not as what we should not do, but in a positive manner as to what we should do to fulfill them. He said he tries to see the spirit of God in everyone with whom he has contact, speaking warmly to strangers like waitresses, postal workers and clerks in stores. A positive attitude with little acts of kindness makes life more enjoyable for others, as well as for us.

The leaders of the Cursillo also stressed that we can talk directly to God in our prayers; there was no need to go through an intermediary—like Dolores and I did when I was in the service and we said the 30-day novena to the Blessed Virgin Mary. I understood this was always the practice in Protestant religions. I was pleased, I liked the idea of talking directly to God in prayer.

Besides discussing the various talks with the other men at our table, the Cursillo was an exercise in happy communal living, showing love to each other. We sang songs while we went to meals, and told jokes after the meals. In the evening the various table groups put on skits, acting out some of the lessons we were learning. Most of the skits had us all laughing until our sides hurt. I was amazed that I could find so much pleasure doing such simple things. I could feel the tension—that I had all my life—leave my arms, talking with the fellows at our table. I hadn't realized how tightly I was strung. I was filled with love and completely enthralled in what I was experiencing. All I could think of was that this must be a little bit of what heaven is like.

The closing ceremony on Sunday night was so moving, with comments by various participants on what they got out of the weekend experience, that tears rolled down my face. We men hugged each other during the Cursillo and when we parted—a Spanish custom. It was a great outpouring of love.

The Cursillo movement recommended that once a week, after the Cursillo, we get together with two or three other men who had made a Cursillo, to talk about our spiritual experiences and how God was active in our lives the previous week. These were called group reunions. Later, when more people in the diocese had made the Cursillo there would be monthly reunions of the small groups meeting in larger groups in each parish or city.

I was surprised to learn that Ralph Martin who led the team (and later led the National Charismatic Movement), the other people presenting the Cursillo, and those who helped in the kitchen to prepare the food and serve it, were all volunteers—people who had made previous Cursillos. I was also surprised no set fee was charged to the participants, only a free will offering at the end.

The morning after the Cursillo, I went to Mass at St. Mary's Church in Appleton and after Mass talked to the assistant pastor, Father Falk, about my experience and gave him a big hug. A somewhat stoic man, he looked like he thought I had gone off my rocker. Later I went to see my friend John Van in Green Bay and with tears running down my face told him how it affected me spiritually more than any one retreat I ever made. I told him that unlike a yearly retreat which continually helps build one's spirituality, this is a one-time shot in the arm that gives you a terrific experience in Christian living.

Father Alcuin wanted to get the movement started in the Green Bay Diocese, so the half dozen of us from the diocese that made the Milwaukee Cursillo got busy recruiting people to make the first Cursillo in the Green Bay Diocese. The Milwaukee group would provide the teaching team and the kitchen help without charge, and would work some of us into the team so that the Green Bay movement would become self-sustaining. It amazed me; these people would have a two-hour drive each way.

I was anxious for Dolores to make a Cursillo and hopefully have a great spiritual experience like I had.

But Dolores was a couple months pregnant with our eighth child, counting John, the child who died at birth. She had gone off the pill some months before.

I had gone on a retreat at the Jesuit Retreat House in Oshkosh. I spoke with the retreat master and told him about the traumatic experience when our baby John died at birth five years before, and how the doctor recommended she take the pill and not have any more children. I told the priest I would ask Dolores to stop taking the pill if I had enough faith that if she became pregnant everything would go all right with her and the baby this time. He encouraged us to go ahead on faith.

When I talked to Dolores about it, after I came back from the retreat, she said she didn't like taking the pill because of its side effects. She said she'd stop taking it, but I would have to have enough faith for both of us. So far all was well with her pregnancy.

During the next couple of months I spent a great deal of time helping to build the Green Bay Cursillo movement. I was taking a lot of time away from my business, but I figured I was doing God's work and He would take care of the business. Not so. The few orders we were receiving were not being shipped promptly, and there were no new ideas in the works to bring in new business. I finally woke up and realized God wasn't going to do it all; the business needed my time, energy, and ideas, as well as His help, to be successful.

Somehow I had to figure out how to use the candy wholesalers to get quality metal vending machines into the grocery stores across the country. The problem was that candy wholesalers wouldn't invest in machines.

I mulled over the problem and discussed it with Dolores. I didn't often discuss business with Dolores; when I did it often ended up in a disagreement of some sort, as she didn't understand my viewpoint, and I didn't have the patience to fill her in on all the details. But she helped me several times with her intuition about people, keeping me from making mistakes in hiring people or taking them into business with me.

Dolores came up with an idea about possibly leasing machines to the candy wholesalers. "Look at Mel Koch with his Rent-A-Truck business. He leases trucks to the Iron Works and the Ariens Company and he's very successful. Why don't you talk to him and see how he does it?" she asked.

"That's a great idea," I told her. Mel was the guy who had our toothbrushes and premiums picked up in New York City ten years before, on back hauls, when he leased trucks delivering farm machinery out east.

I went to see Mel and he was very helpful in explaining his operation. A bank or leasing company puts up the money for the cost of his trucks. In some cases the leasing company owns them, in others they lease the trucks to Mel to sub-lease to various companies.

I went to the Valley Bank to see the president, Gus Zuehlke. He had been very friendly and helpful since we moved to Appleton, also loaning us money at peak inventory times. He had me talk to the officer in charge of consumer loans.

I showed the loan officer the one-page lease agreement I intended to have our candy wholesaler customers sign for the machines we would ship them. It called for monthly payments, but to make the deal more palatable to the wholesalers we charged them 75 cents additional for each box of machine refills shipped to them. We applied this against their monthly lease payments. If they purchased enough refills each month their purchases would take care of their lease payments in full; if not, we would bill them for the balance due us. If for any reason they were unhappy with the program, they could return the machines to us and owe us nothing. The loan officer said it sounded okay and began to accept our leases.

I asked Dick Hare to move to Appleton to supervise the candy brokers, who would talk to the candy wholesalers about leasing our machines. Dick was finishing with the CARE program, and said this new program sounded good to him, so he moved to Appleton with his family. Dick was excited about selling the program. The candy brokers would do most of the traveling and he would be home more with his family than when he was working on the CARE program.

We purchased 500 Northwestern 10-cent capsule machines. Due to continuing inflation, 10-cent toys in capsules were now selling well in the trade. We would use these 500 machines as a test to see how well the program worked. We also purchased floor stands that would each hold two machines so there should be no problem finding space for the machines in the stores.

We discontinued our packaging operation in Brillion and contracted with Sheltered Industries, a workshop for the physically and mentally impaired in Green Bay, to do our packaging and shipping for us. This would help us control costs; we would have a fixed cost on each box of the capsule refills they shipped out for us.

There was now a good assortment of 10-cent toys available for our capsules from Hong Kong. The Beatles were popular with kids of all ages. We would have liked to use pictures of the Beatles rock group on flicker rings as we did with the Three Stooges, but the royalty they commanded was much too high. But even soft plastic beetle insects sold well as long as we used the word "beetles" on the front of the machines.

The 500 test machines moved out fast and the loan officer at the bank seemed happy to loan us the money for the leases the wholesalers signed, which enabled us to pay Northwestern for the machines. We needed more machines, so I flew to California and talked to Harold Probasco, who manufactured the King Koin machine. He gave us the very competitive price of $10 each for a 5,000 machine order. These moved out steadily.

Since it looked like this would be a successful program, we decided to manufacture our own metal machine. Eclipse Manufacturing in Sheboygan agreed to help us design a machine, do the metal stamping of the body, paint them, and assemble and ship them for us. We called the machines Toy 'n Joy.

After shipping the 5,000 King Koin machines and shipping our Toy 'n Joy machines for several months we noticed that some of the wholesalers were not purchasing as many refills as they had been for the machines. The extra 75 cents per refill we were charging them was not enough to make the full payment each month to the bank, on many of the leases. We had our candy brokers check on the problem and they said the refills were slowing down in sales and many of the stores were neglecting to keep the machines full, therefore were not ordering refills from their wholesalers. Many of the machines were standing empty in the stores. The brokers didn't get into the stores themselves so they couldn't do anything about the empty machines.

Things didn't look good. The amount we owed the bank was approaching $100,000.

The Valley Bank soon said we had reached our credit limit with them and they were unable to finance anymore machine leases for us. I contacted several other banks and was turned down by all of them.

Even though many of the wholesalers were not buying enough refills to cover their payments, we were still able to make our payments to the bank for a while because we were making a profit on the leases to the new customers to whom we were shipping machines. Now, since there were no longer any new customers, we were running short of money to make our monthly payments to the bank.

We were in a dilemma. If we wrote the customers and asked them for the money they were short on the lease payments, they would likely use the option in our agreement to return the machines to us. If they did that, we would have to buy back their leases from the bank and have to pay the entire balance left on the leases, not just the payments due each month. In my mind I blamed the bank for accepting the leases, they should have realized it wasn't a true lease. Then I blamed them for continuing to give us money for the volume of leases we brought to them. Finally I realized that I was the one that made up the stupid lease agreement, that put all the burden on us, and none on the customer, who signed the lease.

I went to the bank and talked to Gus and told him the best I could do was leave the machines out there in the stores, as they were bringing us some sales. Even though I wouldn't be able to keep up with all the payments when they were due, I would pay him what I could on the leases. The alternative, I told him, was that we bring back the thousands of machines out there. He agreed he had no choice but to give us more time, but he wasn't happy about the situation.

Then Chuck Buckman came to the rescue, or at least I

thought his new idea was my salvation. Chuck said he had an idea that was so fantastic I had to cut him in on the profits, if he told me about it, and I used it. I quickly agreed to do so.

Punchboards were illegal nationally because they were a gambling device, since a person didn't get something every time a number was punched out of the board. Chuck said he had a legal punchboard we could sell anywhere in the country, and the L. M. Becker Company had the sales force that could sell it. "Well, tell me what it is. It sounds too good to be true," I said.

"What you do Back-er, is make up a punchboard about one inch thick with 50 one-inch round holes in it, probably out of several layers of corrugated cardboard. You glue a sheet of thin cardboard on the front and on the back with dotted lines and perforations matching up with the 50 holes. In between the front and back sheet of the 50 holes you put an assortment of 10-cent toys similar to the ones you now put into your 10-cent capsules. You provide a one-inch wooden punch with each board so the kids can punch out the toys. You sell these to your candy wholesalers and they sell them to the grocery stores all over the country. They charge the kids 10 cents a punch, the kids get a toy every time, so it's legal. The store makes a profit, and you give me a commission on sales for the idea. It's like a disposable vending machine made out of cardboard; when it's empty they throw it away and buy another one."

"I think you're a genius," I said. "I can't believe it's so simple." I was very excited. I knew it would sell and it was easy and inexpensive to make. "I can't see any problem with it. The only thing I would add is a small display area in the center of the board, covered with cellophane, where we could glue in samples of some of the toys in the board."

"That's a good idea. I'm glad I thought of that," he said with a laugh, always the joker. "You should be able to sell a million of these boards with your sales force. We'll be sitting under the palm trees in Hawaii, Back-er, clipping coupons and sippin' mai tais. When are you going to get started?"

"Immediately," I said. "I'm going to have a corrugated box company make up a few samples so I can put them out around here to make sure they sell as good as I know they will, then we'll get into production, probably in a month or two."

I went to the corrugated box company and explained what I needed. They said they should be able to make up a few samples for me. Then I went to a building supply company and bought a one-inch diameter wooden closet pole and had it sawed into two-inch lengths for the punches.

When I got the sample punchboards, I had Ray Hudson dress them up in bright colors with the Poke A Dot name we planned to use, at the top of the boards.

I took one of the boards and gave it to a small grocery store owner I knew in Appleton. He put it on the front counter where he would accumulate the groceries the person was buying. Supermarkets were taking over the grocery business in most cities, but there were still some of these Mom and Pop stores around. I came back the next day, and the board was completely empty. I was sure I had a winner. That was all the testing I wanted to do. I didn't want people to see it, and possibly copy the idea.

Instead of making the production boards out of cardboard, I considered Styrofoam. I figured it must be less expensive than cardboard as it was used to protect breakable products in corrugated cartons for shipping. I located a Styrofoam molder in Milwaukee and they quoted us an attractive price on a one-piece molded Styrofoam board with 50 holes and a small display area in the center of the board. All we had to do was glue the back piece on, fill the holes, then glue on the front piece of cardboard as we did on the corrugated sample boards. I contacted a wire bending company to design a wire easel so they could stand the board on a counter in the store. We found a company in Maine to make the wooden dowels we used for punches.

Dick Hare and I showed the Poke A Dot boards to our candy brokers at the next candy convention in Chicago. We had a suite in a motel across the street from the Hilton, where the candy convention was being held. Our Chicago broker, Ralph Lee, was so excited when he saw the sample board, he couldn't contain himself. We walked out by the pool off our suite and he kept telling me how fantastic it was while we walked around and around the pool. Ralph was one of our best brokers and when he said, "Lyle, you'll never be able to make enough of these boards to keep up with the demand," I knew we had a winner. I went to bed with dollar signs dancing in my head. This was going to be the answer to bailing us out of the mess we were in with the metal vending machines and be a highly profitable business for us for years to come.

With Ralph's enthusiasm added to mine I could see hundreds of thousands, even millions of dollars in sales from the Poke A Dot boards. I didn't think there would be enough small imported toys in stock in the U.S. to take care of our needs—to fit the one-inch holes in the boards—among the dozen or so New York toy importers.

Mel Nadel, the New York toy importer from whom I purchased most of our vending toys, was making a buying trip to Hong Kong in a few weeks. I told him about the Poke A Dot boards and he too was excited about their sales possibilities. I told him I needed new and different toys and I suggested that I go with him to Hong Kong to help select the toys.

He agreed, and said he would meet my plane in Hong Kong when I arrived.

Never having been to the Orient before, I was excited, but a little nervous about the 24-hour trip from Appleton to the other side of the world. But there Mel was, waiting for me in the crowd outside of customs. At 6-feet tall, with dark-framed glasses, and a moustache, he was hard to miss. We took a taxi into the city. What a culture shock. The signs on the buildings were only in Chinese characters even though Hong Kong was a British Colony. Mel said it was impossible to find an office or a restaurant even if you went into the neighborhood and looked around for it because you couldn't read the Chinese characters on the signs. He said the only way to get around Hong Kong was to have the hotel clerk write out the address of the place you're going in Chinese characters, as well as the address of your hotel, to show the taxi driver so you can get there and back to your hotel again.

We drove past ten-story apartment buildings with laundry hanging out the windows to dry. Poverty was evident in the dilapidated structures that housed the people, quite a contrast to the beautiful stone-faced structures of the prosperous banks and hotels in the business district.

I saw rickshaws for the first time, other than in the movies, and was disturbed by the degradation I felt seeing one human being running down the street pulling another in a two-wheeled cart. However, I was fascinated by the physique of the men pulling the rickshaws. They had muscles like the men on the covers of body-building magazines, except these were old men. Mel said the reason younger men were not pulling rickshaws was because the Hong Kong government was not giving any more licenses and when the present drivers quit or died, there wouldn't be anymore rickshaws.

Mel knew how to live. I stayed with him in his twin-bedded room in the Peninsula Hotel, the most prestigious hotel in Kowloon, the mainland part of Hong Kong. Our room overlooked the beautiful Hong Kong harbor and at night the lights of Hong Kong island across the harbor were captivating. Mel said it was reputed to be one of the most beautiful harbors in the world.

Chapter 14

After a good night's sleep and breakfast, Mel and I walked the two blocks to the Kowloon ferry, paying the equivalent of 2 cents in U.S. money for the ten-minute ride to Hong Kong Island. There were U.S. destroyers, freighters, Chinese junks, and sampans in the harbor, the smaller boats dodging the ferry as they moved toward the freighters to unload their cargos of merchandise destined for countries around the world. Then we walked to Clem's office, one of Mel's agents. Clem was a young Chinese man in his twenties. After we were settled at a table, in a room surrounded by walls filled with toy samples, Clem called in the manufacturers, called makers, one at a time, in order of their arrival at his office. Men of all ages, also a few women, brought in their toy samples, some of the larger manufacturers with black sample cases, but most of them carrying their samples in worn corrugated boxes tied with a string.

They would empty their boxes of toys in a pile on the table and Mel and I sorted through them. Mel looked for toys for the carnival trade, who were his main customers, and I looked for the small one-inch toys that would fit into our capsules and the Poke A Dot boards. There were no fixed prices.

The agent was the interpreter, speaking Chinese to the makers, and English to us, negotiating prices between buyer and seller. Mel considered himself a good buyer. If he wasn't, he said he couldn't compete with the other importers who bought the same toys on their buying trips. There were sometimes long conversations between Clem and the maker when Mel said the price was too high. Mel told me later he didn't know whether Clem and the maker were talking about the price or the weather, because he couldn't understand a word they were saying. He said that was why he used several different agents. He sometimes would see the same makers at different agents and be quoted different prices.

At noon we went to lunch at the Manderin Hotel grill, the most exclusive hotel on Hong Kong island. At lunch Clem told me that most of the small inexpensive toys were made in small family businesses with the entire family helping to assemble the toys. Some of the toys were molded in ancient presses with men jumping on them to keep them closed while the hot plastic hardened inside.

One family made nothing but small plastic parachutes, tying strings to each of the four corners with the other ends tied to the plastic parachutist, a very labor-intensive toy which we purchased for a penny apiece. They would cost ten times as much if made in the U.S.

On Sunday one of the agents invited us on his yacht for a cruise around Hong Kong island. We stopped at Aberdeen, halfway around the island, where many of the poorest people worked and lived. Many of the junks in Aberdeen Harbor were owned by the boat people who lived on the boats and fished for a living. This was their home, raising their children on the boats, their children often marrying children of other boat people when they grew up. Mel said many of the toys he buys were also assembled by the boat people.

One evening Mr. Fung, an agent Mel said was quite wealthy, invited us to dinner at a high-class restaurant he owned on Hong Kong island. When Mel told me some of the unusual foods the Chinese eat I was reluctant to go, but when printed formal invitations arrived at our hotel for Mr. Nadel and Mr. Becker, how could I refuse?

Mr. Fung ushered us into a private dining room where he introduced us to his wife—Mel told me later it was one of several he had—and two young beautiful Chinese women who Mr. Fung told Mel were dinner companions for us. This made me a little nervous. They spoke a few words of English, but mostly laughed, when they couldn't understand what we were saying.

Mel warned me, before dinner, not to ask what the waiters were serving in the various dishes, until I had tasted and finished eating them, because, if I knew what was in them I might not want to try them, and that would offend our host. Each of the six or eight courses—I lost count—were placed in the center of the table. Mel had suggested I try at least a little of each dish, and if I didn't like it, not to finish it, because if I did the waiters would keep giving me more.

The first course was a cup of what looked and tasted like chicken-noodle soup. It was good, I ate most of it, then found out it was rattlesnake soup. Then we were served what looked like charcoal broiled tiny crisp pieces of chicken. They were good but crunched when you ate them. No wonder, Mel said they were baby birds, bones and all. The drinks flowed, served from a cart by waiters, with the choicest of American and other imported whiskeys and brandies.

But the surprise of the evening was when a young man came in with a burlap bag with something moving inside. He sat on the floor, opened the bag, reached in and pulled out the head of a live snake. He then took a sharp knife, slit open the necks of three rattlesnakes, took out the green gall on his knife, and put a little of each into several small china cups. Then the waiter poured some brandy into each cup and mixed it with the gall and offered it to the men in the group. Mel declined. By then I was feeling no pain from the drinks. Mr. Fung clinked cups with me saying, "Down the hatch." We drank it, and they all laughed. Mr. Fung said the snake bile was good for a man's sex life, and part of the ritual was to take it from three different snakes. Then I really got suspicious as to why the two young women were with us.

There was shrimp with walnuts in a red sauce, steamed fish, lobster in a white sauce, pea pods, plus many other dishes. We ended the meal with rice and a dessert, birds-nest soup. It was so extremely sweet I ate only a little of it. I'm glad. They then told me it was made from the saliva collected from swallows nests; the Chinese considered it a delicacy. I missed bread; rice was their substitute.

After dinner Mr. Fung told Mel the young ladies were from Kowloon and asked whether we would take them back to Kowloon on the ferry with us. Mel, being very gracious, said we would. Mel excused himself to go the men's room, I followed him.

"What do we do now?" I asked him.

"Don't worry. This happened once before when Mr. Fung invited me to dinner. I just walked with the girl until Mr. Fung was out of sight, then I put her in a taxi and told her I was tired and was going back to my hotel. Mr. Fung would have been insulted if I refused her company," he added.

We took a taxi to the ferry and when we got to Kowloon Mel and his girl got into a taxi. The girl I was with spoke enough English to tell me she worked at the Playboy Club. I remembered seeing the Playboy Club's huge neon sign in English, undoubtedly to attract the tourists, one night when I was walking with Mel. Mel said it had no connection with the Playboy Clubs in the States. I knew it was only a few blocks from the ferry so I said I would walk her to the Club, but then I was going back to my hotel. When we got to the Club I thanked her for a nice evening and said good-bye. She said I must come in for "one drink, just one drink." I didn't want to be rude, so we went in and down the stairs. I don't think there was an upstairs to the place. We sat at a table and the waiter came over. I ordered a beer and the girl ordered a champagne cocktail. The room was quite dark with a dozen tables of which only one other was occupied. Rock music blared from the stereo speakers. After sitting there awhile, she asked me to dance. We danced. I thought it would help pass the time as we sat there smiling at each other, conversation being difficult due to the language barrier. After the dance we came back to the table and she asked the waiter for another drink. I told her I was sorry, but I had come for one drink and now I had to go. I asked the waiter for the check. He brought it; I looked at it and was astounded by the amount. Outside I had seen the sign that said there would be no cover charge. I had a few words with the waiter, complaining about the bill, and immediately the table was surrounded with four big fellows, either waiters or bouncers. Like a fool I opened my wallet, then realized they could see all my money. I hurriedly paid the bill, excused myself, and got out of there as fast as I could. I was scared, looking back, as I practically ran back to my hotel.

I told Mel about my experience when I got back to the hotel. He laughed and said I was in a clip joint, where the girls order champagne. They charge a fortune for it, but give the girls plain soda water. He said I didn't follow his instructions. I was to take her where she wanted to go and then leave. He said he and his girl went back to the Peninsula Hotel in the taxi; he had her stay in the taxi and paid the driver to take her home. I had met his wife Clare in New York, a very lovely woman. They seemed much in love. I believed him.

Soon after I returned from Hong Kong we started production on the Poke A Dot boards and sent samples to all of our candy brokers so they could start selling them. The orders poured in. We made some shipments but then ran into a production problem. We couldn't get the cardboard facings to stick to the Styrofoam boards. It seemed to be the hot humid August Wisconsin weather that was causing the problem. We tried various kinds of adhesives, but none of them worked. As we struggled with the problem for several weeks, orders for several thousand boards were stacking up in our office.

By the time we got the glue problem solved we heard some rumblings in the field. The brokers said the wholesalers wanted to return their shipments, not because of any quality problems, but because the supermarkets wouldn't buy them. Besides a lack of counter space, the checkout person didn't have time to stand there to see how many punches the kids took on a Poke A Dot board. There were very few Mom and Pop neighborhood grocery stores left around the country. I then realized why these same stores took our vending machines; they didn't have to stand there while the kids played them and payment was collected by the machine. I had tested it in a small grocery store. I never thought about it not being a supermarket item.

We stopped selling the item and never shipped the orders we had on hand, which was fortunate, as we would have gotten those back, too. We knew we would get most of them back because there was an implied return policy in the candy trade. We were lucky for the glue problem or we would have had thousands more boards coming back to us. The Styrofoam boards, printed cardboard facings, easels, and wooden punches I had ordered, all in large quantities, would all be worthless. And then there was the problem of what I was going to do with the tens of thousands of dollars worth of toys I had just ordered from Hong Kong.

Now we had two failed programs of gigantic proportions to contend with, the $100,000 worth of vending machines on leases, and people calling us to get paid for the various parts we purchased from them for the Poke A Dot boards.

I wasn't concerned about Mel Nadel dunning me for the toys he ordered for me in Hong Kong, as in the ten years I had dealt with him, he had always been very understanding and would give me months to pay if I needed more time. But what was I going to do with the toys now that the vending machine business, in which I could have used them, was also in deep trouble!

The guy that made the wire easels for us had thousands of them ready to ship, and he threatened to sue me if I didn't pay for them promptly. And Nat Boland, the New York importer I dealt with for years and thought of as a friend, and from whom I had purchased many of the toys for the boards, got very nasty over the phone. He called and harassed the people in the office, sometimes several times a week. He even called me at home early one morning and said, "This is Nat Boland," then he spelled it out, "N-A-T-B-O-L-A-N-D," and said, "I want my money, and I want it now." I hung up on him.

I was despondent, I even had fleeting thoughts, seeing myself walking off a roof! Over the weekend, I sat at home in the living room with a blanket around me, shivering, concerned about how I was going to keep from going bankrupt. I sat there worrying and praying. I said my Jesus prayer over and over in my mind, each time emphasizing a different word, "JESUS loves me, Jesus LOVES me, Jesus loves ME." It seemed to help somewhat so I was able to think.

By Monday morning I had an idea. I made a list of my creditors and what I owed them. Then I took a 12-column spreadsheet and started writing in payments across the page for the next 12 months, figuring which ones I had to pay right away and which companies would probably work with me on extended payments. I then wrote promissory notes, bearing 6 percent interest (which was then the going rate) and sent them to my creditors with a letter telling them we were temporarily low on funds, asking them to accept our promise to pay later.

Then I went to Valley Bank and talked to Gus, the president, about my financial problems and how I planned to handle my creditors. He said that was well and good, but what about the $100,000 to buy up the bank's leases when our wholesalers returned the machines? I told him I needed at least a $10,000 loan to stay in business to have any chance of paying him back, and I offered to have him take a second mortgage on our home as security for the loan. "Otherwise," I said, "to which door of the bank would you like me to have 'YOUR' machines delivered when they come back from our customers?" He gave me the loan.

Other than the guy who sold us the wire racks, and Nat Boland, whom I had to pay, not one of our creditors called or wrote me for money after they received the notes I sent them. A few even complimented me on what I had done, saying that no one else had ever offered to pay them interest on past due accounts.

I worried about finding a solution to my business problems as the loan we received from the bank was in no way going to solve my problems. It would only help to keep our creditors from throwing us into bankruptcy. I had to come up with a new idea for a vending machine program fast.

I was worried and so was Dolores. We both prayed and tried to have faith that the Lord would help us.

Peter, our eighth child, entered the world, another beautiful healthy baby. Dolores had no complications with this pregnancy. I guess the faith the priest suggested we have on my retreat helped. However, she was on a strict diet to avoid gaining any weight. She was confined to the house, unable to drive, or carry out any of her responsibilities, other than to cook the meals, during the last six months of her pregnancy. Paul, eight years old, was the next youngest. Michael, now nineteen, our oldest, was away from home, attending Georgetown University. The older children helped Dolores with the younger ones and with the housework. They were all excited about the new baby in the family.

The Cursillo didn't have the immediate impact on Dolores that it did on me; she said she hated every minute of it. She had a three-week-old baby at home she wanted to be with, and felt she had been railroaded into attending by Father Alcuin and me. She was probably right.

But the Cursillo grew on her as time went on. She later joined the diocesan leaders' group, gave talks on Cursillos, as I did, became the leader of one of the women's Cursillos, and began writing the monthly newsletter. The Cursillo Movement pretty well dominated our lives. Besides one of us working about once a month on the Cursillo weekends and her involvement, I was busy organizing group reunions to keep up the spirit of the Cursillo in the various cities of the Diocese. On many Sunday evenings we attended Cursillo meetings while our older children minded the younger ones. At one of those meetings a doctor in our group said something that many in the group related to: "We'd rather be meeting, talking about how we can help other people's families and kids, than staying home and being with our own." (We learned in later years that our children resented our being gone so much on Cursillo work.)

I tried, but couldn't come up with a new idea, to again get us into the vending machine business on a profitable basis. Staying around the office depressed me, so I decided to take a job selling toy ideas on commission basis to major toy manufacturers. I would be working for John and Pat Mercorelli, the creative brothers from Newark, New Jersey, who designed and produced the molds for some of the small toys we used in our gum and toy vending machines. Although I still wasn't comfortable selling face-to-face, I liked the challenge of selling toy ideas for the Christmas season. Dolores wasn't happy about my decision, since I would have to fly out East a couple times a month where most of the toy manufacturers were located, rent a car, and pay my own expenses. Money was short, especially now that Michael and also Kristine were in college. I told Dolores I hoped we might strike it big with a couple of toys selling in the millions of dollars, on which we would share in the 5 percent commission John and Pat would receive from the toy manufacturers. That would help us pay off the bank.

I showed a board game to the Parker Brothers and Milton Bradley. They weren't interested. Milton Bradley said they had lots of good ideas for board games, and could come out with one anytime they were willing to spend the $300,000 in advertising it took to get one going.

I showed Hasbro Company models of a demolition derby, where wind-up plastic cars slammed together and flew apart, then could be easily reassembled to crash again. I thought I had it sold when I left them, but when I called a couple days later, they said they had dropped the idea because they were afraid demolition derby toys might be on their way out. They didn't want to take the gamble.

I flew to California and showed Mattel a board on which kids could turn a couple hundred six-color beads to make various designs. They weren't interested but said I should come back if we ever came up with a toy that would defy gravity. I think the guy was serious.

I was successful in selling Ideal Toy Company on a toy we called Tap A Sketch, similar to the popular Etch A Sketch which Ohio Art Company sold by the millions. Our board was circular instead of rectangular, and while turning it you could tap the board on the side and the iron filings under the glass would form a sketch of your own design. I attended the New York Toy Fair to see it displayed in Ideal's Show room, but they dropped the idea after the toy show. Evidently most buyers intended to stay with the old reliable Etch A Sketch.

The only partial success we had was a Mickey Mouse camera, about six inches in diameter, in the shape of Mickey's head. I sold the idea to Child Guidance Company. I saw it in some of the stores that Christmas and we got a few small royalty checks, but it was not a hit and they dropped it from their line. It was cute, but I wouldn't buy one for my kids because of the expense of the film and the processing.

One summer evening when Dolores and I were out to dinner at the C&C Club in Door County, she let me have it with both barrels. "I can't understand why you're spending so much time and money selling toy ideas for the pizza brothers"—the endearing name our family gave the Mercorelli brothers. "We're always running out of money in our household checkbook and you keep flying around the country spending money and not getting paid for it. I think you should quit." She was pretty angry, and I knew she was right.

"I have so much time and money invested in the project, and I guess I continue because I don't want it to be a failure," I said.

"But don't you think you've tried it long enough? You've been throwing away money on it now for over a year."

"You're right," I finally agreed. "I'll call the pizza brothers tomorrow and resign."

We still didn't have a new idea that would pay off the machine leases at the bank, and get the company back to profitability. I prayed about it, and meditated, because new ideas sometimes popped into my mind in meditation. I tried to figure out why our last machine program failed. I concluded that neither the wholesalers who placed the machines, nor the retailers who put them in their stores, had much incentive to make the program work. Neither of them had any investment in the machines and didn't have to concern themselves with whether the machines were kept clean and full of merchandise. If the wholesalers tired of the machines they could return them to us, and that's what they were doing.

What if we could sell our machines to the grocery stores instead of leasing them? Then the store owners would have an incentive to keep the machines clean and full. Dick, our sales manager, and I talked about how we might devise such a program.

We knew that independent grocery stores bought their groceries through grocery wholesalers. I knew Ralph Moehring, who headed S. C. Shannon Company, the grocery wholesaler in Appleton. Ralph and I served on the Xavier High School board where both of us had kids attending high school. Dick and I decided to talk to Ralph and see if he could help us design a program to sell our machines to grocery stores. I called Ralph and he said he'd be happy to talk with us.

Dick and I went to his office, showed him a picture of our new six machine floor stand unit, which contained two 10-cent and one 25-cent capsule machines, and three penny and nickel toy, candy, and gumball machines.

"These are the toy and gum vending machines we manufacture. Are you familiar with these kinds of machines?" I asked Ralph.

"Yes, I've seen them in some of our stores," he said.

"Ordinarily the commission the stores get on these machines is about 25 percent," Dick told him. "If the stores purchased the machines from us they can make over 50 percent on sales through the machines. Do you think they might be interested in buying their own machines with this kind of profit?"

"Our member stores average less than 5 percent on groceries; I would certainly think they would be interested," Ralph replied.

"We have a promotional deal that includes enough merchandise with the machine sale so they get back the money they paid for the machine when they sell the merchandise included," Dick added.

"That sounds very interesting. I think they might go for a deal like that," Ralph replied. "Who would sell the machine to the stores?"

"Do you have sales people who could sell them?" Dick

toy 'n Joy
CENTER

Cosmic Quest

toy 'n Joy
toy 'n Joy talking machine
toy 'n Joy

asked. "We're not familiar with a wholesaler grocers' operation."

"No, we don't. We provide a warehousing service for the independent grocers who don't belong to chains. It might be possible the food brokers who call on the stores could offer your machines to the stores. They usually get 5 percent commission, or less, from the manufacturers on the groceries the stores buy from us, but they don't usually sell equipment. If you could pay the brokers an ongoing commission on the refills that we would buy from you, for our warehouse, for sale to the stores, they might be interested in the deal," Ralph explained.

"That's exciting," I said. "We want to try to give the retailer at least a 50 percent profit on the refill sales through the machines and still have room for your profit and that of the food broker. How much would you charge for handling our refills?"

"We take very little profit. We warehouse practically all the items our member grocery stores carry in their stores and deliver what the store needs once or twice a week depending on their volume. We mark up the prices we pay you for your product only about 3 percent. We are profitable because of the tremendous volume we do." Ralph explained.

"It sounds like a great deal for us," Dick said.

"Yes," I agreed, "we could probably even pay the broker 10 percent on your purchases of refills to keep him interested."

"How do we get in touch with these food brokers who call on the stores?" Dick asked.

Ralph thought about it, as he tilted back his desk chair for a few minutes. "I suggest you contact Frank Schultz. He's a young hardworking guy, started in the food brokerage business not long ago, in this area. He might be interested in taking your line of machines and refills. I'd be happy to give you his phone number. Frank's a nice guy. You'll like him," Ralph said. "If Frank's interested, as soon as he sells 20 machines we'd start stocking your refills and then start shipping refills as needed to the grocery stores."

"That sounds wonderful to me," I said. "If it all works out, it will be our pleasure to have you as our very first wholesale grocer customer in the country," Dick said.

"It would be a pleasure," Ralph replied.

We thanked Ralph for his help, telling him about our plans to sell our machines nationally if the program worked for him. He wished us success.

Dick contacted Frank Schultz and he came to Appleton and had lunch with us. Frank was a good-looking fellow in his early thirties, again a guy with laughter in his voice. I figured this must be the mark of a good salesman. Dick told Frank about our machine deal and how the Shannon Company would handle the refill sales for us. Frank said the program sounded great to him. He was surprised at the deal on the machine, where the free refills included would bring back enough money to the grocer to pay for it. He said it was almost like getting the machine free. I told him it's the old Gillette safety razor trick, you give away the razor and make your profit on the blades. Dick told him he'd make 10 percent on machine and refill sales plus $25 for each rack of machines he sold and set up in a store. We would ship the machines and the free refills directly to the stores.

He was excited, especially about the $25 he would make on each machine deal. He was ready to go. He took some colored photos of the machines with him and said he'd get started right away.

The following week Frank called and said he had gotten a couple of orders that he would be sending us, and more should be coming each week. I hoped and prayed we finally had a new program that could pay our debts at the bank and turn our business around.

Dick asked Frank where we could get a list of food brokers. He gave us the address for the National Food Brokers Association. We were now ready to build a national food broker organization, the same as we had done with candy brokers some years before.

Dick and I then picked the Kansas City area, as we thought people would be more receptive to buying machines in a smaller city than in a big city like Chicago. Dick flew to Kansas City and contacted Dave Harrison, a medium-sized broker who had several retail salespeople calling on the stores in his area. I was anxious to talk to Dick when he returned to see if he had been successful.

"I showed the photo of our Toy 'n Joy unit to Dave. He is a nice guy, but he said I was in the wrong place. I should go to the vending company down the street; he was in the food business. Then I told him how easy it was to sell the machines because of the free merchandise deal and the 10 percent commission rate, which he admitted was double what he got on most food products. He really got interested when I told him about Frank Schultz's success in Green Bay and the $25 bonus for each unit his salesmen sold. So he went for the deal," Dick said, with a big grin on his face. "Then we went to see Associated Grocers, and just like Ralph Moehring, he said they'd be happy to bill the machines to their member stores and stock our refills in their warehouse provided Dave could sell enough machines to make it worth their while. Then I had a sales meeting with Dave's salespeople and got them all fired up to go out the next week and start selling machines."

"That's great Dick," I said. "I knew you could do it. Can you imagine the business we'll have when you get food brokers all over the country doing this?"

"I don't see any reason why not. If it works for Frank Schultz and Dave Harrison I don't see why I can't find a good food broker in every territory in the country." Dick was really excited, and so was I!

Frank Schultz sold his 20 machine units and Ralph Moehring ordered refills from us. In a couple of weeks Dave Harrison's men had 25 units sold. We shipped the machines directly to each of the stores with the initial refills we promised, and billed the wholesaler for them. The wholesalers billed the machines to the stores and collected for them, which was great. We had no credit problems; wholesalers usually paid in ten days. Then they began stocking our refills on a regular basis. We were off and running.

I talked to Eclipse who manufactured the Toy 'n Joy machines for us, and they agreed to re-manufacture the machines that were being returned from the candy wholesalers by stripping the paint on the cabinets, repainting them, and replacing the internal parts, so the machines were like new when we shipped them out again.

I invited Gus Zuehlke out to lunch to tell him the good news. I told him we had a way to use up the machines we were getting back from the candy wholesalers and turn them into cash by selling them through our food brokers. We could also start paying off the leases at the bank. He was pleased that we were selling the machines, no longer leasing them. I also told him these machines were going into large grocery stores and supermarkets, compared to the smaller stores the candy wholesalers sold to. We now had a use for the tens of thousands of dollars' worth of toys I bought in Hong Kong for the Poke A Dot boards. We would be able to use them in our 10-cent capsules for the food broker program. I said I expected to have the leases paid off within a year.

I know Gus considered me a friend, as I did him, and we were both pleased we had found a solution to our problem.

Then I said I had a little problem with our home finances. I told him that Dolores and I were both writing checks from one joint household checking account and that it wasn't working out. I asked him for suggestions.

He said, "Helen Jean and I each have separate checking accounts. She's responsible for certain expenses like the groceries, utility bills, clothes for herself and the children, and gifts.

I'm responsible for the house mortgage, car payments, entertainment, taxes and things like that. We agreed on about what her monthly expenses are and I give her a check for the same amount each month to cover what she's responsible for. I've been doing that for years and it seems to work well."

When I got home I suggested this to Dolores and she thought it was a great idea, so we started the following month. She reminded me how I controlled the money after we were married and she didn't have 15 cents to buy a *Ladies Home Journal*! She said it was very frustrating for her to always run out of money in our joint account.

Dick Hare continued to appoint food brokers in other territories and our business began to grow again, and it was growing on a solid footing. I thanked God for our success. We made a small margin of profit on the machine sales, but a substantial margin on the continued refill sales through the wholesale grocers. Dick would not stop appointing food brokers until he had the entire country covered.

Dolores and I needed a break from the tension caused by our business setback. We took our first real vacation together since I returned from the service. With no children along and no business to take care of on the trip, Jackie and Jerry, my niece and her husband, drove with us to Florida and we stayed with a friend of Jerry's for ten days in a mansion that J. C. Penney had once owned on Key Biscayne. We had a great time.

Chapter 15

Father Vincent Dwyer, a Trappist monk with a doctorate in theology from the Catholic University, on medical leave from his monastery in Spencer, Massachusetts, became a member of the National Retreat Board. He brought with him a theory on spiritual growth based on the Swiss psychologist, Jean Piaget's, studies of the intellectual and cognitive development in children.

In a one-day retreat for the national board members and their wives at Marydale Retreat House in Kentucky he went through the steps of spiritual growth he felt were possible in a person's life. He said spirituality can be developed just as our mind and body develop, but some of us get stuck and we don't grow spiritually as well as we could. This interested me. I was never conscious of the spirit within me. I thought about right and wrong and in Catholic school learned how sins can stain our soul and we'd have to go to confession to have it cleaned again, but to think about the Spirit of God within me and that this spirit could grow was exciting. Father Vince said we are all on a spiritual journey.

Father Vince talked about God being everywhere and in everything, and that when He talks to us, we should listen. "How does God talk to us?" I asked him.

"He talks to us in various ways," he said. "He could talk to us through another person, a spouse, a friend, or even a stranger. God can talk to us through the media, a magazine article, a movie, or a TV program, or He can talk to us in the silence of our mind and heart."

Father Vince went on to say that we need to listen and discern from all this input how God is directing us in our daily lives. It brought back thoughts about the discernment of the Spirit Father Alcuin taught me on my 30-day retreat years before. Father Bill said we must learn which of the thoughts that come into our mind we are to act on. I had asked him how we know which thoughts are God's will and which are our will. He said we'll know; the ones that bring us peace are from God.

Dolores and I also became involved in prayer meetings in the Charismatic Movement. We first went to a few meetings with a protestant group in the Appleton area that met in people's homes. But it was a little too much of a fundamentalist group for us. The Word in the Bible was very important in charismatic meetings, but we had trouble with the literal interpretation some people gave to the passages. We also felt pressure from the group to speak in tongues. Speaking in tongues is mentioned in the Acts of the Apostles in the Bible as one of the gifts of the Holy Spirit. Many in the group said they spoke out loud in foreign tongues, while not understanding what they were saying. No matter how hard I tried I couldn't do it. I finally realized I hadn't been given that gift, but this group seemed to imply that if you didn't speak in tongues you didn't have the Holy Spirit within you. Another gift of the Spirit mentioned in Acts is the interpretation of tongues, but no one in the group seemed to have that gift.

What most fascinated me, however, in their prayer meetings, was people witnessing openly to the group on how God made his presence known to them in various ways in their daily lives. It may have been only a simple thing like having an urge to phone a friend or relative and find that person in dire need of your phone call. They talked about a personal relationship with God, which I found exciting.

Catholic Charismatics then formed a group in the Appleton area as an outgrowth of the Cursillo movement and Dolores and

I attended some of their prayer meetings. I was quite impressed with the use of the Bible, because prior to Vatican II, Catholics were discouraged from reading it. The church felt the people needed the priests and bishops to interpret it for them. One of the great changes resulting from Vatican II was the encouragement the Catholic Church now gave to laypeople to read, meditate, and then interpret the passages for themselves, to see what the Bible says to each one of us in our daily lives.

One year after we started selling our Toy 'n Joy vendors through the food brokers and wholesale grocers, we had our debt paid off at the Valley Bank. Gus was happy and so were Dolores and I. We thanked God many times during that year.

The large food brokers have retail sales people that go into the stores, in many cases every week. We worked out an incentive program where they would check our machines so they didn't go empty. We gave the food brokers what we called "Becker Bucks." They were designed like play money, and the broker retail sales people could redeem them for gifts such as kitchen appliances, TV's, or golf and fishing equipment. Each "Becker Buck" was worth about 50 cents in premium value to them and cost us about 30 cents at the price we paid for the premiums. The retail people loved the program. One man saved enough "Becker Bucks" for a grandfather clock kit, and assembled it himself.

Every December, Dick Hare and I attended the National Food Brokers convention, along with the three regional sales managers Dick had hired for the various areas of the U.S. We would wine and dine our food brokers at these conventions and hold meetings with them in San Francisco, New Orleans, or wherever the conventions were held. We encouraged them to push our machines and refills and get as many sold in their territory as possible.

Our business ran like clockwork for several years. We made a lot of money, but at that time the top federal income tax rate was 70 percent, plus 10 percent for Wisconsin. Dolores and I tried to give 10 percent of our profits, after taxes, to charity. All these taxes took the incentive out of making more money, as there was so little left. Peter Lettenberger, our tax advisor from the Quarles and Brady law firm in Milwaukee helped us with the tax problem by setting up a family limited partnership where Dolores and I had a total of 50 percent interest in the business; the other 50 percent was divided equally between our children. Trusts were set up for the children, so the money would stay in the business and they could not draw on it until age 25. It also included a provision for trusts for any future children we might have. This cut our income taxes as Dolores and I then paid taxes on only 50 percent of the income of the company. Each trust for the children filed a tax return and of course, the trusts paid taxes at a much lower rate on the children's profits from the business. ("S" corporations were not then permitted.)

I often wondered how other businessmen ran their businesses and what I could learn from them. Since I had no formal business training I wanted to meet with other businessmen to learn what they knew about running a business. Large corporations had the benefit of a board of directors to give advice to the head of the company, I only had my employees to consult.

In looking through some old McGraw Hill business management books I had purchased through the mail years before, I read about how small unincorporated businesses like mine—that didn't have a board of directors—could get this kind of help by forming an advisory board for their company. It sounded like a great idea. I gave some thought to the people I would like to have give me advice on running our company.

I decided to ask the men I considered friends who were more financially successful than I. I didn't offer to pay them for attending meetings—which was usual on corporate boards. I told them we would pick up the hotel and air travel expenses for them and their wives for one winter meeting a year, a weekend in a warm climate at a resort hotel. We would also have two half-day meetings during the year in Appleton.

Mike Ariens, president of Ariens Company in Brillion, took over the company from his father and uncle after graduating from MIT, and built Ariens into a national company employing hundreds of people, manufacturing yard and garden power equipment. Mike and his wife Mimi were good friends for years, part of our couples dinner group when we lived in Brillion. Mike thought the advisory board was a good idea and agreed to serve. I asked John Van, my friend from the retreat and Cursillo movements. John always had several businesses going in addition to the Downtowner Motel in Green Bay—which at that time was his main business. He was happy to come on board.

I asked Gus Zuehlke, president of Valley Bank, and he agreed to become a member of the board. I thought it would be good for him to keep his eye on the money the bank lends the business. Peter Lettenberger, our tax attorney with Quarles and Brady also joined us. Then Ben Hauserman, a fellow national retreat board member also accepted. Ben and his brothers owned a successful company in Cleveland, Ohio, manufacturing moveable partitions, in the U.S. and Europe, for offices and schools. These five men, plus Dick Hare, our national sales manager, Ed Kettner our office manager, Dolores and I, comprised the advisory board.

We had a short organizational meeting and dinner at the North Shore Country Club near Appleton that Mike Ariens, who was a member there, arranged for us. The first winter meeting was held at the Doral Country Club in Miami, Florida. Since it was in February and all the members of the board were from the midwest, they and their wives were happy to spend a three-day weekend in the Florida sunshine. The board met for a half-day on Saturday morning. We played golf and socialized the balance of the time. Everyone had a great time and I benefited from the advice and counsel of this experienced group of business and professional men at a minimal cost.

At the meeting I gave the board members complete access to the financial records of the company. If we expected to get their advice, we had to give them all the input they needed to help us.

The meeting went well. I valued their help. I kidded them when I sometimes didn't agree with one or more of the members, saying, "Remember this is an advisory board, I'm only asking for your advice." They liked the idea that since they were not a part of a corporate board, they had no legal responsibilities, and could not be sued, as sometimes happens on corporate boards.

Dolores formed a women's group called the Teresians, organizing a chapter with women from the community. The purpose of their monthly luncheon meetings was to promote religious vocations for women. They established communications with the nuns in the area and provided vocational programs for young women who might be interested in a religious vocation.

She made her first plane trip without me, to attend the National Teresian Convention in Boston, Massachusetts. When she returned she told me how nervous she was taking care of her luggage, getting a limo and cabs, checking into the hotel, all the things she took for granted when she traveled with me. It was in the middle of the week and her sister Leona took care of Peter while she was gone.

When she returned I decided to have a talk with her about her involvement in the Cursillo and now with the Teresians. I felt lonely and neglected.

"How can you keep up with all this Cursillo and Teresian work besides keeping the house, making the meals and caring for the children? It's consuming all your waking hours. You don't have any time for me. Our only social life is the Cursillo meetings we attend." I was sitting on our bed while she was unpacking her bags from her trip.

"I need this involvement. I need to have some value as a person and a feeling of accomplishment in my life," she said.

"You practically raised the kids by yourself and you're doing wonderfully with them. Don't you see the value in that?" I asked.

"That's my job. It's what I'm supposed to be doing as a mother. But I'm capable of doing more than changing diapers, wiping noses, chauffeuring kids, and going to PTA meetings."

"Is it the Feminist Movement that's driving you to take on all these extra responsibilities?"

"No. My liberation started back when I went to Dr. Kalina and he told me in my therapy sessions that I was first dominated by Leona, then after our marriage by you, and that it was my responsibility that this was happening to me. I let you make all the decisions until then. You always said I couldn't do things for myself. That's why I went to the Teresian convention and why I'm working on Cursillo. As you know, I was even the leader for one of the Cursillos. I need these things to give me confidence and help me make decisions for myself. It felt good that I was able to handle this trip by myself. Now I could do it again in a breeze."

"I'm pleased you're doing these things to gain confidence. I know all about that. I gain confidence by running my business. But you seem so obsessed in these new things you are doing," I said.

"You mean like you are obsessed with your business?" she asked.

"I guess you're right. Like Dr. Kalina said years ago, we criticize others for the faults we see in ourselves," I said.

"I'm not in favor of the Feminist Movement if it means going out and getting a job to prove my worth. I love being a homemaker and mother. Sure I miss the secretarial jobs I had before we were married, but I want to raise our kids myself and because you support the family, I have a choice whether or not to do so. All I can see the Feminist Movement doing for women is giving them two jobs, one on the outside and the one they come home to every night."

"But with all your involvement, I don't feel we have any time together. We don't go out to dinner or a movie nearly as much as we did when we lived in Brillion. I miss the dinner group we had there, too." I said.

"Do you realize how much you were involved in your business and your retreat work then? In the last year of our monthly dinner group in Brillion, the only times we got together with the group were the two times we had dinner at our home. You were gone every month that one of the other couples entertained. That wasn't much fun for me," she said. "And it isn't that I haven't tried to get a dinner group started here in Appleton, as you know, but nobody seems interested."

"There are no friends like the old friends. I miss our Brillion friends," I said.

"I do, too. Being 20 miles away and with both of us being so busy with the Cursillo Movement, it's more difficult to keep up those friendships."

"There have been a lot of changes in our lives since we left Brillion," I said as I went over and gave her a big hug.

But Dolores's involvement with the Teresians and the Cursillo Movement didn't subside after our talk, it increased. After she led one Cursillo, she was asked to lead another one. She found leading the first one frustrating because all she had to work with were a few notes and an outline. Very little was written down on how to conduct a Cursillo. Dolores liked to be organized; she decided if she were to lead any more Cursillos she needed a leader's operations manual, so she spent several weeks writing one.

After the manual was finished she led several more Cursillos, each Cursillo requiring team meetings once a week for six weeks before a Cursillo, plus the Thursday night to Sunday night Cursillo itself. Besides this she was still writing the monthly newsletter. I felt she was running herself ragged. One night she was so rushed as she left a parent's meeting at Xavier High School that she was stopped by a policeman for speeding on her way to the office to mimeograph the newsletter. She arrived home at one o'clock in the morning.

I stayed at home with the five children most of the evenings and weekends she went to these meetings, and I wasn't very happy about it.

I became unhappy and depressed and we argued a great deal—about little things, like who was right about some minor thing one of us said. Each of us seemed to have a need to be right. We would even kid about our need to be right when we were with our friends, one of us saying, "I was wrong only once. That's the time I thought I was wrong but I was right."

Dolores didn't seem to look to me for her enjoyment in life. She had the Cursillo and Teresian work, and with taking care of the kids and the house she didn't have time to get bored. But I looked to her for my enjoyment, and my social life had suffered since we left Brillion. I wasn't happy with the way things were around home. In Brillion I was away from home almost every night that Dolores and I weren't going somewhere. In Appleton, I was home most every night, bored.

Dolores and I had very different personalities. I attended a management seminar some years before and a psychologist talked about these different personalities. He classified people primarily as "chunkers" or "wingers". Where the "chunker" dominated in a person they tended to be perfectionists, wanting to keep their ducks in a row, which for me described Dolores' personality to a T. I felt I was definitely a "winger", a gambler—in business anyway. I more or less let things flow with the wind.

The psychologist said the personality we develop in childhood is practically unchangeable for life.

I don't know where that put Dolores and me. We just didn't seem to fit with each other and sometimes we talked about it. We even wondered whether we were meant for each other. At one point, I was so terribly unhappy I considered separation, but when I thought about the damage this would do to our kids, I put the thought out of my mind.

I complained to Dolores that she was too sensitive, that she was too easily hurt. Her reaction was that if I didn't like her to be sensitive, she would become insensitive.

And that's what happened. She seemed to stop caring about anything and blocked her feelings about everything. It seemed to bring on depression in her. Now we could both be depressed. I felt she was more unhappy than I was. I feared that some day I might find her on the bathroom floor with her wrists slashed!

This went on for months and I finally talked to her about the change I saw in her, and that I didn't think it was healthy for her or me. She agreed she had become insensitive to her feelings and that it was not good for either of us. As Dr. Kalina told us years before, everyone is entitled to their feelings—no matter what they are.

After that, our relationship made a turn for the better. But I'm sure our problems also affected our children. Besides reading self-help books, Dolores and I took a relaxation exercise course and courses to help us communicate better with each other and our children.

Dolores noticed an ad in the Appleton paper for a Relaxation Exercise course to relieve tension headaches, even migranes. She told me about it because I suffered from migraine headaches that made me ill for a couple days at a time, starting with double vision and then a severe headache, usually above one eye. I had suffered with them several times a year since I was a kid.

She decided to go with me and learn the exercise too because of the stress in her life, raising so many kids and, I guess, putting up with me.

It was a simple exercise to learn, but it took practice, twenty minutes a day, twice a day, to perfect the technique. We both learned how to do it in two evening sessions over a weekend.

All we had to do was to sit in a comfortable chair with our backs straight and our head bent forward. Then we were to close our eyes and be conscious of our breathing—just listening to ourselves breathe. While we were doing this, if our mind wandered and we started to think about something, we were to gently go back to being again conscious of our breathing.

When I tried it, my mind was going a hundred miles a minute, which is probably why I got migraines—it was overloaded. So I found myself many times, during the twenty minute exercise, going back to being conscious of my breathing again. They said we could look at our watch to find out when the twenty minutes had passed.

I tried doing the twenty minute exercise shortly after I got up in the morning, as recommended, to clear out the cobwebs, then at five o'clock when I returned from the office, as they also recommended. Sometimes I didn't find time for it in the morning, but I tried to do it at least once a day to try to leave behind my business thoughts—and worries—and be able to relax my mind.

Believe it or not, that simple exercise did wonders for me when I got proficient in it after a few years. Sometimes I got so relaxed that I went to sleep sitting up. My neck muscles got sore, but soon they strengthened and I'd sleep in that position for as much as an hour. I felt thoroughly refreshed when I woke up, but sometimes I had a little headache coming out of the sleep. The instructor said that was normal, that if this happened, to go into the relaxation mode for a few minutes again and the headache will go away.

Dolores was also able to learn and benefit from this exercise. We told others about it and they were able to master it just by following our instructions and practicing it till they were proficient in it.

I had the opportunity to try it when I felt a migraine headache coming on. They said for headaches, you should stay with the exercise as long as it takes to relieve the headache. I found that I could eliminate the migranes before they became painful. I have never suffered with one since.

One of the communication courses we took was Transactional Analysis, based on the book, *I'm Okay, You're Okay*. Both of us, not having the best image of ourselves, took the course one night a week for several weeks at the Congregational Church Hall. It got us talking together about helping each other with our problems and our self-esteem.

After finishing that, we took the Parent Effectiveness Training course together. I chided our dynamic pastor, Father Janssen, at St. Bernard's parish, telling him how great these courses were for family life, and we had to go to a protestant church to get them. I told him I felt anything that helped families get along better had to have something to do with spiritual growth. I couldn't blame him. He worked unbelievably hard in his huge parish, holding weekly religion classes for hundreds of children, plus ministering to prisoners and the homeless.

Peter came to be known in our family as our "PET" kid since he was the first of our children to benefit from our "PET" skills. We began listening to our children and including them in adult conversations, even with friends. We used active listening skills to feedback what our children were saying to us, to prove we were listening to them and to salve their hurt feelings. It's amazing the change that took place in them once we began treating them like young adults.

I remember Father Vince Dwyer telling us in the retreat Dolores and I made with the National Retreat Board members, that anything that helps us grow in love is spiritual. He taught us to tell our kids we love them; after that Dolores and I never ended a phone conversation with any of them without an "I love you." It took some of them awhile before they felt comfortable saying, "I love you, too." He also taught us to hug our kids. I remember how difficult it was for me the first time I hugged my oldest son Michael when he came home on vacation from college. It seemed difficult for him too, he looked startled.

I showed little affection for our children up to the time they were older and out of the sitting-in-the-lap stage, but it got easier and more comfortable for them and for me, as time passed.

Tom Wolf, and his wife Nola, whom we met through the Cursillo, became close friends. Tom and I got together with a couple of his friends every Friday noon for a fish lunch at Bleier's Tavern, where the drinks flowed along with foolish talk. We usually killed the afternoon with a bridge game, a sauna at one of the local motels, or sailing in Tom's boat on Lake Winnebago. Friday was my big social outing for the week.

One Friday afternoon after our fish lunch at Bleier's, Tom and I stopped at my home to pick up my swimsuit so we could take a sauna. Dolores was with Peter, now four years old, in the car in our driveway. I could see something was wrong. Dolores looked disturbed. I got out of Tom's car and walked over to her.

"How are you doing?" I asked.

"Okay," she said

"You don't look okay. I hope it isn't anything I've done," I said. She cracked up, like I had just told a joke.

"What's with you?" I asked again.

"I'm pregnant!" she told me in a low voice, "Don't tell Tom. Peter and I are on our way to the Dairy Queen and I'm going to have the biggest hot fudge sundae they've got."

Now I could understand why she cracked up.

I got back in the car with Tom. I was stunned. She was 49 years old! Evidently she was as shocked as I was. This would be number nine.

When I got back to the house from the sauna Dolores and I went out on our glassed-in porch to talk about this new surprising event in our lives. The afternoon sun sparkled on the river. It was a beautiful day.

"When I saw you and Tom I had just come back from Charley Dungar's office," she said. Charley was an obstetrician and a friend of ours from the Cursillo. "He examined me and said I was three months pregnant."

"Three months. You must have been shocked."

"Not really. I thought I was pregnant three months ago when I first went to see my regular doctor. I told him I had missed a period, was gaining weight, and thought I might be pregnant. He said he didn't see how I could be pregnant at 49 and that it must be my change of life that caused me to miss a period. He put me on a diet and told me to come back in a month. When I went back the next month I hadn't lost or gained any weight and had missed another period. He then sent me to the hospital for three days of X-rays and blood tests, as you remember, but he couldn't find anything wrong, so he told me to stay on the diet and come back in another month. I still hadn't lost any weight and I reminded him that now I had missed three menstrual periods. I told him again that I still thought I was pregnant. He said he was sure I wasn't when I came to him two months ago, but if I wanted, he'd run a pregnancy test."

"It's amazing that he didn't give you a pregnancy test a month or two ago instead of the X-rays and the other tests," I said.

"He just couldn't believe I was pregnant at my age. He called me this morning and told me the test was positive, but he said sometimes the test results are not accurate. He still couldn't believe it, but he suggested I go to see an obstetrician, as he didn't deliver babies anymore. I suggested Charley Dungar, and he got me an appointment this afternoon right after lunch."

"Charley examined me and then looked at the X-rays my doctor had given me to show him. 'You're right, you're pregnant. How pregnant do you think you are?' he asked.' I told him three months.' He said, 'That's exactly right.'"

"Charley knew I was upset so he talked to me for about 20 minutes. He told me that if I went to Johns Hopkins hospital at 49, having had X-rays in my pelvic region, they wouldn't let me out of there without trying to persuade me to have an abortion. He asked me how I felt about abortions. He added that he didn't perform abortions, which was no surprise to me—Charley was a strict Catholic. I told him it was something I thought my daughters might have to make a decision on someday, but never thought I would. He asked me how I felt about having the baby. I told him abortion was out of the question, that I like little babies, that I'm pregnant and I'm going to have the baby. But I said I felt like I wanted to go away somewhere before anyone knew, have the baby, then come back and tell people it was adopted. I was embarrassed. I hated to look forward to remarks like 'don't you know what causes this?'"

"I know, it embarrasses me too when people make those remarks." I said.

"Then Charley asked me if I didn't realize how unique I was to have a baby at my age. 'Of course,' he said, 'it will change your lives, you and Lyle. When your friends talk about retirement you can tell them you won't be able to talk about that for a while.' I told Charley what a blessing it would be for Peter to have a baby brother or sister five years younger, otherwise he would have to be raised like an only child, as Paul was eight years older. I told him we would be raising Peter anyway, so this would add just five more years to our being tied down with kids. I said my doctor admonished me for not losing any weight in the last two months on the diet he put me on, although I had been very religious about following it. I told Charley I was going out to get the biggest hot fudge sundae I could find. I didn't have any money with me, so I came home to get some and that's when I saw you and Tom in our driveway."

"How do you feel about it now that you've had a little time to think about it?" I asked.

"I loved having every one of our children. I was cut out to be a mother, I guess. I dearly love babies. But it was a shock. How do you feel about it?" she asked.

"Well, let's see, you'll be 65 when this one gets out of high school and I'll be 63. So we'll go from child rearing right into social security. I can see what Charley Dungar was talking about. Most people have at least 10 or 20 years without kids at home before they start drawing social security. We have great kids, I'm sure this one will be great, too." We hugged each other. I knew it wouldn't be easy for me to have kids around that long.

Dolores told me later she had read about the dangers of late-in-life pregnancies and the danger to the fetus from X-rays in the pelvic region. She said our baby could be physically or mentally impaired, possibly born with Down's Syndrome, be blind, or a dwarf. I said we both must have faith that this wouldn't happen. Dolores said the child could also be a genius, as sometimes occurs in late-in-life children.

After several years on the National Retreat Board I was elected president of the National Laymen's Retreat Movement. My goal and what I worked toward as president was to establish regional retreat house organizations that would elect a man from each of their areas and finance their travel to represent their houses on the national board. In this way each retreat house could have input through the regional to the national board. Most of the laymen now on the board were men like me who had helped their local retreat houses set up recruiting programs to attract retreatants, and also had the time and the funds to attend national meetings. They really only represented the house they worked for, not other retreat houses in their area.

As president I would also head a committee of priests and laymen from the board to look at retreats, whether they should be silent or not, as well as other spiritual programs that could be held in retreat houses.

Dolores was happy for me. I felt honored to have been elected president, but she was not pleased about the additional travel the committee meetings would entail. She also was unhappy about board meetings that occurred on Mother's Day and holiday weekends. Evidently, Father Middendorf, the national executive secretary of the movement, was not aware these were family weekends when he set the dates for our meetings.

A year later Father Tom retired as executive secretary and there was no one at or near the Covington, Kentucky, office to take over his job. Even though I'm more of an idea man than an administrator, with never any desire to be executive secretary, something inside me changed. Maybe it was God's grace; I felt a desire to volunteer for the job and the board appointed me. I then had two jobs, president and executive secretary.

The total yearly income for the national office from retreat house dues was $15,000 a year, not much money with which to rent an office and hire a secretary in Appleton.

I asked my secretary at the Becker Company to run an ad in the Appleton newspaper for a secretary for the retreat office. We rented two small rooms on the second floor of the Becker Company for the retreat office.

Jo Lyons was a natural for the job. Mature, college educated, a good writer, a stickler for detail, she was willing to work for the retreat movement for much less than she could have commanded elsewhere. She took over the administrative duties completely, and I was free to concentrate on ideas for the movement.

God had to be looking down on the retreat movement to find Jo to run the national office. Things went smoothly and she got busy helping Henry Balling set up the National Retreat Convention for the following year in Buffalo.

It was a normal pregnancy and birth and our ninth child, a baby boy, was perfect. He was as alert and beautiful as all the others. I thanked God and I know Dolores did, too. We decided to call him Jonathan, which meant "gift from God," in honor of our baby John, who only lived a day.

Dolores told me how concerned her friends were that she had a baby at 49. They figured it could happen to them, too. She frightened them even more when she told them that a doctor in the same offices as Dr. Dungar had delivered a baby to a woman at the age of 52.

The tension between Dolores and me had settled down somewhat. She had slowed her involvement in Cursillo during her pregnancy to help insure a healthy baby. We had both come out of our depressions.

The business went fairly well the next couple of years, even though it had slowed down from its peak when Dick Hare had completed the appointment of food brokers for all 50 states.

However, problems for the future of the business were occurring. The price of sugar went from 10 cents a pound to 60 cents, due to a sugar shortage. Since gumballs are about 60 percent sugar, the price of gum skyrocketed. Our only recourse was to vend smaller gumballs, but there was only a certain amount we could cut the diameter of the gumballs, or the machines would vend two balls instead of one, and that wouldn't be profitable.

Chapter 16

Another Christmas had passed and I again dreaded the cold January and February weather. I was in my usual winter moody mood. I suggested to Dolores that we pack up the car and take Peter and Jonathan with us on a motor trip to see if we could find some warm weather. I thought, too, that the togetherness of a trip for several weeks might be good for our relationship. Dolores liked the idea of finding where the warm weather was, so we could decide where we might move for the winters someday. Paul was away at college and Patrice had a job at Aspen, Colorado. Only Peter and Jonathan were at home.

We had a pop-up camper-trailer that I thought we might use when we got into a warm climate, so I hooked it on the car and we took off with the kids, each in a booster chair at a window in the back seat. It was a terribly cold January day. We had driven less than 20 miles when Dolores and I made our first and best decision of the trip; we made a U-turn, went back to the house and put the camper in the garage. I planned to stop to see some of our food brokers in the various states we would be traveling through, so I felt justified in charging the motel and other travel expenses to the business.

It was an exceptionally cold winter, even northern Texas had icy roads; we saw semis turned over in the ditch. From there we headed west to San Diego, stopping to see our food brokers in Dallas and El Paso on the way.

Peter brought his school books along and we helped him

with the homework his teacher lined up for him. We tried to make the trip as educational as possible by stopping at various places like a cotton gin, the plaza where President Kennedy was assassinated and the Dallas football stadium where we bought a souvenir sample of the astro turf, the new "grass", they had just installed on the field.

It was too cold in San Diego to use the outside swimming pool at the motel. The tiny town of Alpine, west of San Diego, was just like its name, a beautiful Alpine village, but it was in the mountains and there was snow on the ground. That wasn't for me.

We had already been away two weeks, which meant 42 meals in restaurants with a two-year-old who still was in diapers. After raising seven children Dolores was tired of potty-training kids. Peter, now seven, was a perfect older brother to Jonathan. Some nights we would get them something to eat in our room and Peter would stay with Jon while Dolores and I had a peaceful dinner in the motel restaurant. Peter would invariably call the restaurant to talk to us to make sure we were there if he needed us.

We then drove north to San Francisco and saw our food broker there. We heard it was a nice place to live, but it wasn't warm enough there for me, either. The kids especially enjoyed the clowns and mimes who performed near the pier. On to Las Vegas where we stayed at Circus Circus so the kids could enjoy the ongoing circus acts. Then we headed for Florida and agreed we would keep going south until we found some warm weather, even if it meant going all the way to the Florida Keys.

Dolores was a saint on this trip. We had to stop at a couple doctors along the way, as Jonathan had a cough that lasted for a couple of weeks. It was diagnosed as a croup. Most of the motels had outdoor pools, but it was too cold to use them. While I was in Memphis one day, having a meeting with one of the food brokers, Dolores sat at the motel while Jonathan was crying because he could see the swings through the window and couldn't understand why he couldn't go out and play on them. It was raining. Dolores was anxious to get to the Florida sunshine, too. She didn't realize I was going to have so many business meetings along the way.

Then on to Disney World which was fun for all of us. But the next day we lost Jonathan at the Howard Johnson motel in Orlando. It was late afternoon and we asked Peter if he would watch him for a while so Dolores and I could have a drink and relax. We left him in the game room with coins for the pinball games. Peter was as shocked as we were when we came back in a half-hour and noticed that Jonathan wasn't there with him. Peter said someone must have let him out the door. The first place we looked was in the outdoor pool area; we were concerned he might have fallen in. What a relief, no sign of him around there. There was some heavy equipment being used for construction at the rear of the motel. We hoped he hadn't walked into that area. We checked the corridors and the lobby and finally found him out front where the cars pulled up to check in. He could easily have been hurt. We thanked God he was safe. He wasn't frightened; he enjoyed exploring the motel.

Six weeks and 9,000 miles after we started on our trip we were back home. We were glad to be back. It was quite an experience for the kids, as well as for us, but a little too much togetherness for all of us.

That evening, at home over a drink on the porch, Dolores and I reminisced about our experiences, especially about the day in the Arizona desert when Jonathan was so sick of riding in the car that he kept crying "out, out, out." He knew how to say "out" and "tain." He loved the trains we saw along the way, but also wanted us to produce one on demand. I stopped the car and Jonathan got out. I took his hand and we walked toward the sunset. I tried to turn back to the car several times, but he kept pulling at my arm to keep going. Finally I had to pick him up, kicking and screaming, and carry him back to the car. Poor little kid, he was so tired of that car and that long ride. Dolores laughed and said she though he and I were just going to walk off into the sunset.

We stopped for dinner one evening with Susan and Patrice at a supper club near Appleton after doing some shopping for the girls in Green Bay. Susan was going back to college in Beverly, Massachusetts, in a few days. We had quite a long wait for a table, so we had a couple of drinks and some snacks in the bar area.

During the dinner Dolores was talking about her 5-day trip the following week to Chicago to attend an instructor's course on Parent Effectiveness Training. She was so pleased with the results of PET in raising Peter and Jonathan that she wanted to learn how to teach the course to other parents. But she was concerned about leaving Peter and Jonathan with Leona. She said Peter had always been happy to stay with Leona when he was the only one and received all the attention, but now since she also took care of Jonathan, Peter didn't feel he was being treated nicely and didn't want to stay with her anymore.

Susan piped up and said, "Dad, haven't you heard about the Womens' Movement? Why don't you take some time off from the office and stay home with the boys? That's what Dads are supposed to do these days."

"The boys would really like that, Dad," Patrice chimed in.

"That would be totally unproductive," I exploded. "We'll just have to find another sitter."

"I have no idea where we would get another sitter," Dolores said. "We've used Leona for years. I don't know of anyone else. I think the girls have a good idea. It would be nice for you and the boys to spend some time together."

I didn't like the idea at all. I had more than enough to drink and I was fuming. I called the waiter over and yelled at him for some insignificant thing. I was outnumbered and had to take it out on someone. "There is no way I can take five days off from work. Dick and I have to get together on some plans next week," I said.

"You could have Dick come over to the house and meet with him there." Dolores wouldn't let me out of it.

I brooded for the rest of the meal and couldn't wait to get out of the restaurant. I couldn't imagine that Dolores would expect me to do this. I had never taken time off from work before to take care of the children. When we got home I continued sulking and went right to bed.

The next morning I realized I had been pretty selfish and that there was no other choice. I told Dolores I would make some arrangements so I could stay with them.

Dolores was excited about her experience in Chicago and was happy she went. I was pleased to see her take these initiatives and I told her so. I told her things worked out okay. Dick came over several times while she was gone and we got more done than we would have in the office with all the usual interruptions.

Dolores was pleased that all went well. She then told me how concerned Susan and Patrice were the night we came back from the restaurant and I went right to bed. "What have we done to Dad?" Susan had said. They worried they had hurt their relationship with me.

That summer when we were at Sand Bay Beach, our friends John and Jan Van asked us if we might be interested in buying the lot next to them on Moonlight Bay in Door County. We went to look at it. It was a beautiful lot with white birch bark of a dozen large birch trees peeping through the evergreens that covered the lot. We loved it and I told John we'd buy it. Dolores was thinking we might build in a few years, but as soon as we got back to Sand Bay I started sketching a cottage for the lot. By the end of the summer we hired an architect, with plans to build the following spring.

Our son Paul graduated from high school and was attending Berkeley College of Music in Boston, so we were finally able to spend part of the winter in a warm climate. We decided on Florida.

Before we left for Florida, I got the top three people in our company together and told them they would share in a 10 percent bonus each year on the profits of the business. Ed Kettner would be in charge of the office, Bob Knueppel the purchasing and production, and Dick Hare the sales. I felt this might stop the slide in sales we were experiencing.

We spent Christmas and New Year's in Appleton, then left for Florida with Peter and Jonathan.

We went to St. Petersburg, on the west coast of Florida, at the suggestion of Father Vince Dwyer. He said he had a friend, Monsignor Michael Dwyer, who had retired there and knew the area. He could help us get the children into a school in the middle of the school year.

We called the Monsignor and made a date for dinner with him. He was just as Vince described him, a delightful gentleman with twinkling Irish eyes, a ruddy complexion and a little graying goatee. He suggested the Little Red Schoolhouse, a private one-room school for Peter. It had two teachers and an enrollment of only 15.

Jonathan entered kindergarten at the public school near our rented condo. Dolores and I and the kids enjoyed the sunshine, the warm weather and the pool at the condo. I was fascinated by the fact that the *St. Petersburg Times* gave their evening paper away free any day the sun didn't shine sometime during the previous 24 hours. We never received a free paper all the time we were there.

To occupy her time while we lived at the condo, Dolores

gave a free Parent Effectiveness Training Course for some of the parents and teachers at the Little Red Schoolhouse, the first one she tried since her training course in Chicago, They liked it.

We were there until the end of May, when school was out. Then we headed back to Wisconsin. We were anxious to see the progress the builders had made on our Moonlight Bay cottage.

We drove from Florida to our home in Appleton and unpacked our things, then we left for Sand Bay where we would stay until school started again. As soon as we were unpacked at Sand Bay, we drove to Moonlight Bay to take a look at our new cottage. The carpenters were finishing installation of the cabinets and the trim. We were pleased how everything turned out, especially the huge fireplace which dominated the combined living, dining, and kitchen area.

Leona's husband Steve, a Hungarian immigrant who fled the uprising in Hungary some years before and a very accomplished stonemason, built the huge fieldstone fireplace. It was 15 feet wide and from 12 to 15 feet high, due to the cathedral ceiling that extended over the loft overlooking the living area. The fireplace opening, 5 feet wide and 4 feet high gave plenty of room for the large logs we intended to burn. It was beautiful. The chimney also serviced a fireplace in the master bedroom. There were two other bedrooms and two baths. We were pleased with it all. When James and Paul came home from college for the summer they would help me do the staining and painting so they could earn some money.

It was 1976 and Dolores made a decision to go to New York City for a couple of weeks to visit Kristine and to see the ships that would be coming into New York harbor to commemorate 200 years of our country's independence.

I was concerned, as this was the first time either of us had taken separate vacations, and I felt she was unhappy with me.

We had taken along a high school girl to Sand Bay to care for Peter and Jonathan so Dolores could leave and I could help the boys paint our cottage.

It was the Fourth of July; the boys had taken the day off from working on the cottage. I made the 20-mile trip to the cottage. I loved it and I wanted to get the feel of it, drink in the beauty of the setting, and just let it all soak in. I was lonely with Dolores being away. I missed her. I thought back to the Fourth of July picnic in Brillion years before when my friend Jim brought her to the dance and I first danced with her. Then I remembered how I got into trouble with my friend Florence, when she and I rode back to Appleton with Jim and Dolores from the dance, and she became angry with me because after dancing the first dance with her to the jukebox at the Diana restaurant, I danced all the rest of the dances with Dolores. Now I felt Dolores and I were drifting apart and fear came over me that I might be losing her.

The cottage Pat Mangan, the architect, designed was more like a two-story home. The basement was at ground level because of the sloping lot and looked out over the bay. We eventually intended to finish it into an apartment. The living room and dining area that faced the water on the second floor had glass on three sides and served as an indoor deck for use when the flies and mosquitoes were around. From there we had glimpses of the water 75 feet away through the trees. We had cut down only enough trees to make room for the cottage, the nearest ones only a few feet away. On either side of the enclosed deck were two outdoor decks. We were pleased with the design.

Dolores returned from her vacation rejuvenated. I heard her tell the older kids about some fellow in a cab who flirted with her when she rode into the city in the airport limo. I guess it gave her ego a boost, but it didn't help mine. She told me she worked in a boutique for a couple of days, where Kristine occasionally worked, and sold some clothes to the wife of a foreign diplomat. Then she worked in an office for five days for a friend of Kristine's, transcribing audiotapes. She told me how she enjoyed doing these things. I told her I was afraid she liked New York so much she might want to move there. She assured me it was just a fling; she was reliving the things she enjoyed doing before she was married and doing them in a big city like New York. She told me of the nice time she had sharing a picnic lunch with Kristine, watching the tall sailing ships come up the Hudson River. Her vacation was good for her and I was happy she was in good spirits when she returned.

At a meeting of both the men's and women's retreat boards, Father Vince Dwyer recommended we try to establish the retreat office and a Summer Institute at Notre Dame. The board members decided on Notre Dame because of its national appeal, and they thought this would attract people to the proposed Summer Institutes. Henry Balling from Buffalo, New York, a very active lay member of the board who helped in the negotiations with Notre Dame, was elected the first president of Retreats International, the name we chose for the new combined organization, which would now encompass about 400 retreat houses in the U.S. and Canada, men's and women's, mostly Catholic but some Protestant as well.

Father Tom Gedeon was appointed Executive Director of the national office. He would also be in charge of the Summer Institutes which would be sponsored by Retreats International.

Moving the office out of Appleton to Notre Dame at that time worked out well for me. I needed to give up my position as Executive Secretary as I intended to spend the winter months in Florida in the future.

Father Tom drove to Appleton, picked up the stock of literature the retreat office made available to the retreat houses plus the few pieces of office equipment owned by the retreat movement and moved it all to Notre Dame in a U-Haul trailer.

The first Summer Institute was a success with attendance of 90 people and it broke even financially. (Presently 800 people attend and Retreats International earns $50,000 in profit.) Scholars from various parts of the country give one-week courses to the priests, nuns and laypeople in attendance. The courses were spiritual updates for professionals and laypeople interested in spirituality, similar to what doctors and lawyers do to keep abreast of the latest knowledge in their professions.

I felt good about the progress the retreat movement made since Father Tom became the Executive Director. I was also pleased that the organization had developed along the regional lines I had envisioned.

We left for St. Petersburg the day after Thanksgiving that same year, as we thought a six-month school session in Florida would be less disruptive for the boys. We rented a beach house in St. Petersburg Beach for the winter and spring season. What a great experience to live on the Gulf of Mexico with the Pacific Ocean for our backyard.

The evening we arrived we sat on our thatch-covered deck for a drink with the rental agent and his wife, overlooking the ocean and watching the waves break on the sand beach in the moonlight. We couldn't believe this beauty would be ours to enjoy for the next several months. I would need meditation time to figure out what I was going to do to reverse the trend in our business. This was the perfect place for it.

We enrolled Peter and Jonathan in Canterbury School, a private Episcopalian school, as we thought a Christian education would be best for them.

It didn't take long for our friends and relatives to decide that a Florida beach house would be a smart place to visit during the cold Wisconsin winter. We had numerous visitors, Dolores spending a good part of her time in the local coin laundry washing sheets and towels, as we did not have a washer and dryer in the house. The house was old and sparsely furnished with antiquated furniture, but there was plenty of room for guests, having two separate apartments under one roof. However, we nor the guests could ever get used to the huge roaches that invaded the house.

We made friends with the young dentist and his German-born wife who lived next door. Dolores and I played some tennis, which we hadn't done since before we were married. We also maintained friendships with some of the teachers and parents of the school Peter had gone to the previous winter.

The business continued to deteriorate in spite of the incentives I offered the managers I put in charge. Sales were down from the previous year. I guess I had to realize that I could not expect Dick, although a good salesman, to have the marketing expertise to turn the business around, and I was going to have to be the one to come up with that plan.

I started drinking heavily, anxious about the business and unable to come up with anything to solve the problem. Not only did I have a couple of manhattans in the evening, but now it was before lunch, too. One day the German lady next door said to Dolores, "Don't you know your husband is an alcoholic?" Dolores asked me to cut down on my drinking; she said I wasn't very nice to her when I was drinking. She was right, any underlying anger came out after a few drinks.

One morning I awoke at four o'clock worrying about the business and couldn't go back to sleep. I went into the living room and started a fire in the fireplace. In a little while Jonathan got up, not feeling well, and we sat together in a chair cuddled in a blanket before the fire.

All at once the thought struck me that I probably needed to take over the sales department myself. We were primarily a sales and marketing company and our business was now in trouble in the marketing area. I didn't hire Dick for that purpose. He had fulfilled his sales manager's job by appointing food brokers throughout the country. We had to cut expenses, as profits were almost at a break-even point and we were headed for a loss.

This would also solve my problem of how I could live in Florida in winter. I would move the sales department with me. I always thought before I would have to move the entire business if I wanted to be active in it, and I knew that wasn't possible. The three regional sales managers live in the areas they manage; the only person in the sales department living in Appleton was Dick. He managed the three regional managers by phone and mail. If I took over the position of national sales manager, I could do the same from Wisconsin in the summer and Florida in the winter.

It was an exciting concept. I was bored and anxious sitting around Florida seeing the business go to pot. I needed and wanted to be involved in the business 12 months a year, and this could be the answer.

There was only one big problem, I'd have to let Dick go. That would be difficult for me to do. He was a hard-working faithful employee that had done a fantastic job for our company and was married to my niece. He was good at selling the food brokers on the marketing plan he and I developed in our conversation with Ralph Moehring years before and he made a national business out of it. But he finished that development some years ago and now the business was falling apart. I had changed marketing plans several times since I started in the peanut vending business 35 years before, and I hoped and prayed God would help me again.

Dolores felt being involved again in the business would be good for me. She said she knew I was bored and that my boredom and worry about the business was probably why I was drinking more. So I made the decision to let Dick go, but I would wait until I got back to Wisconsin in early June to talk to him.

Dolores and I were looking for something to do evenings in St. Petersburg. She suggested we invite some of the young couples we met the year before through Peter's school to join a discussion group. Father Dwyer developed a very successful spiritual growth program called Genesis II that we helped him finance with some of our tithing money.

Several couples were interested and we moved the weekly sessions around to each of our homes. After a very moving session in St. Petersburg on one of the nights when we were driving back home across the causeway to St. Petersburg Beach, I told Dolores I knew she was concerned about my heavy drinking and I was going to cut it back. I felt it was the help of God coming through our meeting that night that gave me the willpower to resolve to do something about the problem. The next day I found it fairly easy to cut out the drinks at noon and only have one in the evening. Things improved between Dolores and me as I felt better about myself.

When we returned to Appleton at the end of the school year, I had a talk with Dick. He was aware of the financial difficulty of the business. I told him I needed to work out a new marketing plan for the business and I wanted to take over the sales management of the company so I could work directly with the three regional sales managers to implement it. I also said I needed to be active in the sales of the business while I was in Florida during the winter months.

The new plan probably involved finding a way to provide distributor service for the Toy 'n Joy machines around the country which meant we had to somehow take the responsibility for the machines away from the food brokers and find distributors who would call on the stores, change over the merchandise wheels where necessary, and fill and keep the machines clean like Dick Haas, our regional manager in California was doing in his spare time business.

I suggested Dick talk to our Wisconsin broker Phil Coffero in Milwaukee and see if he could arrange to remove the Toy 'n Joy refills from Roundy's, a wholesale grocers' warehouse in

Milwaukee, and then start his own business of going around to the stores in Wisconsin giving full service to the machines. I told him that was the best I could offer him under the circumstances. It seemed like a good deal to me; Dick would not have to buy machines, he could just start filling and taking the money out of those that were already out there.

Phil was a very successful broker and a good friend of Dick's and so he gave up the commission on the refills and convinced Roundy's it would be to their advantage to no longer stock our refills as we found it necessary to go into a full service program to take proper care of the Toy 'n Joy machines in their member stores.

Frank Schultz, our Green Bay broker, agreed to do the same in the northern Wisconsin territory. Both brokers realized they couldn't afford the time and expense to make the changeovers the machines needed so as to vend the proper portions of merchandise.

Dick wasn't pleased about giving up his paycheck and going into the distributing business for himself, but he agreed to give it a try. It was frustrating for him. The machines were spread all over the state and he had to stay overnight in motels to cut the miles he had to travel. After trying it for a few weeks Dick decided he wanted to continue to be a salesman, not a serviceman, so he gave it up and took a sales management job with Direct Vending, the company that had copied our idea and was competing with us in many states throughout the country. Things could only get worse, not only did we have Direct Vending competing with us, now we also had our former sales manager working for them. I couldn't blame Dick, he needed a job and he knew the vending business.

Living in a beach house in St. Petersburg Beach was a great experience but not something either Dolores nor I wanted to do again. It was like living in a cottage, with people tracking in sand from the beach. And it was too cool for me. We considered the east coast of Florida which is warmer than the gulf coast but too much of a tourist area.

Dolores felt it was too disruptive for Peter and Jonathan to start school in Wisconsin, then transfer to a Florida school for the remainder of the school year as we did the two previous years. I agreed. She knew how adamant I was about living in a warm climate in winter, but she was concerned about the children's education, too. She agreed to try living in Florida for the next school year, realizing that if we did this every year and came back to Moonlight Bay in the summer, we wouldn't be living in our Appleton home anymore, which she dearly loved. We decided on an unfurnished home for nine months in Naples, Florida, about 100 miles south of St. Petersburg, as it would be warmer there.

This was a difficult time in our relationship, as I was forcing my will on Dolores. With our furniture being moved to Naples there wasn't much hope that she would ever live on her beloved Fox River again.

We moved into our rented home on Neptune's Bight, a pleasant three-bedroom ranch with a screened-in swimming pool off the family room and an inland waterway at the back of the lot. The kids were excited about the pool. We were not pleased with what we heard about the public schools in Naples, with their drug problems and the need for police on the school grounds, so we sent the kids to a private Episcopal school in Fort Myers, which necessitated an hour bus ride each way.

Naples was hot, really hot, in September. I asked the neighbors when it cooled off. They said maybe by the end of October. I knew then we had make a mistake in moving there, as we would also face some very hot weather in May and June before we could go back to Moonlight Bay.

Shortly after we arrived in Naples we got a call from Father Myron Wagner, a Salvatorian priest from Wisconsin we knew in the Cursillo Movement. He had a new program he though we might be interested in. It was called Focusing and he described it as self-help psychotherapy. This was something we both thought we could use, I with my business worries and Dolores with the adjustment of possibly never again living in her dream home.

We flew back to Wisconsin for the weekend in Racine, near Milwaukee, and met Fathers Ed McMahon and Peter Campbell, two Jesuit priests, both with doctorates in psychology, who were putting on the conference. Father Myron had assembled about 20 people for the weekend.

Fathers Pete and Ed based the program on a concept for self-help therapy developed by Eugene Gendlin, a doctor of psychology at the University of Chicago. Doctor Gendlin's approach was strictly scientific, and Fathers Ed and Pete said they had added a spiritual dimension to it.

Doctor Gendlin came to the conference for a half-day on Saturday and told us how he developed the Focusing technique by recording the initial psychotherapy sessions of his patients, then comparing the first five minutes of each initial session with the success and failure rate of his patients. He was able to find a common thread in his therapy sessions which could tell him in the first five minutes whether a patient had a chance of success.

He said it had something to do with the openness of the person and his willingness to be helped. With this information he developed a technique for ordinary people to lead other people through their own psychotherapy. The helper takes a person through a step by step process to find out what is bothering them—sometimes we don't know—then asks them to focus on the problem and be with it in a loving and caring manner. It is not necessary for the person being helped to reveal the problem to the helper.

The object is for the person being helped to experience what Doctor Gendlin calls a felt-shift, where they experience some relief from the problem. They can then go deeper into the problem, but if it is frightening or too painful they can choose to leave it—put it on the shelf, so to speak—and revisit it at another time. Doctor Gendlin maintains that if a felt-shift is experienced, the problem may not be cured, but each time you focus on it again, the problem becomes less threatening. We formed teams to help each other focus. Dolores and I both experienced the felt-shift. We planned to attend future weekend programs with Fathers Ed and Pete to learn more about the spiritual connection they found in Focusing.

I rented a small office for the business, and since Peter and Jonathan were in school all day, Dolores agreed to work with me in the office, doing my typing.

I decided to write an instruction manual for vending machine distributors who would make a business out of servicing the Toy 'n Joy machines which were owned by the grocery stores in their area of the country. The machines were not being taken care of properly by the wholesale grocers and food brokers, due to the mechanical changes that had to be made in the machines because of the change in size of the gumballs we were supplying. These new distributors would be in the same business I had suggested for Dick Hare, and which he tried in Wisconsin. The manual I was writing would explain all the details of how to succeed in that business.

I would then advertise in business opportunity columns in newspapers for distributors to go into business for themselves. The main difference in this and the CARE program that failed, is that sales of gum and toys in these locations were probably five to ten times as great as with the CARE machines and there would be no investment required in machines.

Because of our financial problems in the business, to save money I called off the winter company advisory board meeting which was usually held in Florida, telling the board members I thought it very important that I call a meeting in Florida with our three regional sales managers, and the business couldn't afford both meetings.

I was concerned that since I had let Dick Hare go the regional managers might think they were next. I wanted to go over my new plan with them for appointing distributors to take over the food broker machines. I also was concerned one or more of them might jump ship and go to work for our competitor, Direct Vending, now that Dick was working for them. To help keep their support I suggested they bring their wives along to Florida for a mini-vacation for a few days.

The meeting with the regional managers was successful and they liked the new distributor program.

A couple weeks later the doorbell rang one evening, and I was served with a notice of a lawsuit against our company for $100,000 by Direct Vending, claiming we were violating federal law by "restraint of trade!" They were asking for the case to be tried in a Texas court. If we were found guilty, federal law called for triple damages of $300,000! I was devastated. I not only had a business that was failing, now I had to worry about a lawsuit bankrupting the company. I was looking forward to our next Advisory Board meeting in the summer for advice on handling this new development.

Besides the oppressive heat and humidity, Naples was stifling for other reasons. It seemed to be a country club community of wealthy retirees and Dolores and I weren't wealthy or country club people. We looked out along the waterway in our backyard, and even on cooler evenings nobody was outside. We thought some people might be barbecuing, like people did in Wisconsin, but everyone seemed to either be at the country club or locked into their air-conditioned apartment cubicles. There also seemed to be a high incidence of alcoholism in the city; it was the only city I new with drive-up windows in their liquor stores.

We both agreed we wouldn't want to come back to Naples the following year. It was too hot and we didn't like the kids spending two hours a day on the school bus, not being able to be with their school friends, even on weekends, as most of their school friends lived in Fort Myers.

Dolores came up with a proposal. "If we are going to live in Florida for the nine-month school year," she said, "I think we should buy a house in St. Petersburg. We have friends there and so do the kids. If we get away from St. Petersburg Beach it will be warmer than it was last year at the beach house, but still a lot cooler than Naples."

This must have been a very painful decision for her to make. We had moved our furniture out of Appleton but hadn't put the house up for sale. She must have realized that if we bought a home in St. Petersburg we'd surely never be living in her home on the river again.

That's what we did. Before the end of the school year we bought a beautiful four-bedroom custom-designed home on a lot with at least 30 tall pine trees overlooking a golf course and a creek in the backyard. We bought it at a bargain price because it was in an integrated neighborhood. Dolores fell in love with it, said it was the nicest home she ever had. It had a red brick exterior, large living room, separate dining room, powder room, kitchen, family room, master bedroom, screened porch and two-car attached garage downstairs and three large bedrooms, a sewing room and even a phone booth upstairs. She agreed, and we put the Appleton house up for sale. We expected to get considerably more money for it than we were spending for our new home.

We held our advisory board meeting in June in Door

County. Since we skipped our winter Florida meeting we made this our big meeting of the year and invited the wives. It was a relief for me to meet with these business and professional men to talk about the lawsuit that was hanging over our heads and it was comforting to be able to share my problems with them.

Our Milwaukee law firm recommended a Texas law firm for the lawsuit, since the case would be tried in a Texas court before a Texas jury. Both sides were going back and forth with discovery proceedings to get as much information as possible about the other company. Of course, Dick Hare knew a lot about our company records and was able to tell their lawyers which documents to request that might be beneficial to their case.

One document that looked bad for us was a one-page agreement we asked the retailers to sign when they bought one of our Toy 'n Joy units. It stated they must buy Toy 'n Joy refills for their machines; if they did not, we could require them to sell their machine back to us at a low depreciated price. It was a useless document to us because to enforce it would have meant we would have had to sue each retailer who violated the agreement, and the cost of such lawsuits would have been prohibitive. We never enforced one of the agreements and never intended to. It was foolish of me to have ever used it. But this is where they could legally say we were restraining trade by tying our refill business to the sale of the machine. They said this was unfair competition and against federal law.

I told the advisory board of my fear of bankruptcy, not only for the business, but also personally, as the business was a limited partnership, not a corporation that protects personal assets.

Several members suggested the first thing to do was to change the business to a corporation. That would at least protect our personal assets.

And then there was our Moonlight Bay home. A second home is not protected under Wisconsin bankruptcy laws. They suggested gifting the property to our eight children. They said

Dolores and I could still live in the home and we each are allowed to gift as much as $10,000 to each one of our children, gift and income tax free, once a year. They also said gifting it was good future planning for avoiding inheritance taxes as it removed the property from our estate.

I took their advice and incorporated the business as an "S" Corporation, which gave us the same tax benefits as our family partnership did. Then we formed a limited partnership we called Becker's North for our eight children, and they each became owners of one-eighth interest in the Moonlight Bay cottage. I was relieved. This helped dispel my fears of losing everything if we lost the lawsuit and had to declare bankruptcy.

The summer at Moonlight Bay was delightful, except for my constant worry about the lawsuit. I was called to San Antonio by the opposing law firm to give a deposition giving them testimony under oath, taken down by a court reporter. I then set up a deposition in New York City for the Direct Vending people in the office of a trade magazine for the vending industry, to show that our company had less than 1 percent of the toy and gum vending business in the country and therefore weren't restraining trade from anyone. They had the other 99 percent of the country in which to sell their machines and refills. But the bills from our Texas law firm kept mounting. It felt like I was again carrying that rock in my stomach. I spent a lot of time lying on my bed, depressed.

It was the end of August, time to go back to St. Petersburg and put the kids in school. The ride back to Florida was pleasant. The kids enjoyed the Holiday Inn swimming pools. We unpacked the boxes from Naples and enrolled Peter and Jonathan at Canterbury, a private Episcopal school.

I didn't find St. Petersburg very exciting, too many old people, God's waiting room, someone called it. I found it difficult to make friends. I worked at home, so I didn't meet many people. Monsignor Dwyer was my best friend. Monsignor and I usually had lunch together once a week, and not an expensive one, as our company lost money that year and I was concerned about spending money. It broke my heart when I got back from lunch one afternoon and I called to tell him that I couldn't have lunch with him anymore as I felt I couldn't afford it.

Dolores seemed to enjoy St. Petersburg. The integrated neighborhood didn't bother her. She walked every morning with Ethyl, the black lady next door. She met other women while working in the library at Jonathan's school. We kept in touch with the young adults we had met the first year we were there, but they seemed more like our kids as they were about the same age.

At the next Advisory Board meeting one of the members suggested trying to settle the lawsuit for $50,000, even though we'd have to borrow money to pay it. Direct Vending refused the offer. Six months later I offered them $75,000. They turned that down, too.

The board later recommended that if I offered $75,000 and they refused that, I had better come up with another $25,000 and then hope they would take it and not raise the ante.

It made sense. I had already accepted the $75,000 settlement in my mind. It was worth $25,000 more to get this thing behind me. Our lawyer fees kept mounting and the expenses of a trial could easily exceed $25,000. The downside, if we lost the case, was $100,000, plus possible punitive damages of an additional $200,000, which would certainly break the company.

I called our lawyer in San Antonio the next day to see if he could settle it for the $100,000. Luckily, he got their agreement without them holding out for more. He also negotiated a payment plan for us to spread the payments over a year. Thank God it was over.

A couple of months after our settlement Direct Vending called me to see if we wanted to buy their business. Mainly what they had to sell was a $400,000 tax loss their company had accumulated fighting us in the marketplace and in the courts for four years. I said thanks, but no thanks. It reminded me of the boxing movie where both fighters slugged it out with all the energy they could muster, both falling to the mat at the end of the fight, totally exhausted. It's good that our change to a distributor operation was starting to make our company profitable again so we could pay their claim.

Chapter 17

The heat, humidity, and bugs in Florida were getting to us. Dolores even had roach streaks on her blouses in the closet. I didn't realize how much the roaches loved to live under the pine needles and invade our house. No matter how many times we sprayed the yard and the house, they kept coming. People told us they could make themselves almost paper thin to get in under the doors.

When we arrived at our St. Petersburg home on Labor Day weekend that year the temperature and the humidity were each about 100 degrees and our air-conditioner broke down. We couldn't get a serviceman because of the holiday weekend. Dolores disliked the heat more than I did, and we wondered how we were going to stand the heat, humidity, and the bugs for another six years until Jonathan finished high school. We had to return to St. Petersburg in late August and not leave there until early June, to be there for the entire school year. That gave us only about 10 weeks at Moonlight Bay.

Our son, Michael, was renting a one-room beach house in Manhattan Beach, California, near Los Angeles. Things were not going well for him right then, and he was mellowing out on the beach. He was lonely and I was depressed about living in St. Petersburg. Dolores thought it might be a good idea for me to stay with him for a while and we could commiserate together. A great idea, I thought, living on the ocean again. I was on a flight the next day.

In a few days I was looking at houses in Palos Verdes, next to Manhattan Beach. It is a beautiful, hilly, bedroom community, somewhat removed from Los Angeles with gorgeous homes with panoramic views of the ocean. Dolores had to see this. I called her and told her I thought we ought to consider California for the winters. I told her it was her kind of weather, not too hot and not too cold. I said winters in California were like Moonlight Bay weather in the summer, maybe five or ten degrees cooler in the coldest months.

On the kids' Easter vacation we flew to California with Peter and Jonathan to look at houses in Palos Verdes. We stayed in the one-room Manhattan Beach place with Michael, with the kids sleeping on the floor. We liked the area and even though the houses were priced at two to three times as much as we could get for our St. Petersburg home, we decided to go for it. Profits in the business were picking up, and again we would have to come up with only enough for the 20 percent down payment. I didn't worry about the monthly payments, I figured the business would support them.

Just before we left the beach house at Manhattan Beach, Dolores called our friends, the Holcombes, in Santa Barbara. We had met Chet and Adabeth several years before on a tour of the Orient. We kept up a friendship with them through the years. They visited us in Florida and we stopped to see them in Santa Barbara on one of my business trips to California.

When Dolores told Adabeth on the phone we were considering moving to Palos Verdes she was disappointed. "Do you mean you're moving to California and you're not moving to Santa Barbara?"

Dolores told her I needed to be close to the Los Angeles airport for my business trips, but Adabeth said the Los Angeles airport was less than two hours from Santa Barbara. At the close of the conversation Adabeth said, "Just remember, we love you and we want you." It was a powerful invitation.

Dolores reminded me that Moonlight Bay was almost two hours from the Green Bay airport and we chose to live there. I asked my brothers, Richard and Harold, who were both school administrators in Corona, California about Santa Barbara. Richard said it's a wonderful place to live, no air-conditioning required, almost a perfect climate. He said he would have lived there if he hadn't established himself in Corona. They both thought we'd like it better than Palos Verdes.

When we got back to St. Petersburg we made the decision to move to Santa Barbara, but we would rent there for a few months to look over the city before purchasing a home.

Before we returned to Moonlight Bay in early June we put our St. Petersburg house up for sale and packed our things for the movers—143 boxes—and left them there through the summer. Dolores reminded me this was the third time we had to pack and unpack those 143 boxes in three and one-half years. She is a saint.

In late August, Joan Richards, our friend and real estate lady in St. Petersburg, arranged for the moving van to have our furniture and boxes moved to Santa Barbara. We rented a three-bedroom, two-story house with a swimming pool, and unpacked only the bare necessities. We stored the rest in our garage.

We joined the Newcomers Club, a national organization for people moving into an area. They organized potluck get-acquainted cocktail parties, bridge games, and golf and hiking outings. It was great for making new friends in a strange city.

Beautiful views were everywhere—the Pacific Ocean, the canyons, the foothills, and the mountains, with greenery and flowers everywhere. People told us the weather got up in the sixties and seventies during the day in the winter months, and the seventies and eighties in the summer. They said the warmest month was usually September, because the marine fog covered the city in the morning during the summer, keeping it cool; but starting in September the days were usually clear, making it warmer. Our friends in Santa Barbara told us they like the winters better than the summer. That suited us fine as we would be at Moonlight Bay in the summers. "Another day in paradise" was the native favorite expression when people got up in the morning in Santa Barbara. It looks like we had made a good choice.

I was comfortable managing the business from Florida and now California. Being away from our office gave me more time to think, and since this was an idea business, that was important. I remembered days in my office in Appleton when I had a whole day's work planned, then at the end of the day I realized I wasn't able to get at any of it because of constant interruptions. Also, my being away helped the people in the office grow in their jobs as they had to take more responsibility. I told them I wanted them to try things even if they make mistakes as they would learn from them. I told them I made the biggest mistakes.

Our western regional sales manager Dick Haas had been telling me about a talking vending machine about 2-feet wide and 5-feet high with a large plastic window, showing a toy chicken on top of a mound of multicolored plastic eggs. He said you insert a quarter, the chicken cackles and vends an egg with a toy inside. He said they were selling well, and he thought we should manufacture a machine like it.

Now that I lived only two hours from Brea, California, where Dick lived, I met with him in Los Angeles and we looked at a chicken machine in one of the supermarkets. It seemed like a good idea, so I looked into the possibility of manufacturing one.

Through my contacts in the vending trade I located Bob Glaser, an engineer, in Chicago, who had made an egg-dispensing machine with a Santa theme that was used in a mall at Christmas time. The plastic eggs in the machine contained coupons for free gifts at certain stores in the mall. We hired Bob, on a contract basis, to design a machine for us, and I was pleased with the finished product. Only, I wanted to improve on the chicken idea. We would make the chicken character and the back drop in the machine, interchangeable with a Santa Claus for Christmas, a bunny for Easter and a pumpkin at Halloween, each character giving an appropriate message for the holiday to the kids. We found an inexpensive way to change the voices and assorted messages for the various characters and seasons of the year. We used the same battery-operated plastic record player that Mattel used in its various toys, such as Cecil the Seasick Serpent, like our daughter Patrice had, which is where I got the idea.

Production on the machine took about a year before we started selling them to our distributors. It was an immediate success in the supermarket trade, and the refill business on the plastic eggs, with toys inside, added to our total sales.

A few months after moving to Santa Barbara we bought a three-bedroom ranch home with a panoramic view of the mountains and the city. It cost twice as much as we got for our home in Florida, but I was happy to be in Santa Barbara and Dolores was, too.

It is an expensive city to live in, mainly due to the high cost of housing, but it has so much going for it. We had the ocean and the mountains within minutes of our home. An architectural board closely monitored commercial as well as residential building to keep a Spanish southwestern look to the city. No big McDonald's golden arches here, you had to hunt for the small signs that designated the few franchise businesses.

Dolores and I made friends with neighbors, in the Newcomers group, and through the church. Santa Barbara City College, overlooking the ocean, one of the highest rated community colleges in California, was open to everyone at a minimal fee. I took a basic computer course there as I didn't know the difference between a calculator and a computer. Then came the time for the midterm exams. My brother and his wife asked us to go to Hawaii with them at the same time as the exams. It wasn't a difficult choice. Hawaii was beautiful.

One of the biggest pluses that set Santa Barbara out front of Appleton and St. Petersburg for me, was its excellent adult education program, connected with City College.

Since it was such a great place to live, it attracted more than its share of professional people. Many of the adult education courses were taught by Ph.D.s, and were absolutely free. For three years, when I wasn't busy with the business, I kept going to my weekly self-esteem class and just let things soak in. Any self-esteem I had, seemed to center around my success in business. I learned that to have true self-esteem I must hold myself, not what I did, in esteem. Still a shy guy, I was learning to like myself better and accept my shyness.

The psychology courses by Dr. David Rico and a speaker series on Monday nights at the Lobero Theater called Mind and Supermind were very helpful. I also took classes in writing, gardening, photography and gospel singing.

Besides the adult education courses, I joined the Santa Barbara Choral Society, a 100-voice choral group. Dolores worked with Villa Majella, a home for single pregnant women. We brushed up on our bridge-playing skills at the bridge center and started playing duplicate bridge—a kind of tournament bridge—hoping to someday become bridge masters. I enjoyed life more in Santa Barbara, and Dolores seemed happier there, too. Jonathan attended San Roque Catholic grade school and Peter went to Bishop Diego Catholic high school.

Due to the success of our wooden cabinet talking vending machine, I thought we could revolutionize the bulk vending industry by having Bob Glaser, our engineer, design an entirely new concept in gum and toy vending machines. Instead of the usual machines bolted to a floor stand, we would put four or five gum or toy machines into a wooden cabinet the size of our talking machine. This would make an outstanding unit for the large supermarket chains, with the talking machine unit in the center and a four or five compartment gum and toy unit on either side. We called it a Toy 'n Joy Center. We offered Bob a position in our company, and he moved his family to Appleton. He said he was happy to get out of the Chicago rat race. He did an outstanding job in designing the new machines, on which we were able to obtain several U.S. and foreign patents.

Father Vince Dwyer became a member of our advisory board at the summer meeting that year. I thought he would add a spiritual dimension to our company. When I told him that, he laughed and said "I think I can qualify as a businessman as well, I was in charge of the jam and jelly business for the Trappist monks when I was there."

"Lyle, with all these new machines you're building, I think you need a sales manager to get these machines out making money for you," Mike Ariens said, at the meeting. I agreed. It made sense. I wasn't very good at sales work; I was more of a marketing man.

We placed an ad for a national sales manager in the midwest edition of the *Wall Street Journal* and settled on Tom Evers. His claim to fame, and what sold me on hiring him, was that he had worked for L'eggs hosiery, and was successful in placing racks of their egg-shaped packages in the K-Mart stores through distributors, which is the direction we were headed with our machines. Most of our machines were in independent supermarkets, but I wanted to get into the grocery chains like Safeway and the discount department stores like K-Mart. That's where the volume was.

Now we had the Toy 'n Joy Center that would look great in K-Mart stores and we had the L'eggs' sales manager that had sold them on the hosiery racks. But our Toy 'n Joy centers cost us almost $1,000 each to manufacture. If we wanted to place these machines in K-Marts we would have to invest millions of dollars in machines to service them. This was much too large a project for our company.

So we scratched K-Mart as a prospect and Tom decided to go after some of the smaller chains instead. Shopko, a regional discount department chain, with stores like K-Marts, were headquartered in Green Bay. Tom was able to get a test in some of their Wisconsin stores. We couldn't believe the amount of gumballs, eggs, and capsules with toys we were selling, over $500 per month per store.

We wanted regional discount chains like Shopko, and an opportunity came knocking at our door. Best Vendors, out of Minneapolis, had a unique idea. They contracted with Shopko, and similar chains, to manage all their vending machines for them in their stores. Then Best would sub-contract with various vending companies, like ours, who had gum and toy machines, also companies who had Coke and Pepsi machines, and those who handled kiddie rides, the little cars and merry-go-rounds you see outside stores. All the money these machines took in would be sent by the sub-contractors to Best Vending. Best, in turn, would take the complete responsibility for management of all the chain's vending machines and send them one check each month for their combined commissions. Best would deduct a percentage of the commissions as their management fee.

Best liked our state of the art Toy 'n Joy centers because they looked so much nicer in the stores than several individual machines bolted to a floor stand, which is what were in most stores.

Then our big opportunity came. Best showed our equipment to several regional discount chains, Caldor, Bradley, and Ames in the northeast and Venture as well as Shopko in the midwest, a total of 700 high volume stores in all. It would mean an investment for us in excess of a million dollars, as some stores would need more than one Toy 'n Joy Center.

There was only one problem, and it was a big one. They had a 20-day cancellation clause in their contract. If for any reason they or the chain was dissatisfied with our machines, merchandise, or service, they could terminate our contract with them within 20 days. Our insurance agent also objected to several things in their contract regarding liability insurance on the machines.

Our office manager, Ed Kettner, and I, and our lawyer, got on the phone on a conference call with their lawyers to try to solve the problems. We ended the call further apart than when we started.

The impasse gnawed at me continually for a couple of weeks, as I tried to think of a solution. A pain, like a knife, went through my chest into my back. Those test stores we had with Shopko were doing so well. What Best offered us could be several million in additional sales per year and for me it was also the pride of getting our Toy 'n Joy machines into some of the major discount store chains in the country.

I wasn't as opposed to the 20-day cancellation clause as our lawyer was. I figured we had the best machines on the market, we bought our toys directly from the Orient, so we should have the best values available. We would have to invest in the machines, but it would be a good investment with the volume of business these stores would do. We would have to find distributors to rent the machines from us, buy our refills, and service the machines. We would have no problem getting the distributors to purchase our refills, as our rental agreement with them would legally bind them to do so.

I couldn't stand the suspense, or the pain in my chest and back any longer, so I called Billy Weisman, the president of Best Vendors and suggested I fly to Minneapolis to get together with him, without our lawyers, to see if we could come to an agreement on the contract. He was agreeable to sitting down with me.

The next day I was in his office. In an hour we had an agreement. He convinced me he needed the 20-day cancellation clause, as the stores they would be representing demanded it. But if we did a good job, which we intended to do, there should be no problem. He compromised on some of the insurance problems to satisfy our insurance agent; we shook hands, and had a deal. I had talked to our bank about applying for a Small Business Administration loan and they didn't think it would be a problem to get it approved. For a guy who is uncomfortable losing more than 50 bucks in Las Vegas, this gamble didn't bother me at all. I was elated. I intended our company would do a good job, and everyone would be happy.

The SBA approved the loan. We ran ads for distributors on the east coast where most of the machines would go. Nick Johnson, our new regional manager for that territory, interviewed the prospects and set up distributors there. He also convinced our son Peter, then 23-years-old, who had dropped out of City College in Santa Barbara and was unsuccessful in starting a rock band in San Francisco, to become a distributor for our company on the east coast. Nick told Peter that if he worked in his dad's business, maybe someday he would run it. A few months later, our daughter Patrice, 32-years-old and a single parent, who had been attending college in California but couldn't decide on a goal, decided to move to New York to also become a distributor for the company. Our son Jonathan traveled for a while with the distributors Nick appointed, to train them. Our son Paul and I made trips to the Orient to buy the toys. Paul also designed the toy displays for the machines. Marlene Campbell, a very capable woman, who by that time had been with the company for 20 years, was in charge of manufacturing the machines and refills that would go into them.

It was an exhilarating feeling when we began placing our first Toy 'n Joy machines in these stores. It had been a long way up since the dark days of the peanut business some 40 years before. From sales of a dollar a month we were placing machines in discount stores that should average as much as $500 a month.

Dolores and I visited Peter and Patrice a few times out east. I sometimes spent a couple of days helping them service our machines. I was fascinated by one store in the mall; Patrice and I put $1,000 worth of merchandise in it for one month's sales. Because of the heavy traffic and the length of our route, we were lucky to service a dozen locations a day. With Peter we started later in the morning, and sometimes did not get back until ten o'clock at night.

Patrice had a difficult problem, being a single parent. She had to be home by the time her daughter's after-school program closed. If she was held up in traffic, she would be worried sick trying to finish her route and get back in time. Taking the coins to the bank, as much as $10,000 at a time, was also a problem. She had to run them through a coin counting machine when nobody would see or hear her doing it. She loaded the coins into her van at night, hoping no one was watching. Once, going to the bank, some of the open bags fell off the dolly as she was pulling it into the bank, dimes and quarters spilling all over the sidewalk. She said she just stood there and cried.

We eventually placed 3,600 Toy 'n Joy units—1,200 Toy 'n Joy Centers—in stores in the Best Vendor program, and the rental income we received from our distributors for the machines was sufficient to take care of our monthly SBA payments at the bank.

Peter was fascinated with the business, but after two years put his route up for sale and moved to Appleton to take over Paul's job as merchandise manager. Paul stuck it out in our office for several years prior to the Best Vendor program, I think, because he was the only family member in the business, and didn't want to disappoint me. I had looked to him to possibly manage the business some day, but Paul didn't care for the management responsibility. A music major, he wanted to perform and tune and repair pianos, although he continued to work part-time in the business.

About a year, after many phone calls to Dolores and me, sobbing over the phone, anxious about being able to properly take care of her daughter as well as her route, Patrice decided to quit. We had Gail Lang, our assistant sales manager, look for someone to become a distributor for her territory, and buy her inventory of merchandise so she could go back to college.

We started to hear rumblings from Best Vendors. They said some stores were complaining about poor service. We knew that some of our distributors in the New England area were not doing a good job. People we put into business as distributors were not necessarily always good business people. It was very expensive to find new distributors and to replace them, so we were reluctant to do so. The air fares, car rentals and hotel expenses of our sales managers were very costly, and several trips out east were sometimes needed to appoint one distributor.

Then Best Vendors put on the pressure. They said several of the chains were complaining about poor service on our machines and that other vending distributors were showing them new styles of machines they wanted to put in the stores to replace ours. Many of the distributors who lost the business in these stores, when we took over, were out to get it back.

We didn't move fast enough to solve the problems. Best Vendors finally did the unthinkable—they exercised their option to terminate our contract in 20 days!

Now I had the same piercing pains in my chest I suffered when we went into the Best Vendor deal several years before. This time the doctor even gave me a CAT scan to find out what was wrong with me. I knew what was wrong, I was under tremendous tension.

Our lawyer determined the 20-day cancellation clause was not legal according to Wisconsin law and negotiated a gradual 12-month pull-out of all of our machines. That eased the problem somewhat.

The good news was that the machines were all paid for. We

had paid off the 5-year Small Business Administration loan in less than 4 years. The bad news was that we would have to pay freight of about $50 a unit, about $180,000, to get the machines back, another $180,000 to ship them out again, if and when we could find distributors who could find locations for them, plus probably $100 each to refurbish them, another $360,000—a total of $720,000. I immediately applied for another SBA loan. I thought I had better do so before our credit rating turned sour at the bank, which was sure to happen eventually, when the machines started to come back. Fortunately the SBA and the bank granted the loan as we maintained a good record by paying off the previous loan ahead of time.

I immediately started to cut expenses. Tom Evers and Nick Johnson had to go—our two most expensive employees. I gave them each six months' severance pay. Gail Lang took over as National Sales Manager. I arranged an early retirement package for Ed Kettner, our General Manager, who had served our company faithfully for many years.

Gail Lang, who took over as National Sales Manager, when Nick left the company, realized our business was in trouble, and I couldn't blame her when a few months later she took a regional sales manager's job with a candy company.

We had reduced our overhead 25 percent in a matter of a few months. But we were still not out of the woods; we had the mammoth problem of finding a home for the 3,600 Toy 'n Joy units coming back during the next year, besides a SBA loan to pay off.

Then I think God stepped in again to help as I continued to pray about the problem. A couple years prior to the Best Vendor deal, I personally talked to each of our employees to find out what they did, whether they liked what they were doing, or whether they might prefer some other job with the company. I also asked for any suggestions on changes to make their various departments operate more efficiently. The survey was very informative, and one interview stood out in my mind, it was with Steve Douglas who had been our shipping and receiving manager in our warehouse near Appleton for over ten years. Steve told me he was interested in sales and would like a sales job with our company if there was an opening. He said his father and brother were salesmen. He thought our machines should be easy to put out in stores. He placed a few on his own time for us in Green Bay, where he lived.

I felt there was no hope in selling the 3,600 cabinet machines that would be coming back to us in the following year. The only way to possibly get these machines out in stores again in that short a time, I felt, would be to rent them at a low attractive monthly rental rate to our present distributors, to replace some of our old style racks of machines they had in the stores, as well as to rent them to new distributors for new territories.

I talked to Steve about my plan, telling him he would have to talk to our present and new distributors by phone about renting our machines, as the company didn't have the money for him to travel the country to do this. Steve, in his early thirties, with beautiful black wavy hair and a winning smile, said he liked talking on the phone and was eager to try his sales abilities in this way. He started immediately by calling our present distributors and had some successes with them. I was excited. I was convinced Steve would be a successful salesman for our company.

Peter and I decided we should exhibit our machines at the National Restaurant Convention in Chicago to see if we could drum up some business for our machines from family restaurants. Our largest distributor, had been very successful with our machines in a pizza chain.

Again I saw God's helping hand. We hardly did any business at the convention, but two young ladies stopped at our booth and in chatting with them, found out one of them was a sales lady for a food broker. She called on pizza restaurants. She said she received a $25 bonus from the food broker for each pizza restaurant that switched to the brand of tomato sauce this broker sold. We asked her if she would be interested in a $25 incentive for each pizza restaurant she was able to get to take one of our Toy 'n Joy machines. She said she'd give it a try. She never secured a location for us, but Steve used that $25 placement bonus idea in our ads for new distributors, in food trade magazines and newspapers, and it worked well.

Steve found homes for a good portion of the returned machines as they came back, and we gave him the title of Sales Manager. Within two years from the return of the first machines our monthly rental income from machines equalled our monthly SBA loan payments. That was a relief.

Another lasting influence the restaurant convention had on me was a talk by the featured speaker, General Schwartzkopf. He talked about leadership and how he once was handed the job of personnel officer for the entire army. After giving him this job, his superior officer immediately left on a lengthy trip.

General Schwartzkopf said he ran after him down the hall imploring him to tell him how to do this new job. He said all his superior officer said was, "Just do what's right." Then he said again, "You'll know what's right, just do it, and everything will be fine."

I was so impressed with this simple, yet so profound statement, that it has been my motto ever since. I try to follow it in my business as well as in my personal life.

That brought back memories of that spiritual retreat years ago with Father Vince Dwyer when I asked him how God talks to us. One of the ways he said was through other people—the guy in your warehouse you hardly ever talked to, the woman who stopped by your booth, a General who gave a talk at a convention.

It was again time for our summer advisory board meeting. We held this one at the Landmark Resort in Egg Harbor. Two new members were added to the board to replace Ben Hauserman, who retired, and Father Vince Dwyer, who also retired to the Trappist Monastery, due to ill health.

Marty Leaf joined the board; he was one of the owners of Leaf Gum Company (now owned by Hershey Chocolate Company). Marty and his wife Iris had been our good friends for years.

The other new member was Bill Hoeltke, Mike Ariens' sales manager during the years they built Ariens into a national company. Bill and his wife June had been our friends since our Brillion days, when they belonged to our couples' dinner group.

I was worried about this meeting. Because of all the Best Vendor machines that had come back and the cost of refurbishing them, plus the freight in and out of our assembly plant on them, we were $400,000 in the hole through June of that year. What would our banker, Gus Zuehlke, think of this? We had borrowed a good portion of the SBA loan I had arranged from the Valley Bank, to pay these costs.

It was 8:00 a.m. and we were ready to start the meeting, but Gus hadn't arrived. Gus had never missed a meeting in all the years he was on the board, and he was usually one of the first ones there. We waited awhile, then decided to begin. That morning, I got up my courage and opened the meeting with a prayer. We needed help.

Fortunately, John Van, who had several businesses of his own and was a stockholder and member of the loan board at the Kellogg Bank in Green Bay, analyzed our company statement. He said the correct accounting procedures were to capitalize the refurbishing expenses on the machines and not take all these costs as immediate expense. We could depreciate them over several years. Marty Leaf, who had been involved with finance at Leaf Gum, agreed. This almost eliminated the loss on the books and I was relieved. (Our outside accounting firm also agreed that capitalizing these assets was proper.)

Gus never showed up for the meeting. I called him the next day and he said he was sorry, but he forgot about it. He said he was at his Door County home and could have come. I felt God had to be involved in this to spare Gus the shock when looking at our statement. He had enough of those jolts through the years with the ups and downs of our company, I think God spared him this one.

Chapter 18

My son Peter and his wife Karen were doing a bang-up job of merchandising our toys through our capsule machines. They traveled to the Orient together to select the toys they thought would sell best in our Toy 'n Joy machines.

A big change had occurred in our industry over the previous few years. Tens of thousands of charity machines, vending everything from gumballs to M&M's, were being placed in every possible retail store up and down the street that would take them. No longer vending penny gumballs, most machines were a quarter a play. Each machine had a label stating the merchant was donating the space for the machine and that a portion of the proceeds—the commission usually paid to the retailer—would go to a charitable organization like "Jerry's Kids" or "Hugs Not Drugs." Our trade magazine said there were 375,000 of these machines in stores across the country, some stores ending up with two to as many as five machines, as retailers didn't want to offend any of the charities that offered them machines.

Naturally, this took business away from the gumball machines in our Toy 'n Joy units. Peter's response to this was to get our distributors to change more of their Toy 'n Joy machines from candy and gum, to vend capsules with toys. Consequently, our sales of refills to our distributors eventually changed from 40 percent gum and 60 percent toys to 15 percent gum and 85 percent toys, most of the toys in 50-cent capsules. This actually helped sales, as we eliminated most of the 5- and 10-cent gumballs and kept the 25-cent size, which was competitive with the charity machines. Our distributors were pleased, as their sales increased substantially.

I talked to Peter about his future plans and whether he might be interested in taking over the business when I retired in a couple of years. I told him I had confidence in him and felt he could do a good job in running the company. He was pleased I asked him and told me that this was his goal when he gave up being a distributor and moved to Appleton to work in the office. He said he was fascinated with the business. I said I planned to retire on my seventieth birthday, which was less than two years away. He said it would be a challenge for him to take over, but he looked forward to it.

Peter, Marlene our production manager, Bob our engineer, Steve our sales manager, and I, were sitting around the conference table discussing the business in the new office we had recently rented in an industrial park in Kimberly, a few miles out of Appleton. It was September and Dolores and I were leaving soon for Santa Barbara.

Steve said the candy claw machines were the hot new vending machine out in the field and our distributors were asking for them. I was aware of the claw machines in bowling alleys and arcades where kids and even adults would put in quarters to operate the overhead claw device to try to pick up a plush toy. These machines had come out some years before and were declared a gambling device in some states because you didn't get something every time for your money. Steve got a copy of a trade magazine to show me a picture of a candy claw machine, where you played until you won, and received a portion of candy or toys.

I always remembered my fascination with the claw machine as a kid at the Brillion Firemen's picnic and how I begged nickels from my mother to play it. I had talked for years to Bob Glaser about eventually making a claw machine for our company, and had our patent attorney send Bob copies of all the expired patents for claw machines for ideas. But I didn't want a gambling machine. I wanted one where you got something every time for your money.

Bob said one of the local supermarkets had a candy crane that you could play until you won. I wanted to take a look at it, so we all hopped in our cars to go see it. It was a quarter machine, but it was out of order with a toy stuck in the claw. It didn't look very exciting to me; it contained an assortment of wrapped hard candies and toys we can buy for a penny apiece from China. I told Bob I would like to be able to give the kids a nice toy each time for their 25 or 50 cents. The only problem with my idea was the claw could pick up more than one toy at a time or maybe a few pieces of penny candy. That's why they had to put such cheap toys in the machine. There was no control on what they could pick up.

The wheels started to turn in Bob's head and he said, "Maybe we could use a suction device, like a vacuum cleaner uses, to suck up a toy in a plastic capsule."

"That's a great idea," I said. "We wouldn't even have to use a capsule. We could put the toys in a cellophane bag. It would be a less costly package and we wouldn't have to confine ourselves to toys that fit into a capsule."

Then Peter said, "Why don't we have a little spaceship the kids can control with a joystick, like they have on video games, and have the spaceship dip down and pick up a toy?"

"That's it," I said. "We'd just have to make sure the suction tube doesn't pick up more than one toy at a time."

"I think we can control that," Bob said, "by having a small diameter suction tube, possibly only a quarter-inch in diameter, then control the amount of vacuum in the tube."

"That's terrific. Where did you ever get the idea of using a suction device?" I asked Bob.

"They use suction devices to move parts with robotic arms

in assembly machines," he said.

"Now that you mention it, I also remember a suction device being used to feed paper into a platen type printing press," I added. "We could put in a nice assortment of toys every time for either 25 or 50 cents, or even $1, depending on the value of the toys we want to vend.The kids will have more fun fishing for them than simply turning a handle on our capsule machines and taking what they get."

"We might be able to get a patent on the idea," Bob said. "I have never seen a suction device used in a claw machine."

"Wouldn't that be great? We'd have the greatest non-gambling machine on the market. Mothers would like it as the kids would get a toy every time they played."

The next morning I came into the office and Bob was there sucking up toys in cellophane bags with a tube off of a vacuum cleaner on which he had stopped down the suction. The concept worked. Now all Bob had to do was design the machine.That wouldn't be easy with all the electronics necessary in a claw machine; also it would be the first electric machine we ever produced.

In a few weeks Bob had worked out enough of the design with drawings to meet with our patent attorney at Quarles and Brady. They wasted no time in applying for a U.S. patent. They said it would take about a year to know whether it was approved.

Dolores and I and our family celebrated my 52 years in the business at my retirement party. Chuck Buckman, my partner 52 years ago in the peanut vending business was there. Vern Vechart and Dick Hare, the first two sales managers of our company, were there to celebrate with us. Vern took our business national in the candy trade, and Dick did the same with our Toy 'n Joy machines in the supermarket trade. Our eight children and their spouses were able to make it, along with our employees and friends. It was a great evening. I felt good about having been able to build a national business without ever having to give any part of it away to investors for money to finance it. It was still owned 100 percent by our family. I would still remain Chairman of the Board.

I received the usual engraved gold watch, packaged in a gold-plated talking-machine egg. It wasn't a Rolex, but one of the digital watches we used as a prize in our 25-cent capsule assortments. The engraving on the back thanked me for my fifty-two years of service to the company. I shall cherish it always. I also received a beautiful mahogany Monopoly set with gold and silver-plated houses, hotels, and playing pieces, Monopoly being a tradition in our family.

After dinner I represented Peter with a gavel inscribed, *To Peter, with full confidence in your ability to lead the company into the next century.*

Dolores and I celebrated our Fiftieth Wedding Anniversary that same year; we had a wonderful party in Appleton at Butte des Morts Country Club—Gus Zuehlke got us in with his membership—with about 300 guests. All of our children and grandchildren were able to attend. We celebrated on a Saturday night, July 23rd. I told people, facetiously of course, that we had it a couple days early as we might not make it to the 25th, which was our anniversary.

Peter needed to take over completely and spread his wings in the business, now that he was president; so he and I agreed to cut off my day-to-day phone and mail contact with the business. I was glad to be away from the daily routine.

Although, I had spent the last 15 years with my primary residence in Florida or California, almost like an absentee owner, I would now rely on the monthly financial statements to see how the business was doing. I did promise to come into the office from Santa Barbara or Moonlight Bay for a couple of days every few months, and would always be available for consultation by phone, or in person, if and when Peter might feel the need.

Peter, now 28, organized the business to free himself of the details, and be more able to concentrate on helping our distributors to be successful, by supplying them with the best machines, products, and marketing expertise in the business. He appointed Marlene, in her forties, who handled purchasing and production in the company for over 20 years, Executive Vice President in charge of the day-to-day operation of the company. We now had a young eager group to run the company.

At our next advisory board meeting, where Peter took charge, I presented a plan put together by Peter Lettenberger, the attorney on our board from Quarles and Brady, and Paul Werner, a partner in Schenck and Associates, our accounting firm. The idea of the plan was to make it possible, for estate tax purposes, for Dolores and me to gift 95 percent of the value of the company to our children. It would get most of the value of the business out of our estate, but still keep 50 percent of the voting stock in the company for Dolores and me. Peter Lettenberger said it was important to do this while the value of the company was not too large, because of limits on tax-free gifting. By law, Dolores and I were each able to gift $10,000 per year to any person, gift tax and income tax free. This allowed us to give a maximum total of $160,000 per year, without any tax consequences, to our eight children.

This plan was accomplished by issuing a second class of stock, a non-voting stock. Enough non-voting stock was issued, so that over a period of years we would be able to gift 95 percent of the non-voting stock to the children, leaving us with 5 percent of it. But we would still retain 50 percent of the voting stock. The eight children would also own 50 percent of the voting stock, split eight ways. We still operated the company as an "S" corporation.

According to our agreement with the children, the company is required to pay them only enough of the profits to cover the taxes the company would pay as a regular "C" corporation. The children are then able to keep any excess money they receive from the company over and above the taxes they must pay, which should be less than the corporate rate.

Also, with their combined 50 percent of the stock, the children are unable to change the rules on how much money the company must distribute to them. This allows the company to keep the money it needs for expansion. With only one of our eight children voting with us, Dolores and I still have control of the company. This means we can make the decisions, as to who is to run the business and how much, if any, money the children are to receive from the company over and above that needed for taxes.

Peter Lettenberger also set up a family foundation for Dolores and I and our children. Dolores suggested we call it the Caliana Foundation with the purpose of helping the less fortunate in the world, in loving memory of Callie and Anna, her mother and mine, who were very caring women.

I finally found a place I enjoyed living for the 9-month school year. Daytime temperatures in Santa Barbara were usually in the high sixties to the low eighties, with possibly a ceiling fan, but no air-conditioning necessary. We had similar weather, maybe five to ten degrees higher, in the three summer months we spent at Moonlight Bay. We lived in paradise 12 months of the year.

The new friends we made in both areas complemented the friendships we had made in Brillion and Appleton. Dolores and I were getting along better than when we lived in Appleton and in Florida. We still had some of the same problems, my impatience, raising my voice and Dolores taking it as anger, both of us feeling we are right in a dispute, and both of us wanting to be in control.

It seemed now it was Dolores' turn to be depressed about our problems with each other. She decided to see Sue Fajan, a family therapist we got to know through the Focusing Movement with Fathers Ed and Pete. She sometimes used Focusing in her therapy sessions.

Dolores went to a couple of therapy sessions alone with Sue, then she suggested that she sit down with both of us as she felt Dolores had a lot of pent-up anger toward me. I agreed, as I wanted to help Dolores in any way I could.

Sue suggested Dolores and I face each other and talk to each other.

"What are the things in your marriage to Lyle that you still feel angry about?" She asked Dolores.

"Lots of things. It dates back to when we lived above Maggie Pritzl's and she yelled at me for not keeping Michael quiet. He cried a lot and I didn't know why. You never offered to hold the baby or sympathized with me. You even took sides with her and thought I wasn't doing enough to keep him quiet," she said, looking me in the eye. "I remember I shook out the dust mop on the porch one day and accidentally hit the railing and you told me I should be careful because even that noise might bother Maggie."

"I know you had a lot of problems keeping Michael quiet, but I didn't think I sympathized with Mrs. Pritzl about it," I said.

"Yes, you did."

"I'm really sorry about that. I know, now, I should have helped you with Michael but I knew less about babies than you did," I said as I looked at her.

"And it really angered me in our Dewey Street house when you'd sleep on the living room floor at night, while I did the dishes, gave the kids a bath, and put them to bed. Then you'd wake up about 9:30 when I was walking up the stairs and want to talk. I was tired and going to bed after a long day with the kids. When I told you about it, you said I should get a high school girl to help me with some of my work. Then you had a dishwasher installed in the kitchen."

"I remember going to sleep on the floor in the evening," I said. "I know I told you we had departments, yours was the kids and mine was the business."

"I loved being a mother, having children, and keeping a nice house, but it was overwhelming. There was so much to do. I didn't want the dishwasher—it took up what little cupboard space I had in that tiny kitchen. I would have liked for us to do the dishes together, and for you to help me with putting the kids to bed. I didn't need someone to come in and help me. I needed a husband, and our kids needed a father," she said, with tears in her eyes.

I got up and put my arm around her and hugged her. "I'm sorry, honey. I'm really sorry. I should have helped you. I was tired, but I'm sure you were even more tired than I was with all you had to do."

Sue told us we were going through a healing process, and it was healthy to talk to each other about our pain and disappointments in our relationship.

Dolores said that was about all she could handle in this session, but that she had a lot more things she wanted to let me know about. Sue said she felt we were making good progress and set up another appointment for the following week.

During the week, we didn't talk about the session we had. I guess we both felt more comfortable with a mediator present. I didn't have any pent-up anger toward Dolores. There were some things that bothered me in our relationship; they were minor compared to the pain I had caused Dolores in our marriage.

The following week at our appointment with Sue, she asked Dolores how she felt about the things we talked about the week before.

"It was like a cleansing," she said. "I felt better."

"How did you feel, Lyle?"

"I felt like a heel. Looking back, I never realized I was that inconsiderate. I felt she had a right to be angry."

"Do you have more that wants to come out, Dolores?" she asked.

"Yes, I've been thinking of quite a few other times that I really was disturbed by the way you treated me," she said, looking at me. "Remember the time I was hysterical when you came home real late from a trip when there was a terrible storm outside, and you hadn't called to tell me you'd be late? You held my arms and shook me and yelled at me that I shouldn't worry about you."

"I don't remember that either," I said.

"I was so worried that something had happened to you."

"I should have been pleased you were concerned about my safety. All I can say is I'm sorry about that, too. Seems I've got lots of things to be sorry about."

"I love you, and I was worried something had happened to you," she said again, with tears in her eyes.

"What else?" I asked. "I didn't realize that you were carrying all these things inside you for all these years."

"Then there were two times you wouldn't take off work when I had to take kids to the hospital. You went to a meeting in Chicago with Dick Hare and then on to Hong Kong while I went to the hospital with Jim for surgery on his leg. The doctor thought he had a bone spur on his knee, but when the doctor operated, he found a large tumor. I was afraid it might be cancer. You never wanted me to call and bother you at your business meetings, so I just worried about it myself. Besides, Jim was so angry because the doctor had cut his whole leg open. He didn't expect anything like that. He was in the hospital for two days."

"I never remembered much about that," I said.

"I know," she said, "I never told you about it until you got back from Hong Kong. By that time, I knew it wasn't malignant, but I worried for a week about it until the doctor's report came back."

"I can't believe I wasn't more considerate of you."

"Well, I had no idea he was going to find a tumor and you didn't know that, either."

"What was the other time you had to take one of the kids to the hospital?" I asked.

"Kristine was home from New York and someone had to take her to the plane in Green Bay, so she could return. There was a terrible snowstorm. Patti complained about her stomach and needed to see the doctor. I needed you to take care of one or the other, but you said you were too busy and couldn't get away from the office," she explained.

"Really? I don't remember that at all."

"Your business was everything to you, Lyle. Nothing stopped you. Your business was always more important," she said, sadly.

"What happened with Kristine and Patti?" I asked.

"I took Kris to the plane and had a terrible time of it through the snowstorm. Then when I got back, I took Patti to the emergency room and she had to be admitted to the hospital immediately to have her appendix removed," she explained.

"I can't believe how inconsiderate I was. You had a right to be angry with me and I can see why you're still angry, because you've kept this inside all these years. I'm really sorry Dolores. I'll try to make it up to you some way. Please forgive me." I said, as I hugged her tightly.

"It helps me to let you know what I have been carrying around all these years. I think these are most of the things that needed to come out.I'm sorry to have to load all this stuff on you like this."

"It's okay with me honey if it relieves you of the burden," I said, as I hugged and kissed her.

The therapy sessions seemed to help us all. Dolores told me that Sue convinced her that she wasn't going to be able to change me. Sue said a person's personality doesn't change very easily. Sue suggested Dolores and I try to work out our problems with each other.

Dolores and I golfed together once in awhile. We were on the sixth hole on a nine-hole course when I said I enjoyed golfing with her and hoped we could golf together at least once a week. I said I was bored and looking for something to do that I enjoyed. She told me she'd golf with me once in awhile, but I shouldn't depend on her alone for my happiness. Dolores had made quite a few friends with the women she was involved with in supporting Villa Majella, and usually was not looking for things to do.

I was hurt when she told me I shouldn't depend on her to golf with me, but after I thought about it I realized that I needed to find some activities I could do alone or find some male friends to do them with. I remembered years ago when Dr. Kalina told Dolores and me that a healthy relationship for a couple was for each of us to have our own activities, as well as some we shared together. I found some adult ed classes I could take in the afternoon, and started golfing mornings with Ray and Jack who lived across the street from us. Dolores and I now had three couples we enjoyed playing bridge with, and played with each of them occasionally in the evenings in each others homes. Dolores and I also had occasional dinner parties with our friends in each others homes.

The real estate market was booming in Santa Barbara, especially with its prominence since President Reagan's visits to his ranch, which was actually in Santa Ynez, about 25 miles away. Real estate values increased as much as 15 percent a year, several years in a row.

Dolores spotted a beautiful Spanish style house, on her daily walk, being built a few blocks from our home. We weren't looking for a new place to live, but she told me I had to see this one. When we went to see it, I could see why she was so fascinated with it. Two stories, with an open clay tile stairway off the huge entry doors in the center of the house that split at the landing, one stairs leading to a large master bedroom overlooking the mountains, with a huge bath. The other stairs led to the bedroom wing with two bedrooms and another bath.

Next to the living room on the first floor was a study with an outside entrance. There was a formal dining room between the open stairway and a large family room and kitchen, with a half-bath and a dinette separated from the kitchen by a counter. The door in the kitchen led to a two-car garage. It was a beautiful home, quite pretentious on the outside as well.

Two of our friends, Jesuit priests Ed McMahon and Peter Campbell from the Focusing Movement were visiting us for our yearly board meeting, as Dolores and I had been active since our first focusing experience ten years before. They had put us on the national board of the movement and appointed me president of the Institute for Spiritual Research that taught the focusing technique.

"Buy it," Ed said, after we all looked at it together. "You can't go wrong. You'll love it, and it'll be a good investment." It was more than Dolores and I had ever envisioned owning. It was priced at a little more than double the cost of the home we were living in, but that house had also appreciated in value, enough to give us the equity for the 20 percent down payment on the new one. So we bought it.

We lived in it for three years when Dolores developed a minor heart problem and it exhausted her to walk the stairs. We searched for a year for a ranch house, and we finally found one we liked in the foothills of Santa Barbara, overlooking the city and the ocean. The three-bedroom home was very comfortable, not at all pretentious, and it had a pool. We were satisfied. We had made our splash in the big fancy house. This one was more suited to our lifestyle, and it was considerably less expensive. The wrap-around deck in the rear was in constant daily sunshine with spectacular views of the sunrises and sunsets, and overlooked a canyon.

Ed was right, the Spanish house was a great investment. It appreciated a remarkable 60 percent in the four years we had lived there. I finally redeemed myself with Dolores for the poor real estate deals I had made in Brillion 40 years before.

Chapter 19

The first two years after Peter took over as president of the company, he spent his time building our distributing business. At our advisory board meeting Mike Ariens suggested that Peter determine where we get the bulk of our business and give special attention to our best distributors. He said the usual rule of thumb in most businesses is that you get 80 percent of your business from 20 percent of your customers, and Peter found this was about the way it was in our business. Mike said most managers do not spend enough time on the 20 percent, they spend most of their time trying to build the 80 percent into better customers. Mike felt that many of the smaller customers don't have the money or the ability to grow in their businesses, where the big ones do. So Peter went to see some of our larger customers and some of them visited our office and assembly plant. He worked out a program to make master distributors out of our largest distributors. In some cases, where the master distributor contracted with a supermarket chain for their machine business, the smaller distributors were able to take over service of the stores in their immediate areas.

Peter wasn't making any giant steps in the business, but he was strengthening our distributor program and thereby strengthening the business. Having worked as a distributor for our company, Peter was able to more fully understand their problems. He had also reduced our expenses by working with our son Jonathan, who computerized the business enabling

Peter to further cut costs by eliminating some of our middle management people. I encouraged Peter's creativity. He worked hard to move the business forward.

It was seven months since I visited the office in Appleton when Peter called me in Santa Barbara and asked me to fly in from California to discuss a new sales plan he and his "team," as he put it, had come up with. He sounded excited.

I had no idea what to expect when I arrived in Appleton and sat down with him and his people the next morning in the office conference room. Peter and Marlene, Steve and Ryan, an additional sales manager Peter had hired, were sitting around the conference table and I sat down with them.

"We owe the bank over $1 million, including our SBA loan," Peter said. "That costs us $100,000 a year in interest payments. As you know, we own all the rental machines we took back from the Best Vendor locations. First of all, I propose that we sell at least enough of the rental machines we own to pay off the bank to save this $100,000 yearly interest expense."

"That sounds like a great idea, but do you think our distributors will want to buy the machines they are renting from us?" I asked.

"I think we can convince most of our distributors to buy them. They can probably get a loan from their bank and pay the bank about what they are now paying us in rent and own the machines in three to five years. It makes sense for them to own them, then they don't have to continue paying rent forever."

"We've already talked to two of our largest distributors, and they're interested in looking into it," Steve, our sales manager, replied.

"That's only part of the plan," Peter continued. "Steve and Ryan say vending operators call us every day and want to buy our Toy 'n Joy refills for their machines. We're considering offering our refills to the operators out there who own and operate their own toy and gum machines in other areas of the country. We would make them distributors of Toy 'n Joy machines and refills."

"What will our present Toy 'n Joy distributors think about that?" I asked Peter. Up to that time, we had sold or rented our Toy 'n Joy machines and sold our Toy 'n Joy refills only to distributors of Toy 'n Joy machines, many of whom we had started in business years before when we were changing over from our food broker program.

"It's a big country out there," Peter replied," we would only take on new distributors in territories that our present distributors don't cover. As you know, there are some territories like the northeast where we hardly scratch the surface in the market. Our distributors have been with us a long time. We value their business; we don't intend to hurt them in any way."

"It certainly sounds like a good idea. I know you and Karen are finding some great selling items in the Orient and the creative displays that help sell them in the machines are the best in the business," I said to Peter.

"And we don't want to keep all this good stuff under a bushel basket. It deserves to be offered to the kids all over the country," Marlene added, smiling.

"I sure think it's worth giving it a try," I said. "The additional business we get from these new customers will strengthen our business and make us more successful and could make us leaders in the field. People prefer to deal with successful companies. I say go for it."

"We'll make a lot of guys happy who have been calling to buy our refills," Ryan said.

A couple of months later, our engineer Bob Glaser called me in Santa Barbara. What would be one of the nicest things that could happen to us in our business?" he asked.

"I don't know, maybe we bought some tickets for the lottery

and won," I said.

"We received a U.S. Patent today on our claw machine and it gives us an exclusive right to use a vacuum suction device on our Cosmic Quest machine! The patents are good for 20 years from the date we applied for them." He sounded very excited.

"Wow, that's great," I said. "I really congratulate you, Bob, for coming up with that suction idea. As you know I didn't want the machine to be a gambling device. With the suction device the kids will get a good value for their money each time they play the machine. This will keep the Mothers and Dads happy and they will want to go to stores where the machines aren't just eating up their kids' money in those gambling claw machines. That way our machines can bring in other business for store owners. Bob, I think we should apply for worldwide patents as well."

"OK. I agree. I'll look into it right away."

"How are you coming on designing the machine?" I asked Bob.

"We should have a few machines ready for testing in another couple of weeks. I'm designing this machine in modules, just like we did the Toy 'n Joy machines, so that if it goes out of order, all the distributor needs to do is replace the module; he won't have to spend time at the store trying to fix it."

"I'm anxious to get some machines out for a test to see how well they do," I said.

One summer morning I drove to the office from Moonlight Bay. Peter had asked me to come in to tell me how the program was doing, selling the rental machines to the distributors and opening up more territories on our Toy 'n Joy refill business.

I sat down with him in his office. He told me the good news. The sale of the rental machines was going well and with the money they received from the machine sales, they had been able to pay off our SBA loan. He was excited. We had just received a check from a large distributor the day before for $200,000, for the machines he had been renting from us which made it possible for us to pay off the balance we owed on the SBA loan, 22 months ahead of schedule.

"Wow, that's wonderful," I said.

"We've sold a lot of the machines that were rented by the smaller distributors, but this is the first big sale we made so far. We still owe several hundred thousand to the bank, but we expect to have the bank completely paid up within the next six months." Peter said.

"That takes a load off my mind," I said. "Before you launched your new plan, our business was just standing still and that money we owed the bank worried me."

"Our Toy 'n Joy refills are selling well in the established vending trade, too. We're up 15 percent in refill sales since we've started the new program and we're projecting a 25 percent increase in refill sales for the year, so the company should make a nice profit this year."

"So both parts of your program are working well. That's great news. I'm really pleased with how you've taken over this business, Peter."

"When people asked me how I liked retirement, I told them that you never really retire from a family business. I still had a financial responsibility in it. Now with this news I can really retire and not have to think about it every day."

I felt a tremendous load lifted from me. I realized I was carrying this burden for over 50 years. In the prosperous years it was much lighter, but there was always a feeling the good times wouldn't last, as they didn't, many times.

I realized now how great it was that Peter, and not I, discovered a way to help the business grow again. His confidence seemed to soar with his ability to come up with new ideas that worked.

I thanked God for Peter and the insights he gained that were making the business profitable again. My thoughts turned to God's guidance in the business and how this helped me grow spiritually.

God must have been guiding me each step of the way, even when I didn't realize it. New ideas popped into my mind when they were needed. I feel these ideas were gifts from God. I thought about how my relationship with God had developed through the years.

I thought back to God's earliest intervention in my life when as a youngster I prayed on my way to Barnard's Drug Store so I would win some candy bars on the penny punchboard; and I usually did. Then the major boost to my faith in God came through the miracle in the infantry that resulted in my transfer from a front line outfit to an office job when Colonel Cartwright, a total stranger—the only one of 10 million men in the service who could help me—was transferred into my regiment as my commanding officer.

The next milestone I remember, in my spiritual life, was the one-on-one 30-day retreat that Father Bill Alcuin gave me and how on the first day I had an unusual visual spiritual experience that helped me encounter God in a personal relationship as a protective loving father. God was no longer distant. He was a friend, close to me, and I could talk to Him in a thought or a prayer, anytime of the day, and didn't have to get into a prayer mode to do so.

Prayer now was talking to God in my mind, in my own words. I began to feel God's love for me. I found His answers in the good things that came about in my life and in the changes in the things I prayed for. I remembered how hard I prayed driving to the Appleton hospital from Brillion to see our new son Paul, after Doctor Young said he had jaundiced and was in danger of death; and he recovered.

Going on retreats, working on Cursillos and with the

meditation and the Focusing Technique I learned through Fathers Ed and Pete I was able to step aside from my daily life and look at how I was progressing in my spiritual life. With the feeling of God as a companion, in my personal as well as in my business life, I could no longer handle the guilt of my shady business practices, and resolved to be honest and "do what's right" in my dealings with employees, customers, and suppliers in the business, and with my family and friends in my private life.

I came to believe that having faith is much more than faith as a belief system, as in "my Christian faith." I developed a faith that God loves us, only wants good for us, and that He protects us as long as we are trying to do His will in our lives. As Father Bill said, "We know when we're doing God's will; we are at peace with ourselves."

I also came to feel that God doesn't punish. I feel we punish ourselves by our misguided actions. Sometimes He allows what we think are bad things to happen to us, but allows them for a reason, maybe to help get us on the right track or to bring us closer to Him, as I was drawn closer to Him when I was drafted into service, then put into the infantry. I now never pray for myself or anyone else without ending the prayer, "if this be Your will". I no longer try to second-guess God.

I am pleased with the results of my prayers, but I also no longer expect end results overnight. I'm satisfied when I see improvement in the things I pray for. After all, it also takes time for God's flowers to bloom and His trees to grow.

I again learned of the power of prayer shortly after we moved to California and I was working my way out of my depressed state. I decided to start going to daily Mass again as my friend Chuck Buckman had shamed me into doing decades earlier. I prayed for our family and soon all hell broke loose! In a period of a few weeks two of our kids told us they were considering a divorce; I had to fly to Austin, Texas, to pick up one of our sons who had suffered a "psychotic break" and was being held by the police, and an unmarried daughter told Dolores and me she was pregnant with a bi-racial child. Dolores and I were shaken of course, by these events.

After these things happened, Dolores stopped writing her monthly family newsletter "In Touch" that she had been sending to our kids and some of our close friends for a couple of years.

"How can I write it?" she said to me. "What do I say, one kid's in jail, two are getting a divorce and an unmarried one just got pregnant?" I admired her sense of humor, even in adversity.

These all seemed like catastrophes at the time. But not in God's plan. Our prayers were answered in God's time. Both the troubled marriages ended in divorce. Our son who dearly loved his wife was divorced by her, but he is now very happily married to a good woman, with a wonderful son from a previous marriage. They now also have a beautiful daughter of their own.

With the daughter who divorced her husband, it seemed it was one of those cases where they dearly loved each other, but their personalities clashed and they couldn't live together. They continued to be friends, seeing each other regularly even though they lived on opposite sides of the continent. Within the last few months he has had a brain seizure, caused by a cancerous tumor on his lung that had spread to his brain. She rushed to be with him, just in time, or he would have been alone when a seizure happened, and she called 911. He credits her with saving his life. He is now taking treatments to retard the cancerous growths.

Our son recovered from his "psychotic break" and has never had a relapse.

Our daughter told us that having her daughter probably saved her life. Soon after giving birth she left the father as she didn't want her daughter raised in the kind of environment she had been living in. Struggling through college, being dyslexic, she did a wonderful job as a single mother, raising her daughter.

I feel that in God's plan sometimes things have to get worse before they get better. I also believe that sometimes God answers our prayers by doing nothing, because doing nothing is best for us at the time. When looking back on Dolores' and my life and the lives of our children I can't think of a thing that I thought was bad at the time it happened, that I now don't see as good.

Father Chester, pastor at St. Rosalia's, the church we attend in Door County, continually reinforces the thought of God's love for us. One day I heard him say that God needs us. I was surprised, I didn't think that God needed us for anything. As a kid I was taught that God is self-sufficient, He doesn't need anything or anybody.

But Father Chester got me thinking. If God allows us our own free will, which I have been taught and believe He does, He needs us to help others, especially our family and friends, to have faith in Him. He can't just zap us with the faith that He loves us dearly and only wants good for us; that wouldn't be allowing us our own free will to love Him or not.

I believe God needs us to share with people our experiences of His loving presence in our lives, so they too may find the joy in His help and protective care in ways they may not yet have experienced.

This requires risk on our part. Most people don't like others interfering in their lives. I take risks when I suggest solutions, when talking to our children who are struggling with problems and yet I feel this is my duty as their father. I don't think our responsibility for our children's welfare ever ceases. I have found that while sometimes there are hurt feelings when I first approach them, all the long-term results have been positive.

Some of our friends tell us they are concerned about their children's spirituality because they do not go to church regularly. I tell them that most of our kids don't either, but they're all great kids. To prove it I tell them to look at our license plate, "9GT KIDS"—we couldn't forget John who died at birth. I ask them if they feel theirs are good kids. Invariably they say they are. "Why worry then?" I feel the reason for religion is to bring us close to God and help us "do the right thing" in our lives. If we are trying to do the right thing we are certainly doing God's will. It's up to us to help our children and other people be close to God, and if we feel we have a relationship with God in our lives, try to help them also to experience that relationship.

Each of our three children and their families who live in the Appleton area, spend several weekends with us during the summer at Moonlight Bay. We remodeled the basement area into an apartment a few years ago. It has a family room, kitchenette, bath, master bedroom and a bunk area for the grandchildren. Since it is on ground level at the rear of the house, there are beautiful views of the water through the trees.

We also added a one-car garage with a sunroom above it. It's like a tree house on the third story level and looks out through the treetops at the pale blue sky. I use it as my getaway room, quiet, with no entry from the house, only from an outside deck.

Peter and I meet occasionally in this peaceful setting to talk about the business. Peter, like me, when I headed the company, continually has the business on his mind. He brings work home with him on weekends and enjoys spending some of his time talking business with me at Moonlight Bay.

One Saturday morning, several weeks after he told me that the final payment had been made on the SBA loan, he brought his cup and a carafe of coffee upstairs and sat down on the sofa in the sunroom.

"Our refills sales are doing great, Dad," he said with a big smile on his face. "We're up 20 percent in sales for the first six months of the year and now expect to be up 25 percent by the end of the year. We have finally turned the corner and are making a good profit over our expenses. The bank should be paid off by the end of summer."

"That's great, Peter, I'm really pleased with how things are going."

"We have several exciting new 50-cent capsule assortments coming in from the Orient. I brought this display card along to show you. These are the woven hemp bracelets and necklaces from India I told you about, that sold so well in our test machines. We've already booked a lot of them in advance orders, and have a lot more on order. They should start coming in next week."

"They're beautiful, so colorful. What are the pendants made of?"

"They're glass. Karen and I saw similar bracelets and necklaces selling in Appleton for two and three dollars apiece."

"What a tremendous value for 50 cents. No wonder they sell so well. Peter, It's so great to see you take hold of the business like this."

"It get's even better. Our management team and I have come up with a new concept to rev up our Toy 'n Joy machine sales." He was so excited he got up from the sofa and started walking around the room, talking. "As you know we've been anxiously awaiting the dollar coin in our business so we can begin to sell $1 and even higher priced merchandise in our machines, but the government keeps dragging it's feet and it could be years before it's introduced."

"Here's our plan to sell dollar merchandise. We intend to expand our four compartment wooden cabinet Toy 'n Joy unit from four compartments to six, then between two of these six machine units, instead of the talking machine, we will attach a control box with a coin acceptor that will take quarters, and a dollar bill acceptor. The control box will be connected to each of the 12 individual machines. Once you have inserted your coins or paper money, you can buy merchandise from any of the 12 machines in the unit and select items anywhere from 25 cents to $2 per play. How does that sound?" Peter asked, smiling at me.

"Expensive," I said, "but if you can sell $1 and $2 items, the unit should sell enough higher priced merchandise to pay for itself. It's an excellent idea. Did you think of this yourself?"

"Not completely, we improved on a concept that was introduced in our trade a few months ago. I talked it over with Bob Glaser. He said it was the same idea used in candy, and now in food and drink vending machines for years. You insert your money in one slot in the machine and pull a lever, to open the compartment, of the item you want. That automatically blocks the other compartments so you can only get one item out of the machine at a time. It will be a more expensive machine to build; that's why we feel that we need 12 compartments in the machine for a larger selection of items, and the dollar bill acceptor so we can move up to $1 and $2 on some of the items in the unit," Peter explained.

"I don't think there's any question that you could double, even triple, your present business in a supermarket with that machine, this could be even bigger than the Cosmic Quest claw machine, Peter. With these two new units our business should explode, we could become the leaders in machines as well as in refills for the bulk vending industry."

"The business is exciting, Dad. It's nice to be proud of the machines and products we produce and sell. They make money for the distributors as well as the retailers who put the machines in their stores, and it should make the parents happy when their kids are happy with what they get out of the machines.

"Peter, I look at your taking over the management of the business from me as when Mike Ariens took over the management of the Ariens Company family business from his father and uncles and sales exploded into the tens of millions of dollars. For me it's a wonderful feeling not to have to worry about the business anymore."

"I got the fun part," Peter said. "You had the hard part. But it wasn't easy for me either. I worried about the business the last couple of years since I took over. I had a nerve acting up in my leg and I've had to get my neck adjusted by the chiropractor several times. With all the good news of sales and profits the past few months the nerve in my leg doesn't bother me anymore and my neck feels great," he laughed.

"I've had a lot of time to reflect on the changes in the business over the past 56 years, Peter. What a contrast with the business now and what I foresee when these new concepts are fully developed."

"Yes, it's a tremendous change, Dad."

"As I was building the business I looked at what I thought were failures: the peanut vending business, the sale of our 5,000 penny toy and gum machines at fire sale prices, the success and eventual failure of the 5-cent plastic capsule machine in the candy trade, the success and eventual failure of the Toy 'n Joy machine business in the supermarket trade, and finally the demise of the Best Vendor program. But then I thought about how each of these programs improved on the previous one and led to our manufacturing the talking machine, which led to the wooden cabinet Toy 'n Joy machines, which led to the Cosmic Quest machine, and now may bring about your new electronic machine. It eventually dawned on me that these programs weren't failures; each of them was just a stepping-stone to the next plateau of success. Peter, if I only had gotten out of the way and didn't fight the changes— thinking they were failures—it would have been so much easier. Like the saying from my Cursillo, years ago, 'let go and let God.'"

"I've turned to God a lot for help since I took over the

business," Peter added. "I couldn't do it alone."

"I began to see God's help in what happened through the years. The changes for the better didn't result just from hard thought out ideas, even though I scoured my brain trying to keep the old programs going and then find new programs to replace them. When I think about it now, I see that these new ideas were gifts from God that you, Bob, and I and the others connected with the business received. My idea of trying a mixture of gumballs and small toys in a penny machine years ago just popped into my mind. The idea to manufacture a plastic machine to vend capsules came to Chuck in the shower. The idea to use a suction device in the claw machine came to Bob when we were talking to him about how to make a better claw machine. And now the new ideas you are bringing into the business, these have got to be gifts from God. It finally dawned on me as the business changed, each time for the better, that God is co-creating this business with us," I said.

"Dad, I feel you and Mom have passed your faith on to us. I feel God's help in my personal life as well as in the business."

"Peter, I noticed you opened the last two advisory board meetings with a prayer. I commend you for that. In all the years I ran those meetings, I only had the guts to do that once or twice."

"Peter, I've mentioned to you before that one of my goals in making the business successful was to generate some money for you kids, but not too soon so that it killed their incentive to accomplish their goals in life. Our financial success seems to have come at the right time. All of the children have developed a career for themselves and are doing fairly well financially."

"Yes, Dad, the bank debt will be paid off in a couple of months, with profit left over to give some of it to the kids."

"Peter, I hope you don't let the business dominate your life, as it did mine. If I just had enough faith as I went along with my work each day and let God do the worrying, my mind would have been more free to be more involved with you children. Don't let the business get in the way of your family, as I did. Remember, 'let go and let God'. He is there beside us co-creating these successes. God is truly the King of the Gumballs!"

Epilogue

Michael, our oldest at 51, freelances in sound recording for film and television, working out of Santa Fe, New Mexico. His group recently received an Emmy nomination for a *National Geographic* special on the Lechugilla Cave in New Mexico. He was married to Francoise, who we still consider family. They are still close friends, sharing the success of their two sons. Michael A., 29, has his own production company, FilmTribe, in Hollywood. His latest production, *City Scrapes*, showed recently for a month on the Sundance channel. Canton, 24, and his college buddy, Matt, perfected computer software to allow musicians to play music with famous bands in other parts of the world, finding a way to do this in "real time," allowing for the fractional difference in time. Canton and his friend are part owners of a Silicon Valley start-up company called Res Rocket Surfer, an internet band and software company providing virtual music studios where musicians from anywhere in world can "jam" together on the internet. For you computer buffs, their web site is (www.resrocket.com).

Kristine, 49, was married to Eliot. They are still good friends. She lives in Santa Barbara and is working on her dissertation for her doctorate in psychology from the California School of Professional Psychology in San Diego.

Susan, 46, lives in Santa Fe. She's married to Doug Svetnicka. Susan is a school librarian and Doug works for the Cultural Affairs Department for the state of New Mexico, drumming up business for their museums. They have three children, Justin, a senior in high school, and twins, Nicholas and Christopher, who are freshmen in high school.

James, 43, also in Sante Fe, (Michael moved there, the other two visited and decided to live there, too) freelances in TV production under the name Becker Video. He does a great job, specializing in editing, lately doing a lot of work for ESPN television. James has a lovely wife, Mary, a son, Christopher, ten, from a previous marriage and they have a daughter or their own, Joanna, seven.

Patrice, 41, lives in Wrightwood, California. She is in her fourth year as a physical education teacher in Phelan, California. Patrice has done a fine job as a single parent raising her daughter, Talena, a great kid, now entering her first year of high school.

Paul, 40, lives in Appleton, works part-time at the Becker Company, but his first love is the piano—tuning, repairing and playing it. His business is called The Piano Doctor, serving the Fox cities and Door County areas.

Peter, 31, lives in Appleton and is president of L. M. Becker & Co., Inc. He is married to Karen, who had three boys, Dylan, Dustin and Landon from a previous marriage. Dylan is a sophomore, Dustin a freshman and Landon is in eighth grade. They have a daughter of their own, Camryne, who is five. Karen works part-time in the business, traveling to the Orient and on other business trips with Peter, and is head designer of the toy displays for the machines.

Jonathan, 26, lives in Menasha, Wisconsin, and is married to Cheri who works for the Winnebago Welfare Department, finding child care for the counties' new welfare workers. He has adopted her son, Jan, 11. Jonathan is our computer expert for the L. M. Becker Company. In his "spare time" he is in business as the "Computer Guy," doing computer consulting in the Appleton area.

Dolores and I are in good health, enjoying our retirement, visiting our children and grandchildren, and having them visit us at our homes in California and Wisconsin. I feel she and I are reasonably happy together. But as I learned through her "liberation", I can't talk for Dolores. I asked her recently whether I still control her. She said, "Not as much." However, in one spat we had recently she said "look out or you'll need to add another chapter to your book!" It keeps me on my toes. At least now we can kid about our differences.

We are proud of our kids and grandkids. It just occurred to me that all of our male children and grandchildren, of working age, are in business for themselves or working for the family business. I guess it rubbed off on them. If you want to keep up on the latest at L. M. Becker & Co., Inc., you can check their web site, (www.toynjoy.com).

As for the other people in the book I guess we should start with Chuck, Ward, Hermy and my brother Gene, three of the famous stooges on the infamous excursion to place the first peanut machine.

Chuck and his wife, Bernie, are living in Green Bay enjoying their three children and grandchildren. Chuck is as clever as ever, keeping the group laughing at their breakfast club at the Holiday Inn. Chuck, although not in great health, has outlived his brother Ward, who is survived by his wife, Pinky.

Hermy and Gene each passed away a few years ago. I was sorry I didn't get this story written sooner, I think they would have gotten a kick out of it.

My father, Mike, as Chuck called him, died in a T.B. Sanitarium as his T.B. became active again, but he lived to the remarkable age of 82.

My brother Bernard, who was declared missing in action in the Philippines, was eventually declared dead by the U.S. Army. He was the first serviceman to die in World War II from Brillion so now the Legion Post has the name Bloedorn-Becker Post.

Two of Bernie's buddies in the Air Force came to visit my dad after the war and told us the story of how the three of them went through the Japanese lines on the Bataan peninsula and were surprised by the Japanese while they were sleeping. Bernie ran into the tall reeds but the other two were captured and survived the Bataan death march. They assumed Bernie died, as he had malaria and didn't have any medication with him. I listened to this story with my dad. We were happy at least to have some idea of what had happened to him.

My sister, Anita, who ran the peanut route while I was in the service and who married Al, my partner in the Indianapolis route, is still living in Milwaukee enjoying their eight children and grandchildren. Al has Alzheimer's disease and is in a nursing home in Milwaukee.

My brother Harold, now retired, still lives in Corona, California, enjoying his two children and grandchildren. His wife, Sylvia, passed away a couple of years ago.

Don Charles, now retired, still lives in Connecticut, his wife Jackie died suddenly a few years ago.

Vern Vechart went into portrait photography when he retired and lives with his wife, Armella, in Wheaton, Illinois.

Dick Hare works for a hobby magazine featuring classic cars and lives with his wife, Mary, in Appleton.

I think I have been easier for Dolores to live with in the past three years while writing this book, so as soon as I put this one to bed I plan to start another one—just to keep out of trouble.